Rethinking South China Sea Disputes

The proposed book draws on the ongoing South China Sea dispute, and the multifaceted challenges wrought by the South China Sea issue that requires an interdisciplinary perspective. It employs legal-analytical methods to emphasize the nuances of the role and interpretation of international law and treaties by China in different periods, while taking into account policy and strategic concerns, which generally cast great sways in decision-making. The reintroduction of interdisciplinary concerns straddling law and history illustrates that the historical dimension, which has long been neglected, is an emerging concern posing looming dangers that may unexpectedly radicalize the friction. Contributing to debunking the mystique wrought by confrontations between a historical and a law-dominated perspective, these perspectives are supported by a more nuanced analytical framework, featuring theoretical concerns with a tinge of practicality. The South China Sea Dispute aims to unveil a nuanced evolution of the issue with a confluence of inter-temporal law, policy and maritime practices in the South China Sea.

Katherine Hui-Yi Tseng is a research associate at the East Asian Institute, National University of Singapore.

Routledge Studies in Asian Law

Asian Law in Disasters
Towards a Human-Centered Recovery
Edited by Yuka Kaneko, Katsumi Matsuoka And Toshihisa Toyoda

Judicial Review of Elections in Asia
Edited by Po Jen Yap

Rethinking South China Sea Disputes
The Untold Dimensions and Great Expectations
Katherine Hui-Yi Tseng

Rethinking South China Sea Disputes
The Untold Dimensions and Great Expectations

Katherine Hui-Yi Tseng

LONDON AND NEW YORK

First published 2017
by Routledge
2 Park Square, Milton Park, Abingdon, Oxon OX14 4RN

and by Routledge
711 Third Avenue, New York, NY 10017

Routledge is an imprint of the Taylor & Francis Group, an informa business

© 2017 Katherine Hui-Yi Tseng

The right of the Katherine Hui-Yi Tseng to be identified as author of this work has been asserted by her in accordance with sections 77 and 78 of the Copyright, Designs and Patents Act 1988.

All rights reserved. No part of this book may be reprinted or reproduced or utilised in any form or by any electronic, mechanical, or other means, now known or hereafter invented, including photocopying and recording, or in any information storage or retrieval system, without permission in writing from the publishers.

Trademark notice: Product or corporate names may be trademarks or registered trademarks, and are used only for identification and explanation without intent to infringe.

British Library Cataloguing in Publication Data
A catalogue record for this book is available from the British Library

Library of Congress Cataloging in Publication Data
A catalog record for this book has been requested

ISBN: 978-1-138-94272-1 (hbk)
ISBN: 978-1-315-67297-7 (ebk)

Typeset in Galliard
by Apex CoVantage, LLC

Printed and bound in Great Britain by
TJ International Ltd, Padstow, Cornwall

Contents

	Introduction	1
1	The South China Sea under the colonial encounter in the nineteenth century	7
2	Beyond territorial disputes: maritime issues and the revolutionary China	20
3	A neglected dimension in South China Sea: fishing	37
4	From the centre: the dash-line claim as a historical imaginarium or a quest for new course?	53
5	From the centre: a proposal of jurisdiction right upon maritime spaces	76
6	From the periphery: the South China Sea as a frontier and application of the maritime space jurisdiction right	101
7	Echoing the mandala legacy: rethinking ASEAN engagement in the South China Sea	125
8	From the periphery: state succession and the South China Sea disputes	144
	Conclusion	162
	Index	167

Introduction

The general perception is that the story in the South China Sea began when the Chinese government (Republican government, Taiwan) drew the dash-line map in 1947. The region then experienced several eventful decades, and an environment inducive to economic and political development only emerged in the 1990s. Having survived the financial crisis that struck hard in late 1990s, the region was confronted with another challenge, the South China Sea dispute. Before it gradually surfaced China (both Chinese governments across the Taiwan Strait, the People's Republic and the Republic of China) was involved in couples of events, confronting Vietnam in the Paracel Islands in 1974 and Mischief Reef in 1995. Maritime skirmishes drew an inscrutable veil on these remote, barren and uninhabitable rocks spread across the South China Sea. In particular, the rather under-developed-ness of naval capability of coastal countries largely hollowed out their South China Sea claims. Without enough naval resources, their claims could be fortified, let alone implemented in a meaningful way. Yet, amid the growing tension, in the beginning of the twenty-first century, China and ASEAN countries for the first time laid down their projections to a peaceful South China Sea in a document, the Declaration of Conduct. While vowing to seek peaceful resolutions, these outlooks remain lip service that is hortatory, waiting for political will and real action.

It is a long and discursive path to trace the development of the South China Sea issue. Yet the South China Sea is often portrayed as a source of potential armed conflict, most often directly between China and Southeast Asian claimant states but also indirectly as a result of intricate military alliances with the world's major and emerging powers in a bid to maintain strategic influence and control access to the world's busiest sea lanes. A recent dispute on Scarborough Shoal in 2012, and the ongoing arbitration initiated in 2013 illustrate well the perception that confrontation, of all kinds, lies just around the corner. Despite intricate political considerations, the essence of these disputes focused superficially on resource competition. What goes unnoticed is actually confrontation between different sets of values underlying these conflicts, which have lingered into the twenty-first century. It is this theme, more accurately prescribed as re-examination of inter-temporal law and practices in maritime affairs in East and Southeast Asia, that plays a central role in framing discussions in this project.

2 Introduction

This volume therefore includes South China Sea crises which are protracted or seen largely as routine in a country's political landscape that actually illustrates a far more complex picture. The reintroduction of interdisciplinary concerns straddling law and history illustrates that historical dimension, which has long been neglected, but is an emerging concern, with looming dangers that may unexpectedly radicalize the friction. Hard facts aside, this study also attempts to propose new concepts for solutions from a pragmatist point of view. Stemming from traditional and historical maritime practices in this region which have largely been marginalized due to the overwhelming expansion of western international law, new proposals aim not only to break current the stalemate, but to revive these oriental values by reintroducing local and traditional maritime practices. These can fine-tune the contemporary legal regime so that disputants' interests can be better addressed.

The book draws attention to the ongoing South China Sea dispute, and the entailed challenges which are multifaceted and thus require an interdisciplinary perspective. It employs multiple analytical methods straddling various subjects, such as the role of international law and its implications in different periods, while taking into accounts policy and strategic concerns that greatly influence decision-making. Also, attention will be drawn to factual and historical episodes to see how the concept of maritime defence, maritime boundary and limitation and marine affairs management took root in the development of contemporary China and Southeast Asia.

It is with these understandings that in the second part of this book, new proposals are attempted for practical resolutions. The concept of a jurisdiction right upon maritime spaces is proposed, mainly addressing the maintenance of maritime security as the provision of public goods by exercising a jurisdiction right on the great swathes of waters in the South China Sea. By drawing reference to conventional maritime practices and territorial concepts with a tinge of Asian tradition, this jurisdiction right is to draw the attention of all stakeholders on order maintenance and security provision, a goal which nevertheless has long been neglected and overshadowed by sovereignty disputes and resource exploitation. Yet the concept is not to be exercised at the cost of disregard or denunciation of the Law of the Sea regime. Rather, it could only be justified and upheld on the basis of observing the established regime and prescriptions of Exclusive Economic Zone in the Law of the Sea Convention. In this respect, a better mode of operation stems from regional cooperation that can more comprehensively accommodate Association of Southeast Asian Nations (ASEAN) claimant countries and China, with a security focus and instrument of police power on the sea.

Another issue worth of mentioning is a long-neglected actor, Taiwan (Republic of China) due to its special relations with China (People's Republic) and unrecognized state as a sovereign country. As a self-governing polity, Taiwan also claims sovereignty upon all land features in the South China Sea. It was Taiwan (the Republican government) that had drawn the dash line in 1947 and had made initial attempts to replenish the dash-line claim with modern and legal essence in the 1990s. Yet, without a recognized sovereign status, Taiwan's claim has not been formally admitted to the negotiation and dialogue forum for a long time. What further attenuates the credit of Taiwan's claim, as of its own, is the impact of state succession, with which China (People's Republic) can be deemed as a legal successor to Taiwan's claims. In other words, Taiwan (Republic of China) is a de facto polity which officially (at the time of writing at the beginning of 2016) upholds the "One China" principle. Under current international contexts, this "One China" refers to the Beijing government (the People's Republic). Therefore, Taiwan's claims, on the foothold of a de facto Chinese government, are to be subsumed into China's claims, which represents and has been recognized as a de jure Chinese government in the international community. It is in this sense that the Taiwanese government is encouraged reconsider its South China Sea claims. Yet, this re-contemplation is not a corollary that Taiwan is to march forward to more formal independence. Rather, taking into account the fledgling consensus among the Taiwanese public on the direction of future cross-strait relations, to adopt a think-and-move approach on the South China Sea issue is realistic and helpful.

This book contains eight chapters.

In Chapter 1, a trace-back is conducted on the concept of "border" and "territorial rights" in Asian tradition, to provide a sensible explanation of what Asian practices of maritime activities were before the arrival of European hegemony. Confucianist thought suggests that borders should be porous and people should have the rights to move across borders to pursue better lives. Also, the concept of rulings performed by a True King indicates that Asian tradition had different perceptions and practices of how a territory should be administered, and its proprietorship attributed. It is under this concept that Asian perceptions and practices towards "boundary" and "territory" are the polar opposites of those prescribed in the Westphalain system. Accordingly, it was contestable, yet convincing to argue that China's South China Sea is not of a sovereign nature, as presented in the Westphalian system of international order as now construed. Rather, the Chinese dash-line claim should be deemed a defensive characteristic for security purposes. However, the way in which countries with great maritime capabilities and ambitions arrived at a consensus – or at least a common-sense understanding of how maritime activities and rules be conducted and promulgated – indicates that Asian countries are generally excluded from this process. On the China side, what is depicted was a chaos catalysed out of a compound of reasons, such as corruptive governance of dynastic politics, western invasions, lack of knowledge of Westphalian international law and other factors.

The chaos extended on to the revolutionary era. In Chapter 2, China was enmeshed in a rather fragmented chaos that had also led to its incompetence and incapability in maritime policy-making. The lack of knowledge of international law was one root cause, albeit of critical importance, to China's misjudgement and miscalculation. The South China Sea issue also highlighted differences between China and other Asian countries, such as Japan, which was the only one able to stand up to fight against the grandeur trend of colonialism and imperial invasions in this region. China has travelled a rather discursive pattern, in the scenario of developing insights and due consciousness of maritime policy-making, and the build-up of maritime capability. Yet, after the Second World War, the South China Sea issues have become gradually territorialized. International law, while presented both in treaties and legislative law-making, does not lend considerable help in either dispute resolution or conflict alleviation. Rather, a clear-cut boundary concept, focused on the sea but not on the continent, along with a narrowly defined one of "border security", has largely dominated the configuration of the issue. The fact is that the South China Sea issue continues to deteriorate, with a dim outlook for any practical resolutions in near future.

Yet, before efforts are being attempted for possible resolutions in the second part of this book, there remain issues being marginalized because of the intensification of sovereignty disputes in the South China Sea. Fishing is one case, shedding critical light on conflict management and dispute resolutions in this South China Sea conundrum.

Chapter 3 is dedicated to fishing as both a right and duty in the scenario of the South China Sea issue. The South China Sea is confronted with serious depletions of fishery resources because of fishing overcapacity, illicit and unreported fishing and harmful and wasteful harvesting methods. Contributing to this fishing disaster are the yet-to-be-clarified international norms to keep national authorities well-informed of fishing activities of various kinds as well as the lack of effective and efficient regional mechanisms. Amid this institutional chaos and normative confusion, China nevertheless has deemed fishing as a critical component to its historical right claim in the South China Sea issue. Ironically, when these two issues – fishing and sovereignty claims, in and of themselves with two different natures and characteristics – confront, the issue of fishing is likely to be subsumed or subjugated to serve the interest of contesting of sovereignty claims. The result is that risks wrought by disputed maritime zoning upon fishermen's safety are neglected, and their lives imperilled.

Consequently, in a sequence of chapters (from Chapter 4 to 7), efforts are dedicated to re-flesh the dash-line claim with modern contestations that are more sensible to the Westphalian international order and prevailing international practices. Chapter 4 takes up the challenge by first elaborating how this dash-line claim could be meaningfully constructed. Yet, this re-configuration will be proceeded in a creative manner which on one hand, revives conventional regional practices, while on the other, observes the well-established Westphalian international order and Law of the Sea.

Then, Chapters 5 and 6 pick up the thread, proposing a concept of "jurisdiction right upon maritime spaces". Although contemporary maritime order is established on the essence of "freedom of navigation" enshrined in the Grotian idea of "mare liberum", the Law of the Sea system nevertheless contains several structural flaws and legal lacunae. Examples include the relations between maritime zoning in the Law of the Sea and state responsibilities incurred when countries compete in demonstrating sovereign claims in disputed waters. This

Introduction 5

jurisdiction right upon maritime spaces is to fill in these gaps formed, unintentionally but with inadvertent, yet serious effects. The goal of this concept is three-fold, for order maintenance, conflict management and navigation freedom.

In Chapter 6, concept-building efforts continue, albeit from a Southeast Asian perspective. With different concepts of "border zone" and "boundary" inherent in this region, the South China Sea can be deemed as a zone of contact, which actually requires concepts and practices delivering tolerance and deference to various different others, rather than exclusive segregation of spaces with deterrent boundary lines that entail punitive outcomes. It is on this basis that methods of implementing this concept are further unfolded, featuring a regional approach and mutually beneficial, burdening-sharing operation model. China, deeming the South China Sea as the area falling with its inherent zones of influences, logically is to take up the lead to put through this concept. In this sense, historical right and interest, as long contested by China, serve to supplement and fortify the Law of the Sea regime, but not as a dampening factor.

In Chapter 7, the interactions between ASEAN and South China Sea issues are examined. Drawing from a historical-cum-cultural perspective, the regional custom and practice help inform the unique perspective held by contemporary ASEAN countries towards South China Sea issues, and the implications to themselves and the region. The contestation is that echoing the legacy of ancient regional order, which was termed a "Mandala" system, the concept of "ASEAN unity" has been misunderstood in the context of South China Sea scenario. Instead of forming a unified position, which is practically unlikely, this concept actually refers to the consistence and resilience of ASEAN serving as a platform of dialogues between regional countries and their rivalry. In the South China Sea context, the rivalries refer to China, and other intervening extra-regional countries as well. In this sense, the ASEAN unity is presented not so much as a unified position, but in the resilience of all member countries that would stand as a group in the face of crisis.

The last chapter is dedicated to another long-neglected issue, a quiet claimant Taiwan (Republic of China, ROC) which has long been excluded from negotiation forum and international scenarios due to political reasons. Chapter 8 studies how the cross-strait relations interact with the South China Sea issue, and how sovereign claims of Taiwan (ROC) are impacted. The "One China" principle, observed both by the international community and two Chinese governments across the Taiwan Strait, sets the basic tone that Taiwan's claim is to be subsumed into that of China. The logic is that claims by the de jure government are to overwhelm and take in those asserted by the de facto government. It is also under the context of state succession theory that Taiwan's claims in the South China Sea require re-contemplation. Stresses on effective control, featured with consistent and uninterrupted administrations, in contemporary law of territorial disputes, have called for a revisionist view on Taiwan ('s claims.

The South China Sea issue is likely to continuing boiling for coming decades. Becoming highly politicized and intractable, any resolution is unlikely anytime soon in near future. Yet, amid the atmosphere of over-politicization and over-judicialization of the South China Sea issue, the concept of "jurisdiction upon maritime spaces" may provide an alternative for, in the short term, order maintenance and conflict management, and, in the long term, dispute resolution. Yet, one critical lesson of this long quest should not be ignored, and may go far beyond the legal and political wrestling on the surface. The lesson is how this South China Sea issue triggers/induces the consciousness/awareness of re-contemplating and re-treasuring local traditions and rules of engagement, in due course when missions to build a new regional order are yet be accomplished in the contemporary era. Only when this ultimate purpose being clearly recognized and consistently upheld, could this mission be able to achieved effectively and efficaciously.

The writing is finished in December, 2015, before the first arbitration on the South China Sea issue (Philippines v. China) was concluded, with an award issued on 12 July, 2016. A brief sketch of the award and its implication is included in Conclusion.

1 The South China Sea under the colonial encounter in the nineteenth century

I The western winds of colonialism

A An overview of colonial expansion in the Southeast Asia

In company with commencing the long haul of transformation into modern capitalist economies and nation states, Europeans had conducted a process of expansion that led to European encounters with the "others", beyond what the scope of the "barbarian" peoples referred to in ancient periods.[1] This process of expansion, begun in the fifteenth and sixteenth centuries, extended well into following centuries, with expeditions keenly probing around the globe.

During the fifteenth and sixteenth centuries, the Europeans had advanced their explorations in three main areas. In the beginning they concentrated on the Atlantic basin from the Atlantic islands and coastal western Africa to the hinterlands of the American continents. Subsequently, the northern seas fell into the grip of the Europeans, stretching eastward from the Baltic to the White Sea and the Siberian Coast and westward to the coasts of Canada. Then came the Oriental seas and northern Asia. The Pacific region was brought under the European influence during the eighteenth century, when the islands and coastal regions in and bordering the west Pacific, such as Australia, New Zealand, New Guinea and the Pacific Islands, were grabbed by the European explorers.

When Europeans arrived in Southeast Asia as early as in the fifteenth century, they did not come into a decaying and impoverished hemisphere, but rather a wealthy, open and dynamic region. Situations subsequently changed, in both the Europeans' intentions and the overall context, as the growing European interests extended beyond acquiring trade concessions into huge and prosperous markets in Southeast Asia and China. Instead, the desire to obtain minerals and growing crops for export, for further encroachment into the hinterland of Asian continent, and for prestige in both political and legal legitimacy began to overshadow those original mercantilistic commercial activities.

In this context, at the end of the nineteenth century, there was hardly a piece of land in the world into which the Europeans had not exerted their economic and military powers, let alone the more provocative religious and cultural infiltration. These European penetrations around the globe set in motion processes which resulted in a new reality that the world had been defined by trans-cultural and trans-national phenomena. Prescribed by Wolf, with insights and persuasions, these were the encounters and implications between the Europeans and the rest in the post-1400 world. European expansion created a market of global magnitude by incorporating pre-existing networks of exchanges and by creating new itineraries and historical trajectories between continents bridging European and non-European populations and societies. Intriguingly, this pattern of historical process and international commodity exchange had fostered regional specialization and had initiated worldwide movements of commodities. The growth of European trade and the dominion of capitalism, originating in the European continent, had brought about a qualitative change not only in the regnant mode of production, but also in the commercial network connected with it.[2]

In Southeast Asia, western countries came in different periods, but had gradually established a condominium of great powers both in the Asian continent and the bordering West Pacific Ocean. In Indonesia, the Dutch greatly expanded their power between 1750 and 1914, by conducting commercial activities and administrations mainly on two big islands, Java and Sumatra.[3] After consolidating their position in India, the British became interested in, yet had not become deeply involved in the Malay Peninsula until the late eighteenth century.[4] The British also extended their power into the area inhabited mostly by Muslim Malays in Borneo and Sarawak in the middle of the nineteenth century. The French ambitions were in Vietnam, gradually creeping into the Indochina continent in pursuit of a "civilized mission" to cultivate the people by spreading French culture and religion, commercial gain, and control of riverine areas along the Mekong and Red River routes.[5]

B Evolution of intergovernmental maritime cooperation and practices[6]

The European expansion would not have been vindicated without the advancement of maritime technology and the re-envisioned world views. Following the unfolding of the world map from the European continent, expansion expeditions of these empires helped cultivate the classic mercantilist economy, in which its theoretical advancement and operation was underpinned by state policies and practices of mercantilism, along with a row of measures that helped empires to maintain balances of trade.[7] In this sense, it is argued that acquisitions of overseas territories and colonies were effected mainly to increase the wealth of the imperial mother nation by furnishing raw materials at controlled prices to the advantage of the mother country. The kinetics between mercantilist economy and the formation, and even collapse, of empires, could also be verified, as it has been asserted that "wealth is needed to underpin military power, and military power is needed to acquire and protect wealth."[8]

From this line, imperial encounters on the sea aroused issues and challenges both among expeditioners themselves and with local and indigenous communities. Within these empires, raw materials, fresh labour and markets with huge export potentials brought about from overseas occupation triggered fierce competition in political manoeuvring in metropole capitals, and legal brainstorming among European intellectuals. The proposal of a liberal formula for maritime traffic, from which the right for free trade in the newly discovered territories was granted to those equipped with required capabilities, was staunchly upheld by late-coming Dutch colonialist-cum-merchants.[9]

One positive side was that this competition brought to the table the agenda of law-making and conflict management in maritime affairs among these empires. It developed further when maritime communication became an artery critical for continuing thriving of imperial dominance on the Indian Ocean and the Southeast Asian waters. Leaving aside whether certain criteria drawing the line separating the civil and military dimension of these imperial maritime activities had been developed in due course, it was an era where conventions were to be redrawn – and the view re-envisioned – in the scenario of law-making and rule-compounding in maritime communication. Nevertheless, what overshadowed this rosy picture was the differentiation, if not outright discrimination, in the application of rules and institutions to European polities and non-European kingdoms and dynasties in the exotic, non-Christian world. Adam Watson poignantly observed, "The rules and institutions which the Europeans spread to Persia and China in the nineteenth century were those which they had evolved with the Ottomans. . .rather than those in use within itself. . ."[10]

By the mid-nineteenth century, the ideal of international cooperation in maritime affairs was accompanied by sprouting efforts, taking multilateral treaties as a type of international legislation and an initiative for a prosperous outlook. The Declaration of Paris of 1856 marked the beginning of converging a consensus of maritime affairs management at the international level.[11] Despite an aftermath effort in post-war period of the Crimean War, which seemed dedicated more to wrap up the conflict but not to commence commencing international judicialization and institutionalization of rules of maritime affairs, this Declaration laid out protections of vessels and cargos during belligerency.[12] It further advocated the abolishing of privateering and the binding of blockades based on the effectiveness principle.[13]

Subsequent efforts were picked up in 1884, when the International Convention for the Protection of Submarine Cables was signed by 26 nations, aiming to deal with international communication and vessel operations.[14] Later in 1889, the Washington Conference on Safety at Sea was convened to discuss difficult issues, such as rules to determine the seaworthiness of vessels and compulsory sea lanes in frequented waters.[15] Other than these, the Conference had considered creating a permanent international maritime committee, a predecessor of the International Maritime Organization today. These international efforts, as law-making efforts aiming at global uniformity were nevertheless aborted.[16] Yet, they had at least reaffirmed that treaty process, which converged, recalibrated and refined proposals and opinions from participating countries, all of which appeared essential for the progressive harmonization and unification of laws in maritime trade and shipping.[17]

These efforts, however, encountered rather tepid responses from the international community, as international cooperation was suspended during the ferocious maritime and naval competition between the powers in the early years of the twentieth century. The First World War further postponed these important international works, which were not resumed until 1929. The 1929 Conference produced a new convention, dealing with the subjects concerning safety standards and technology of vessels, and lifesaving appliances on the ship.[18] An International Rules of the Road was also included.

The League of Nations, established after the First World War and surviving only 20 years, nevertheless took up some maritime subjects and was able to achieve some success with respect to uniform systems of maritime signals and buoys. However, subjects such as oil pollution of the oceans were less successful and had not seen any breakthrough until after the Second World War in 1958.[19] To a considerable extent, the multilateral treaty process was one critical step in forging and reifying international consensus in maritime law-making and rules-compounding. Despite its overtly idealistic discourses and the lack of political support from members in the international community because of the deteriorating economy and dwindling trade, the League of Nations had demonstrated the feasibility of international cooperation in this early period in international law-making in maritime affairs, only that its system of collective security had failed to achieve the contextual stability and global peace thus required.[20]

II Southeast Asia and the South China Sea in the colonial era: the intermixture of changed-unchanged paradox in colonial policy

A Some critical thinking on the colonial Asia and the maritime law-making

When writing about maritime issues[21] in colonial Asia, one enduring problem is how history should be constructed and recast in the writing. Undoubtedly, history has played a weighty role in regional maritime disputes. Moreover, situations may become more complicated, should they be imbued with frivolous sentiments of national pride, self-determinative justice, an inflated sense of victimization and an insatiable demand for compensation, whether nominally or materially. This has plagued efforts to recast the history of maritime issues in Southeast Asia and China during the periods of colonial and imperial occupation.

From an epistemological perspective, history, in the scenario of maritime territorial disputes, could be reconsidered via three lenses. First, it can be conducted from a national perspective, by retracing the ancestral footsteps of respective countries and reframing contested issues when considering mainly realistic interests of respective countries. The second is from a bipartisan perspective, in which the main examining body would be legal treatises, claims of involving nation(s) and an analytical and chronological discussion of the development of disputes. The third is to deem the issue as a fraction of a general history, and to examine such in the context of the vicissitude of political powers and balances of interests, at both regional and international level. This third approach risks boiling down the subject to merely bland prescriptions based on the right, but dry, analytic instruments of power and politics. However, it tends to outbid the former two approaches, in terms of its academic contributions, because of a bipartisan attitude and a relatively neutral position when treating the presented facts, realities and contestations.

Another issue meriting attention is the need to heed a specific shift in terms of subjectivity and the framing perspective. It can be done by avoiding the misperception of realizing the interconnectivity of local day-to-day activities and events either read or constructed in Southeast Asian waters and Chinese coasts, with the erasure of the civilizational, societal, ethnic and regional boundaries from afar, namely the not so relevant European contexts and perspectives. This adjustment is worth efforts.

On the one hand, it marks the recognition of the continuing struggle of the indigenous people, their uncomfortable response to the thrust-upon "modernity" with the escort of threating forces and discriminatory western mastery. It is from this approach that the very often monolithic history writing of Asia at the helm of colonization and imperialism could be avoided, when voices and concerns of the indigenous people could be meaningfully presented. On the other hand, this plural-dimensional tone in historical prescription is to better present the complex relationship between Europe and the rest of the world in post-1492 era. It is thus one reasonable expectation that the outcome would be a detailed analysis when considerations at the macro-level were also heeded, and one incorporating as many actors as possible so that dynamics in plural dimensions could be more vividly illustrated.

In this sense, Eric Wolf has made a persuasive argument about the necessity, justification and contributions thus brought about. European expansion created a market of global magnitude, by incorporating pre-existing networks of exchange, and by creating new itineraries and historical trajectories between continents which linked European and non-European populations and communities.[22] This pattern of historical processes and international commodity exchange would also foster regional specialization and initiate worldwide movements of commodities.[23] This provides a more informative and contextually relevant explication, when regional incidents or practices of these local and indigenous people, previously tainted with judgmental incriminations and discriminations, could be culturally and meaningfully recast.

It is with these understandings that the re-casting of certain critical concepts would, to their best effect, help decipher the South China Sea conundrum.

B Boundary in the evolution

i Evolution of border, boundary-making and territorial rights in China

It is rightfully asserted that the concept of border, from which a territorial domain of China as a nation state can be referred, developed in quite a late stage – around eighteenth and nineteenth centuries.[24] In particular, its evolution has been mostly catalysed by an imminent and forceful presence of imperialist western powers pressing for trade concessions and political leverages in the Chinese mainland. This, however, is not saying that such concepts are lacking in traditional imperial China.[25] While the prevailing discourse that this concept would be socially embedded – so as to render distinctive, yet culturally informed elaborations – leaves not much room for further contestations, this "border-boundary" rhetoric is one segment of the much prevailing state-centred narrative in the contemporary international legal system, to which dissident international relations theorists and critical geo-politicians have often countered post-structuralist argument. In their discourses, one harshest criticism is the construction aimed at rendering the concept, constituents and practices of the "territorial trap" as "theoretically visible", which were allegedly the traditional assumptions of state territoriality and fixed images of the bordered world of nation-states and identities.[26] In this aspect, Shapiro writes tersely, that "The assumption that bordered state sovereignties are the fulfillment of a historical destiny rather than a particular, and in some quarters controversial, form of political units has been challenged."[27]

In Chinese tradition, the concept of "border" and of boundary-making is relevant to how the world view is delineated and explicated. The dominating Confucian thoughts had dwelled on the narrative of a world order governed by rites (li) and rituals (de), and at the helm of a virtuous ruler. This refers to an ideal moral and political order admitting of no territorial boundary, as it saw no reasoned and reasonable justification towards such need, and thus transcends the narrow-ness of bordered states.[28] One main reason why the Confucian thoughts of the world order and of inert-polity relations are deemed as relevant today is that the era when these thoughts were developed had seen the vicissitudes of conglomeration and separation of local polities and principalities, which resembled the fifteenth- and sixteenth-century Europe from which contemporary multistate system had emerged. It is thus under this context that the seemingly rather ideal Confucian thoughts of world order, and of border (and territorial rights), had actually be blended with practical concerns.

Put succinctly, there are three concerns, which could be termed as general principles of the Confucian thoughts on "world order" and "territory and boundary".[29]

For one, in a non-ideal world full of competing states for limited resources and one sole ruling legitimacy (the mandate to rule over the world), states should be prepared for wars, while getting the people on the side of the ruler as one most effective and ultimate defence means. Boundaries, in this aspect, were thus justified if they helped promote peace, but not a simple outcome of ruthless wars and conquest.

The second was to emphasize "unity", while paying regards to pluralism within unity. In an ideal society, the world was to be unified, while critical thinking was nevertheless promoted and tolerated, as ways of life and fair mechanisms for conflict resolutions. In a non-ideal world, the fact that states, small and large, had competed with each other and was involved in wars and conflicts. This chaos and abnormality should be rectified if rulers could practise humanity, and had resorts mainly and only to virtue. Rules as such, termed as True King, would also seek to spread to the world his humane and benevolent governance. The ultimate purpose was that everyone could be civilized. A tributary system was created to help vindicate this ideal world order and to deliver the projected civilization fruits to all that were supposed to be cultivated and benefitted. It was in this context that the pluralism discourse had been substantiated under the overall context of a unified world order in this depiction, as no restrictions, racial, ethnic or other, were to be discriminated among members in the Confucian community, as the principle of adherence to humanity would be strictly implemented and faithfully observed.

The third principle dealt with virtues of rulers. The ruler needed to perform perfect virtues, so as to impose upon the people a civilizing effect. It would thus be reasonably expected that coercive laws and regulations would no longer required. Yet the reality rendered some flexibility of these applications. When rulers did not perform virtues as required, people should migrate to states with relatively benign rulers.

These principles are not always well performed and duly reciprocated. This Confucian thought, despite its main characteristic of idealism and harmony, allows expediency and flexibility in terms of its application. In this aspect, implications can be drawn in a meaningful sense, regarding how boundary and territorial rights are construed and practiced.

Put succinctly, settlement in a piece of land is not deemed as a requirement to become a true gentleman in the Confucian thought. Rather, certainly mobility is to be retained, for the purpose of seeking for virtuous rulers. Yet for common people to perceive the value of settlement in a certain piece of land, they need to make productive use of land in order to meet the material needs of families and communities.[30] Failure of such would deprive them of the right to claim ownership of the land, and further, to justify the abandonment of the land for more satisfactory economic conditions.[31] Therefore, the settlement of the people is reflective of a conditioned perspective towards the "territorial" right of the people and the ruler. For the people, their pursuit for better economic conditions and a more prosperous future, together with the inertia and unwillingness of rulers to perform virtue and humane governance, justifies the flow of the population between places. In this context, the concept of borders should be interpreted in a way that is distinctive from and opposed to that in the Westphalian system. Borders should be porous, and people have the right to move to places where their economic difficulties encountered in the original places could be redressed. To further refine the thought, it is a virtue for a gentleman to leave the homeland to seek benign foreign rulers, while the common people should have the right to flee from the tyrannical rulers.

Having said such, how could this brief sketch help inform the Chinese perspective of the South China Sea area, including the waters and land pieces, and of the later-consolidated claims?

Yet before delving into recasting the Chinese perspective of the South China Sea in the Confucianist territorial discourse, it is worth considering the Southeast Asian perspective. This helps to reveal opinions from local people and dynasties in Southeast Asia bordering the South China Sea.

III Recasting and refining: the South China Sea as a zone of contact

A *China's claim in the South China Sea was not sovereign in nature*

Elaborations of the Chinese concept of "border" and "territorial rights" in traditional Confucianism discourse help dispel the all too familiar myths of sovereignty veiling contemporary South China Sea issues. Indeed, the modern concept that sees littoral areas and adjacent maritime zones as spaces for both passive defence and active development, is a relatively late arrival. It was argued that not until after 1870s, in the face of Japanese encroachment along the southeast coast of China,[32] that the Qing government in Beijing had learnt about the modern concept of how "maritime" concepts and relevant affairs should be construed, planned and implemented.

Responding to the Japanese invasion of Taiwan in 1874, the Qing government heard appeals for a new strategy of coastal defence.[33] Instead of the recognition that western countries had possessed great powers that cast unprecedented threats to the survival of China, it further suggested that the major battlefield had already moved from the northwest to the southeast coast. The threat to China from the seas had been much more serious than the invasion over land borders as culminated in sum in previous dynasties.

Under the threat from both contingent clashes in the southeast coast and critical situation in northwest defence, the Qing government adopted a dual track when strengthening its border defence policies, when capable military personnel and financial resources were devoted to the northwest terrain and southeast coast. In 1888, the Northern Fleet was formally established, deemed as a revelation to Chinese and foreign naval personnel, which was then one flagship naval fleet among East Asian navies. Its success had become a nine-day wonder, as the First Sino-Japanese War in 1894 to 1895 quickly brought a tragic end to its transitory blossoming. This defeat by Japan marked a watershed moment of the ultimate collapse of the Sino-centric tributary system, which had actually been dwindled steadily since the First Opium War in 1842. This failure was also deemed a revelation of the real thorns in the flesh in China's efforts of maritime development, namely anachronistic maritime concepts and out-of-touch of policy-making and strategy-manoeuvring.

Put succinctly, two characteristics featured in the failure of imperial China's first attempt in naval wars in modern era. First, the Qing government had not changed its traditional land-based mindset when dealing with maritime affairs. Even those who positively advocated coastal defence still stuck to the rather outdated coastal defence concept as a replication of that in the Ming Dynasty. For them, there was naval coastal defence, but no naval battles. In this logic, they paid much attention to coastal defence and security, seeing the navy as one means for territorial protection, but not for a prosperous outlook for maritime expansion and blue-water projections. As such, it is fair to say that the Qing government, even these allegedly heralding figures, had actually no positive sense of sea power, and of how China would continue to be out on a limb, should this maritime dimension be shrugged off consistently. In a nutshell, the Qing government had viewed the Northern Fleet as a means of coastal defence on the one hand and, on the other, the demonstration of China's national glory and the self-perceived superiority, as the overlord suzerain country in the region.[34] Put poignantly, this Northern Fleet served as a placebo, bringing transitory images to the war-torn country of an ostensible revival of China's imperial glory.

This first observation brings us to the second relevant point, that the Qing government had viewed the renovation of naval capabilities and revolution of naval policy-making as an isolated issue, to which it applied a static approach. Because the personnel in policy-making level, let alone those in the front line of deployment, had not developed a clear understanding of the grandeur arising from the growth of maritime competition, the coastal defence construction was limited to an instinctive reaction to western powers' gunboat policy, so it consisted mainly of low-level military and defence measures. It was not surprising that the whole process had been passive, negative, and short-sighted. It was also expected that the Qing royal household had reallocated the naval funds for other purposes, such as renovation of royal garden and livelihoods, once it was convinced that naval construction was capable for coastal defence purpose, and more implicitly, for a showcasing of national prowess and glory. Poignantly, the defeat of the Northern Fleet in the First Sino-Japanese War (1894–1895) not only unravelled many institutional deficiencies in China's coastal defence construction, but also the limitations of its insights to maritime issues and naval strategic polices.

It was thus a fair observation that, even as recently as the turn of the twentieth century, that the Qing government (China) had yet to develop a clear understanding towards of the potential of maritime zones and the capacity brought about from prosperous outlooks in naval development and blue-water deployment. Absent these insights, would the Qing government have then developed the concept of sovereignty over the land pieces and maritime zones in the South China Sea? Put differently, would the observation that China had

16 *Under the colonial encounter*

long deemed the South China Sea land pieces and maritime zones a part of its territory be upheld, when its very original understanding/perspective towards its southeast coast and the South China Sea was mainly out of security concern and defence needs, with the overt lack of a management mindset and ambitions for further developments?

In this respect, two incidents should be considered to complete the picture. In 1909, the government of Guangdong province dispatched naval expeditions to the South China Sea and had landed on the Pratas Islands.[35] The Guangdong provincial government later established an agency in the Paracel Islands, which paved the way for further explorations.[36] Correspondingly, the Chinese people demonstrated unprecedented passions for naval affairs and advocated its construction.[37] In November 1909, people's consciousness of maritime affairs and naval construction had been awakened, prompting significant donations to support naval replenishing and renovation among all walks of life and even overseas Chinese. In particular, financial aid from overseas Chinese not only was directed to the governmental policy-making and the establishment of civil organizations, but also to encourage the booming of revolutionary forces that had long sought to redress the awkwardness and plights that had enmeshed China since the 1840s.

In this context, some argue that this is a rather opportunistic, yet expedient, application of the American naval theorist Mahan's Sea Power Theory.[38] On the one hand, Mahan's Sea Power Theory had been introduced to the Chinese, and more significantly, caught people's attention and directed the required resources for its application in solving the rather dire Chinese situations. On the other, it added a twist in Mahan's theoretic template by revealing that the possibility of a reversal of Mahan's historical trajectory could be actually vindicated, provided conditions met and situations required. In China's case, the merchant fleet preceded the naval vessel, which fitted into the Chinese reality, political uncertainty and military incapability.

It was this background of security concern and defence purpose that led some to argue that the dash line in the South China Sea originated therefrom, and thus should be regarded as a line for security and defence purposes.[39] Apparently, this line of thought had been lived well into the twentieth century, when China had undergone the first revolution and succession in 1911. The new Republican Chinese government was placed in a no less easier position in the turn of the twentieth century, when the imperialist presence remained forceful and threatening in the Chinese continent. What appeared to be different was that the Republican China had forged a clearer understanding towards the concept of its "sovereign terrain" and a strong adherence to sovereign equality and territorial integrity.

Notes

1 For many centuries, the "others" that the European had been encountered referred to the Greeks and Romans, then the Islamic Arabs and the Mongols. Later, for around five centuries, the "others" were the Ottoman Turks. One

commonality was that all these "others" were enemies constituting a direct threat to the Christian Europe.
2 Eric Wolf, *Europe and the People without History* (Berkeley: University of California Press, 1982), 386–389.
3 Craig A. Lockard, "The Western Winds of Colonialism, 1750–1914", in his *Southeast Asia in World History* (New York: Oxford University Press, 2009), Chapter 6, 93–117.
4 Ibid. Also, see, "Colonial Impact and Changing Fortunes, 1800–1941", in Lockard, *Southeast Asia in World History*, Chapter 7, 118–134.
5 See, notes 3 and 4.
6 This section provides a brief sketch of international cooperation and evolution of international law-making in international organizations. There existed efforts in the international community to help advance the development in maritime affairs, such as the Comite Maritime International and the Intergovernmental Maritime Consultative Organization. Yet a detailed discussion of such goes beyond the scope of this project. Nevertheless, the Southeast Asian countries, then colonies to various European imperial powers, and China, were largely excluded from this kind of international community activities.
7 These measures included high protective tariffs against manufacturers of its trading partners; subsidies to its inefficient industries; and monopolies and price-fixing in its domestic economy.
8 Paul M. Kennedy, *The Rise and Fall of the Great Powers: Economic Change and Military Conflict from 1500 to 2000* (New York: Random House, 1987); Arnold J. Toynbee, *A Study of History: Abridgement of*, vols. 1–6, D.C. Somervell (ed.) (Oxford: Oxford University Press, 1988); Oswald Spengler, *The Decline of the West*, Helmut Werner and Charles Francis Atkinson (ed. and trans.) (Oxford: Oxford University Press, 1991).
9 See Chapter 6 for more discussion.
10 For those evolved between European national polities and the Ottoman empire, rules regarding capitulations and mutual consultations with jurisdictions over their nationals were two examples. For those applied between European national polities and on the European continent, free movement and residence virtually without passports could be counted as two illustrating instances. See more at. Adam Watson, *The Evolution of International Society* (London: Routledge, 1987).
11 John C. Columbus, *The International Law of the Sea*, 6th ed. (New York: David Mckay, 1967), 457–463; Joseph C. Sweeney, "From Columbus to Cooperation – Trade and Shipping Policies from 1492 to 1992", *Fordham International Law Journal*, 13:4 (1989): 481–523.
12 Ibid.
13 See, note 11. The effectiveness mandate was vindicated by the display of a force sufficient to prevent access by sea to an enemy's coasts.
14 Convention for PROTECTION OF Submarine Cables, Paris, 24 March, 1884, 24 Stat. 989, T.S. No. 380.
15 See, Final Acts and Protocols of Proceedings of the International Maritime Conference, 16 October to 31 December, 1889, at 51st Congress, 1st Session, S. Ex. Doc. No. 53 (1890).
16 Few nations adopted the Rules enacted by the Conference, even though these nations were leading maritime powers.
17 This spirit of international cooperation had extended beyond, and could be said to encourage such, the realm of maritime trade and shipping. For example, the 2nd Hague Peace of Conference of 1907 dealt with the subject of naval warfare. See, L. Oppenheim, *International Law: A Treatise*, vol. 1: *Peace*, 8th ed., Hersch Lauterpacht (ed.) (London: Longmans Green & Co., 1955), 732–735.

18 *Under the colonial encounter*

18 International Convention on Safety of Life at Sea, 31 May, 1929, 50 Stat. 1121, T.S. 910, 136 L.N.T.S. 81.
19 A conference was convened in 1954 to deal with deliberate discharges of oil and oily mixtures from vessels operating within zones of the high seas in which such discharges would be prohibited. The convention thus produced went into effect in 1958. International Convention for the Prevention of Pollution of the Sea by Oil, London, 12 May, 1954, 12 U.S.T. 2989, T.I.A.S. No. 4900, 327 U.N.T.S. 3, entered into force on 26 July, 1958.
20 Patricia Clavin, *Securing the World Economy: The Reinvention of the League of Nations, 1920–1946* (Oxford: Oxford University Press, 2013); Susan G. Pedersen, "Back to the League of Nations: Review Essay", *American Historical Review*, 112:4 (2007): 1091–1117; Alan Sharp, "From Balance of Power to Collective Security? The League of Nations and International Diplomacy", in *Crossroads of European Histories: Multiple Outlooks on Five Key Moments in the History of Europe*, Robert Stradling (ed.) (Strasbourg: Council of Europe Publishing, 2006), 173–186; Francis Harry Hinsley, *Power and the Pursuit of Peace: Theory and Practice in the History of Relations between States* (Cambridge: Cambridge University Press, 1967).
21 In this project, "maritime issues" is not to be read in a general and thus broader sense, which includes maritime affairs management, rules of engagement, international law, policies and community practices. Instead, it will be used for legal and political elaborations in a stricter sense, covering mainly maritime rule-making and maritime territorial disputes.
22 Wolf, *Europe and the People without History*, 386–389; also, see James Warren, "A Tale of Two Centuries: The Globalization of Maritime Raiding and Piracy in Southeast Asia at the End of the Eighteenth and Twentieth Centuries", in *A World of Water: Rain, Rivers and Seas in Southeast Asian Histories* (Leiden: KITLV Press, Royal Netherlands Institute of Southeast Asian and Caribbean Studies, 2007), 125–152; Warren, *Pirates, Prostitutes and Pullers: Explorations in the Ethno-and Social History of Southeast Asia* (Crawley, UK: University of Western Australia Press, 2008).
23 Ibid.
24 For more discussions on China's border disputes and development in contemporary political and diplomatic contexts, see, Junwu Pan, *Towards a New Framework for Peaceful Settlement of China's Territorial and Boundary Disputes* (The Netherlands: Martinus Nijhoff Publishers, 2009); M. Taylor Fravel, *Strong Borders, Secure Nations: Cooperation and Conflict in China's Territorial Disputes* (Princeton: Princeton University Press, 2008); Allen Buchanan and Margaret Moore (eds.), *States, Nations and Borders* (Cambridge: Cambridge University Press, 2003).
25 Ibid.
26 J. Agnew, "The Territorial Trap: The Geographical Assumptions of International Relations Theory", *Review of International Political Economy*, 1 (1994): 53–80; M. Shapiro and H. Alker (eds.), *Challenging Boundaries* (Minneapolis: University of Minnesota Press, 1996); G. Otuathail, *Critical Geopolitics: The Politics of Writing Global Space* (London: Routledge, 1996).
27 Ibid., see "Introduction", in *Challenging Boundaries*, xvi.
28 See Pan, in note 24, also, Joseph Chan, "Territorial Boundaries and Confucianism", in *Boundaries, Ownership and Autonomy*, David Miler and Sohail Hashmi (eds.) (Princeton: Princeton University Press, 2001), 89–111.
29 See two classic Confucian texts, The Analects of Confucius and The Works of Mencius. Further, for the interpretation, understanding and elaboration of Confucian thoughts in contemporary discourses, see, Wei-ming Tu, "Confucius and

Confucianism", in *Confucianism and the Family*, Walter H. Slote and George A. Devos (eds.) (Albany: State University of New York Press, 1998), 38; Randall Peerenboom, "Confucian Harmony and Freedom of Thought", in *Confucianism and Human Rights*, W. Theodore de Bary and Wei-ming Tu (eds.) (New York: Columbia University Press, 1998), . . .; Daniel A. Bell and Hahm Chaibong (eds.), *Confucianism for the Modern World* (New York: Cambridge University Press, 2003).
30 Ibid.
31 This is vividly reflective of the basic logics of the Chinese emigration. Generally, the Chinese have demonstrated strong preferences and recognition towards their mother lands and Chinese culture. In the occasion when emigration occurs, it is generally because of the pursuit of a better life and more prosperous future.
32 The Japanese ambitious encroachment along the southeast coast of China was best demonstrated via two incidents in quick succession. The first was Japan's invasion of Taiwan (Formosa Island) in 1874, on behalf of Ryukyuan fishermen who looked to Japan for protection. The second was the annexation of the Ryukyu Kingdom by Japan in 1879.
33 Hongzhang Li, "The Memorial to the Throne on Coastal Defence Proposition [Chouyi Haifangzhe]" (1875), in *Li Hongzhang Collected Edition* [Li Hongzhang Quanji], vol. 2 (Haikou, China: Hainan Press, 1997), 825.
34 The Qing government had devoted great amount of financial sources to build the Fleet. With equipments purchased from western countries, the Fleet was deemed the first-class level naval force among East Asian countries. The Fleet had further cruised between Chinese coastal ports and around harbours in pan-Asian area.
35 Stein Tønnesson, "The South China Sea in the Age of European Decline", *Modern Asian Studies*, 40:1 (2006): 1–57; Brantly Womack, "The Spratlys: From Dangerous Ground to Apple of Discord", *Contemporary Southeast Asia*, 33:3 (December 2011): 370–387; Stein Tønnesson, "The Paracels: The 'Other' South China Sea Dispute", *Asian Perspective*, 26:4 (2002): 145–169; also, note 25, Tønnesson, *The South China Sea: Law Trumps Power: A Geographical Description of the Spratly Islands and an Account of Hydrographic Surveys Amongst Those Islands*, Clive H. Schofield (ed.) (Durham, UK: IBRU, 1995). Also, see the IBRU-Centre for Border Research website, www.dur.ac.uk/ibru/.
36 Shicun Wu, *Solving Disputes for Regional Cooperation and Development in the South China Sea: A Chinese Perspective* (Oxford, UK: Elsevier, 2013), 65–69.
37 Lixin Sun, "Chinese Maritime Concepts", *Asia Europe Journal*, 8:3 (2010): 327–338; Yifeng Zhou, "The Introduction to the East and the Influence of Sea Power Theory" [Haiquan lun dongjian ji qi yingxiang], *Journal of Historical Science* [Shixue Yuekan] 4 (2006): 38–44.
38 A.T. Mahan, *The Influence of Sea Power upon History, 1660–1783* (Dover: Mineola Press, 1987), 27.
39 Gungwu Wang, "China and the Map of Nine-Dotted Lines", *The Strait Times*, 11 July, 2012, p. A23.

2 Beyond territorial disputes
Maritime issues and the revolutionary China

I A revolutionary China and a developing Chinese sovereign consciousness

A *The failed attempt in the naval modernization*

The Qing dynasty replaced the Ming in 1644, and had not encountered serious threats from the sea. The Taiwan conquest in 1683[1] was one exception, which still had not provided enough justifications for investing in a modern navy, or to expand the maritime sector. For the first half of the Qing regime, overseas trade grew despite official bans and indifference from the central government. Booming overseas trading business had owed much to the extensive settlement of overseas Chinese in diaspora community in Southeast Asia. However, maritime communication was not received well in the central government, when a row of coastal defence and relevant policies were ordered in mid-seventeenth century.[2]

The 1683 Taiwan conquest shed light on how maritime policies were shaped by a continent-oriented mindset. On the one hand, within certain periods both before and after the Taiwan conquest, policies had much negated the importance of the coast as a battleground. Examples included the prohibition of sailings with unauthorized personnel and onboard resources and the ordering of coastal inhabitants to move inland. Even if the Qing government had established a naval fleet for coastal defence, this fleet appeared to be more an issue-driven institution, from which the central government had soon directed resources to other hot spots of crisis. The Qing navy had not remained on a war footing for very long after the Taiwan conquest in 1683, when the Qing government turned its attention to the land-based expansion of the Russians in northeast part of the Asian continent. On the other, the Qing expansion continued in the southwestern part, seeking progress to the Tibetan plateau and Turkestan. The terrestrial domain of the Qing empire had greatly expanded, as the Qing navy largely remained a coastal defence operation up to the eve of the First Opium War in 1842. The capacity and capability of the Qing fleet was used principally for defence against outside pirates and local marauders.[3]

Even with the enthusiasm of reform-minded intellectuals, the replenishment, renovation and establishment of a modern navy by the Qing government[4] had met serious tests – first in the Sino-French war from 1884 to 1885,[5] and second, during the first Sino-Japanese war from 1894 to 1895.[6] In the Sino-French war, the Fuzhou fleet was almost completely destroyed by the French vessel. Holding other fleets from running to the rescue of the French raid in Fuzhou fleet, China chose to settle the issue with negotiations. Despite a Chinese land victory over the French, the outcome nevertheless was bitter. Inter alia, one profound implication was the French annexation of Vietnam, which debilitated further the consistently withering Chinese tributary system, already at its last breath. The Qing government encountered another harsher strike in 1894, when the Qing and Meiji governments were quarrelling over the dominance upon the Korean peninsula, later escalating to formal hostilities between China and Japan. The war was ended with the evisceration of the North Fleet and the loss of senior commanding officials.

Lessons from these two maritime battles shed poignant lessons about the survival of Qing empire, and broadly, the transformation and modernization mission assiduously undertaken by this ancient civilization.

For one thing, even with technological and material advantages, failures of China in both the Sino-French and Sino-Japanese wars were traced with retrospective eyes, teleologically, back to the failures of the restoration attempt in the mid-1860s. Failures were mostly blamed on the institutional reform, and on the outcome of the learning of the political system among the Qing mandarin. Concerning the Sino-French war, the Chinese committed strategic errors in coordination among the four fleets as well as between land and naval forces during the war, information collection analysis in prewar periods, and negotiation misjudgement in postwar periods.[7] Even with more respectable armaments, technology alone was not the key determinant of the war outcome.[8] However, these institutional shortages had not been redressed efficiently and effectively in the aftermath of the destruction of the Fuzhou fleet in the Sino-French war. This inertia led to another landslide defeat of the Qing navy in the Sino-Japanese war of 1894–95, for which China had paid an enormous and resounding price. In essence, the Sino-Japanese war marked the collapse of the Sino-centric tributary system and the reversal of status of China and Japan. In postwar period after 1895, the meteoric rise of the confidence of Japan constituted a sharp contrast to its Chinese counterpart. Japan had proved to be superior in political and military leadership, governmental reconstruction based on a western template, and strategic manoeuvrability with modern navies. With the reversal of international statuses of China and Japan in both East Asia and at the international stage, it was at this critical moment that China had begun its century-long quest for an identity as a modern nation state, which seemingly has yet to be completed.

A second lesson poses a profound challenge to China. Implicitly, China's failures in these battles had shed reflective light on the relative underdevelopment of its maritime consciousness and ambitions. Succinctly put, it was not the maritime security, or even the integrity of a coastal defence that had been prioritized in the national agenda. Rather, it was how to reclaim authority in many areas then subjugated to western domination that was actually the key to the independence, integrity and superiority of the national sovereignty of China as a modern nation state. The extra-territoriality stipulated in allegedly "unequal treaties" served one example.[9] In other words, the Qing and later the Republican government had been trapped in a dilemma that both were left with only a nominal position as the Chinese sovereign, while the de facto sovereign authority was eviscerated by western powers, with the extraction of almost all economic and financial revenues. While being recognized as the sovereign authority of China as a modern nation state, the Qing throne and subsequent Republican government nevertheless played that role in name only.

Another example was the raid of the Fuzhou fleet in the Sino-French war, which showed not only a good case of the national sovereignty being hollowed out substantially, but also of the lack of knowledge of international law of war and experiences of practices of military activities.

In the Sino-French war, the Fuzhou fleet was almost quickly destroyed, in part due to the vagueness about whether war had been formally declared between the Qing government and French Indochina administration. This diplomatic nicety had allowed French war vessels to sail past the Min River defence and approach the Fuzhou dockyard unchallenged and unimpeded. In other words, without a formal declaration of war, the two would have no justification in blockading the navigational freedom of foreign vessels in inland waters by the Chinese continent. The "unequal treaty" regimes further added fuel to the fire, in the sense that the French had acquired inland water navigation concessions from the Qing government in the Treaty of Tien-Tsin signed in 1858.[10] An institution of formal hostility would debilitate the operation of these treaty regimes, depriving the French of such rights. Further, a war might also generate new opportunities for China, to readjust, via negotiations, diplomatic and political maneuvering, the imbalanced rights-and-obligations structures envisioned in unequal treaties.

It was in this context that the Qing government would not prioritize maritime security, and blue-water maritime strategy in its national agenda. Rather, it was the invalidation and abolition of these "unequal" bilateral treaties – and the entailed unfair concessions relinquished forcefully to western powers under them – that had priority in the national agenda of the Qing and later, the Republican government.

B Budding maritime consciousness at the turn of the twentieth century

The late Qing period and early Republican period – from 1916 to 1928 when warlords had carved up the Chinese continent – had not seen major achievements in building a modern navy or a clear sense of maritime consciousness and projection. Efforts to build up a modern navy were only successful on paper, including establishment of a national Navy Office, a better-organized training regimen and shore establishment, and standardized naval regulations in 1888. In other words, the Chinese navy, unlike its Japanese counterpart, failed to become a coherent national force.

The Republican government had not devoted much of its attentions to naval development, but relied almost entirely on ships left over from the Qing period. Given China's general political and economic disarray, no significant efforts were ever possible to advance the modernization of the naval force.

When boiling down to the micro-level, warlords that had occupied various regions in the Chinese continent also catalysed the chaos in Chinese naval disorder. Individual warlords occasionally made effective use of maritime units, but mainly to augment ground forces. It was in the late 1920s, around the time when the Chinese unification was achieved under the Chiang Kai-Shek leadership, when western observer rejected the allegation that the Chinese navy was a serious battle force.[11] It was suggested thereby that a steady deterioration in the discipline of the Chinese navy since the establishment of the Republic was discernible. Different units were under the control of various militarists. These maritime units were deemed private properties of these warlords, which made impossible a comprehensive maritime strategy for the country.

However, naval actions did occur, but mostly in inland waterways, such as rivers and canals. Many warlords used inland waterways for transportation, to building up military barriers, and as a lucrative source of revenue. But most of these episodes were of no significance as to stimulate coherent maritime thinking or navy building in China. This echoed the previous observation that without a national sovereignty secured in various key aspects, territorial integrity, as in China's case, would become empty and eviscerated. In other words, China was left a modern sovereign in name only.

In this context, two southward expeditions took place in 1909, two years before the Qing dynasty succumbed to the 1911 Xinhai Revolution.[12] This was the only positive interest shown in the islands in the South China Sea. Nevertheless, in the next three decades, China fell apart and was in no position to push through its claims upon these islands in the South China Sea through effective occupation or utilization.

These Chinese expeditions were intriguing, when a contrast was vividly demonstrated between European colonial powers in Southeast Asia (which had shown a lack of interest in these rocks and islands in the South China Sea) and the relatively keen Chinese sovereignty pursuit. A more panoramic view of the regional context is required; in particular, a sketch of these colonial powers' strategy and measures in the South China Sea helps fill in this information gap.

II Maritime consciousness: budding and transforming in the early twentieth century

A In the European colonial context

In the nineteenth century, the South China Sea was a condominium of European colonial powers, which hosted the Portuguese, Spanish and Dutch in a premodern pattern, and the British and France on a new template of modern sovereign states. The former pattern was centred on trade among port cities, local principalities and great trading countries in the north and west, China and India. During this period, business and political interactions were heavily tinged with pre-modern local customs and practices, with trades, a consensus shared among residual colonial powers. However, maritime communication was not guaranteed, although all had committed major undertakings in intra- and interregional trade. Rather, the legal contestation for "freedom of navigation" was held by latecomers, the Dutch, to liberate the maritime routes controlled by the Portuguese and Spanish.[13]

Together with the concept of sovereignty and territoriality, the distinction between land and sea was made. Briefly sketched, the sea was to open to all, while the lands came under the rule of these colonial authorities. What had been, and largely reasonable, was the land features scattered around the great swathes of waters. There had been rare considerations, except the perceptions viewing these islets as impediments to navigation safety. In an era when the concept of national sovereignty was still budding, and when applications of international law to these non-Christian and non-Western local principalities remained disgracefully contested, the importance of the South China Sea was threefold:, that maritime power was mainly volatile, but improving, that the region had seen a confluence of external and local hegemonies, as presented in business patterns when production and commerce were mainly intrinsically confined to local produce and raw materials. The last but not least denotation of the South China Sea was that it was seen as a source of danger.

The British and French later joined this condominium and had reshaped regional terrestrial and maritime order on a new template of national sovereignty. While large portions of the terrain fell mainly under the grip of either the British or French, the Southeast Asian mainland and, to a lesser extent, maritime spaces were redrawn and remapped with "boundaries" and "border lands".[14] In effect, the terrain of Southeast Asia, was carved and marked by boundary lines that defined the different domains under the Britain, France and Kingdom of Siam.[15] These boundary lines were to delineate, in a definite way, various spheres of influences of colonial power and local kingdom. In other words, these lines were to define their various colonial domains and to delineate in a clear way their sphere of interests. In this sense, these boundary lines were mainly marked for colonial power domain and border security, which served the interests of the metropole country and colonial authority. Instead, these lines on the terrestrial domain were less for border control management, which would take into account the local conditions in a true sense. It was in this sense that these boundary lines had been tinged with a conflicting character, and a denotation of boundary skirmishes and territorial disputes.

On the sea, these denotations became more complicated and less obvious, due to the underdevelopment of maritime technology and communication. Human movement on the sea had remained scant and largely depended on small islands and rocks sporadically scattered on the great swathes of water. However, these islands and rocks remained uninhabitable, without a consistent supply of fresh water and basic conditions to realize sustainable human activities. Types of human movements were also limited, as fishing, maritime traffic for inter- and intra-regional trades constituted two main groups. In other words, without frequent human transgressing, there aroused few chances for conflicts over the proprietorship of these small islands and rocks. Without the advancement of technology and equipment for maritime communication, these small islands and rocks only lived in the logbook of fishermen, and had been marked as "dangerous grounds" that ships needed to avoid when sailing through the area. In this context, it was within expectation that the boundary concept would not be applied to maritime spaces, in any sense and at whatever manifestation. The approach stipulated in the Law of the Sea convention for maritime zoning only emerged relatively late in the twentieth century, and when all conditions required were duly satisfied.

On the other hand, it appears to an urgent matter that this "boundary" and "border land" concept now be re-contemplated and refracted on the utilization of maritime spaces. For one thing, only via cooperation among all those holding stakes in the South China Sea would guarantee the most efficient management of maritime affairs. Waters flow and fish swim. In other words, maritime boundary allocation and delimitation may turn out to impede the management process, and cancel off the aspired outcome. Accordingly, intra-regional cooperation would require, to a considerable extent, abolishing maritime boundaries. Meanwhile, the concept of "reasonableness" of claimant countries' behaviours is needed, with an array of determinants duly established. It is only in this way that the real issue – the resource competition, overlapping of claims to maritime zoning and entailed exclusivity of these claims – in the South China Sea can be effectively dismissed, with interests benefitted all those in this region.

B The Chinese claim as a hedging tactic against the Japanese pursuit for an international status

Previous discussions reveal the paradoxical effect of the application of "boundary" and "border" in the scenario of maritime affairs in the South China Sea. Even with the advent of advanced technology, the primary concern in this region remained still maritime traffic for trade and communication. Yet, the whole hydrographical and geographical environment continued to pose considerable dangers to maritime traffic, which significantly had impeded the progress of maritime resource exploration. In other words, exploration and development of maritime resources had not been and could not become the most important concern in the colonial administration, due to realistic limitations.

It was in this environment that colonial administration authorities in this region had shown no keen interest in further development of maritime resources in the South China Sea. One rare example was in the 1870s, when a group of merchants in northern Borneo obtained a concession from the British governor of Labuan to exploit guano on Spratly and Amboyna Cay. These business outreaches had led to formal territorial claims by the British crown claimed in 1877. This was the first-ever territorial claim in a modern sense laid upon these islands and rocks. It was recorded that from 1891 to 1933, the Spratly Islands and Amboyna Cay of the Paracel Islands were mentioned annually in the annual list of the British Colonial Office list. Nevertheless, the British governor of Labuan had done little to demonstrate British sovereignty.

It was at the turn of the twentieth century that changes of power structures and balances had set in, when two additional actors joined the colonial competition in the South China Sea. The U.S. took the Philippines by defeating the Spanish in 1898 and Japan acquired Taiwan (Formosa) after the First Sino-Japanese War 1894–95. This power condominium contained the Britain, France, Netherlands, Japan and the U.S.A.

Generally, the five powers had demonstrated no keen interest in the South China Sea. Britain, France and Netherlands had established and focused on colonial administrations and their interactions with China, while the other two, Japan and U.S., had also directed their eyes on mainly trade with China. It was not until after the 1930s that certain moves towards these rocks and islands were triggered by expansive ambitions of these powers. Inter alia, the Japanese example drew a picture with polarizing differences from other powers. Put tersely, it was one Japanese "China Dream" that had motivated and justified its expansive ambitions in pan-Asian area, with the South China Sea a nodal point of its dramatic encounter with the western colonial powers.

Japan's pursuit for a national identity: the South China Sea as a litmus test

After acquiring Taiwan (Formosa) in 1895, Japan's power was enhanced step by step at the turn of the twentieth century. Beginning with its alliance with Britain in 1902, a victory over the Russian navy in 1905 and the annexation of Joseon in 1905, Japan's efforts culminated in the First World War, when it made a judicious choice by standing with western allies. However, even by defeating a traditional Asian power, the Qing Court, and one European imperial power, Russia, Japan found itself been bitterly rejected from the club of the top rank in the power condominium in Asia. This was reflected in the 1920s, when power relations among them were regulated at the naval conference in Washington and a later generated convention. The number of ships and tonnage allocated to Japan was far lower than traditional European powers, such as

Britain and France. However, another new member, the United States, was granted equivalent status in terms of ship numbers and tonnage with Britain. In other words, Japan came out as a loser, diplomatically and militarily, by being forced to relinquish its newly obtained territorial possession in China, the Liaodong Peninsula, and to restrict room for its naval development.

The result had much confused and angered the Japanese, arousing resentment against its western imperialist counterparts, which later also triggered the booming of an Asianist ideology. This ideology had put Japan in the forefront and also the centre of a struggle against Western domination in Asia, by adopting an array of policy instruments to further its advancement. Militarily, Japan adopted a chauvinistic expansive approach, by which the right-wing had dictated the prewar policy-making in Tokyo. This right-wing tendency had overshadowed the Japanese politics, thus leading to a highly militarized mindset in Japan's overall national policy-making. Economically, Japan actually had tried to improve its position mainly through a modern production-commerce approach. One strategy was to develop projects to exploit guano from reefs and islands in the South China Sea. Its newly acquired colony, Taiwan (Formosa), served one expedient base for this southward expansion. After the world economic recession of 1929–30, which also hit Japan hard, Tokyo shifted to a military-themed expansion, as shown by the occupation of Manchuria in 1932, and the Second Sino-Japanese War from 1937. This thriving military expansion projected a crisis in the South China Sea, so as to trigger a row of reactions from colonial capitals to stem this tide of Japanese expansionism.

The Japanese expansionism stirred up the waters in the South China Sea, driving France to claim the Spratly and Paracel. Different from the first attempt in 1890s,[16] while some Frenchmen had proposed to erect lighthouses and make sovereign claims on these islands, the fears towards Japanese expansionism had driven the French formal claim, finally being substantiated, in 1930–33.[17] The French also took possession of some islands in the Paracel group. Britain had stayed in communication with France regarding the new development in the South China Sea, and chose not to oppose the French claim.[18] Britain did not pursue its own claim made in 1877 either. This nevertheless should not be deemed an abandonment of its claim. However, both Britain and France had agreed, although the consensus being archived and kept confidential, that China would have a better legal position on these islands and rocks against the Japanese encroachment. The Republican Chinese government had fallen apart due to regional separatist forces and warlords, and was not in a position to uphold its claim. The French Foreign Minister had not registered opposition from then Republican Chinese government.

After Japan waged the Second Sino-Japanese War in the 1930s, its southward expansion had become substantially felt in the South China Sea once it acquired Hainan Island. A military base was established in the Spratly Islands, and the administration was placed under the Governor General of Taiwan. These Japanese moves set in motion the already brewing hostility between western powers and

Japan. Southeast Asia soon became enmeshed in dense fights, turning the South China Sea into a sea of war and conflict for coming years.

This sketch of the Japanese move in the South China Sea since the late nineteenth and early twentieth centuries shows that the South China Sea had not been brought to the front burner until the 1930s. In other words, territorial competition had not emerged since the very beginning when the South China Sea entered into sailing diaries of local people and official gazettes of western colonial powers. Furthermore, the nature of the dispute was not rooted in a competition for territorial rights, but more as a conflict of interests and of the possible overlapping of their zones of influences. In other words, disputes in the South China Sea reflected the inherent egoistic character of imperialist colonialism in foreign lands. Such colonial administration would show the predilection for a cost-saving pattern of dispute resolution, which relied on use of force, political and strategic tactics, and aimed at serving the interests of European ruling classes in colonial capitals, but not people residing in local communities. The pattern was generally provocative rather than conciliatory, destructive to the societal environment in the long run, with short-term resolutions imbued with issue-driven considerations.

To some extent, this echoed one phenomenon that, generally speaking, disputes in Southeast Asia, when tracing their origins back to colonial era, had demonstrated a high degree of over-politicization, at whatever manifestation. In other words, these territorial disputes were not a socialization outcome of intra- and inter-communities exchanges in the region. Rather, they were the result of the rupture of the political, societal and cultural orders of local communities imposed by colonial rulings. These disputes were thus refractions of a distortion of the evolutionary process of the local order. It was in this sense that colonial rules were deemed to be destroying old processes of cultural interaction, as new patterns of economic activity and boundaries were drawn to suit the needs of European colonial administration. Poignantly put, colonial rules had destroyed ancient economic and cultural relationships, replacing them with extra-regional economic, political and cultural alliances and dependencies.[19] Historical arguments and nationalistic sentiments thus emerged in local communities at a later stage, as what were necessary in order to overthrow/eliminate the suppressive colonial administration. In a reasonable sense, disputes now vigorously debated in the South China Sea scenario were not legal in nature, as their judicialization would not be acquired until the adoption of the Law of the Sea convention in 1982. In this sense, the revelation was that judicial means may help to thaw the tension in due course, but should not be overemphasized. In other words, over-judicialization of the South China Sea issue would not help in crafting peaceful resolutions, in any sense.

It could also be argued from one perspective that the Japanese move had managed to create a pan-Asian regional order, to break the fetter imposed thereupon by western powers. In this sense, it represents another type of struggle different from the Chinese one.

The two struggles nevertheless both represented Asian countries' continuing struggles against western suppression. The Japanese struggle was no easier than the Chinese one. If the Chinese effort was for due survival, to reconstruct the country based on the western template of a modern nation state, the Japanese one would be for the meaningful presence of the country in the international community dominated by western powers. In short, the Chinese efforts were for the survival of the people, country and civilization from a total demise, while the Japanese were for an ascendency of the physical survival to a respectable presence that acquired corresponding respects and due regards. Under this context, a modern Japanese nation state turned to pursue wars to realize this goal. Precisely, the Japanese were persuaded that a modern nation Japanese state, with respectable national prowess and armaments, could only earn due respect from western counterparts via a more grandeur scale of predation and military expansion. In other words, war served one most effective and efficient way for the demonstration of national capability.

It was in this context that the South China Sea had been put in the frontline of conflicts, and had been turned into a sea of conflict. Until the end of the Second World War, the South China Sea issue had not been catalysed further, with which heavy tinges of sovereignties and territorialities remain a separate category of considerations. Yet, with Japan's defeat in the war, it was fair to say that the Japanese effort in its pursuit of establishing an identity of a modern Asian state had failed. In this sense, both China and Japan shared similar bittersweet experiences, despite their assiduous efforts. Both also shared one commonality that they had started another arduous journey, in pursuit of this yet to be finished quest for a national identity as a modern independent Asian sovereign in post-WWII era.

III Becoming territorialized: international treaties and the South China Sea disputes

General context

Between the late nineteenth century and 1945, China had not shown any interest in launching sovereign claims in the rocks and islands in the South China Sea. The country was imbued with a series of revolution, warlord separatist forces, the Japanese invasion (the two Sino-Japanese wars, 1894–95, 1937–45) and civil conflicts. Even if the French occupation in 1930s had aroused public attentions which thus pushed the Republican government to heed the South China Sea issue, China was not in a position to uphold and implement its sovereign claims. The Chiang-led Republican government was defeating one warlord after the other, which in due course had created a government with a legitimate claim to represent China as a whole. Along with this gradually converged unification process, the South China Sea tension due to Japanese expansionist movement did arouse intellectual interests. Beginning in the 1930s, efforts to conduct hydrographical surveys and cartographical studies were rife, leading to the first map depicting these land features in a general way.[20]

Limited by underdeveloped technology and scant equipment, these land features were classified under four general groups: the Pratas, Paracels, the Macclesfield Bank and Spratly Islands. Yet the Republican Chinese government had not made sovereign claims until the end of the Second World War. In 1947, naval fleets were sent by the Republican government to reclaim its sovereignty over these islands, and to erect monuments acclaiming sovereignty contestation.[21] It was also for the first time that the Chinese government had made sovereign claims officially and openly in the South China Sea. The Chinese efforts were later re-confirmed in the Treaty of Peace with Japan in 1951, which had started to remould the nature of the South China Sea disputes as sovereign and territorial.

The trend of territorialization of the South China Sea disputes in postwar era

It was not until the end of the Second World War that local indigenous people in this region had started to reinterpret/retrofit these foreign concepts, sovereignty and territorial rights (territoriality), through local practices. European powers had loosened their controls and eventually declined in the region. Meanwhile, local communities had succeeded in gaining self-governance and independence respectively in the next two decades. This shifting geopolitical context then set in motion a process of transformation of the disputes in the South China Sea, a transformation that saw these disputes becoming tied to the formation of modern nation states in Southeast Asia. In other words, these disputes have, in one sense, served evidentiary effects for state-building and identity-formation of the involving Southeast Asian claimant countries. It was under this context that a trend of "territorialization" of the South China Sea disputes is taking place. The process has continued to the present day. The China-Philippine arbitration serves one critical nodal point in this regard.

This process had begun with the Treaty of Peace with Japan in 1951[22] (also known as the San Francisco Peace treaty, SFPT, or the Treaty hereafter), which formally ended the state of war between Japan and the international community. Among claimant countries involving in the South China Sea disputes, only the Philippines ratified the Treaty and became a member.[23] The two Chinese governments (The Republic of China in Taiwan and the People's Republic of China in China) were not invited. The Republican government in Taiwan later negotiated a separate peace treaty with Japan in 1952,[24] in which the treaty text had echoed that of the San Francisco Peace Treaty.[25] Other claimant countries were yet to become independent sovereign countries and had remained one component of the British colonial empire in Southeast Asia. Vietnam was soon enmeshed in a row of wars, first against the French (1946–1954), and then civil wars later catalysed into a proxy of the East-West confrontation in the Cold-War context.[26]

Malaysia had begun its independence process, with Singapore, Sarawak and North Borneo merged into or separated from the Malaya Federation. This process was completed, in name, in 1965, when Malaysia solidified its contemporary sovereign domain after several episodes of territorial session and annexation.[27] China was in a similar process, albeit a prolonged one which has not yet come to a complete stop.[28]

These developments show that countries in Southeast Asia involved in the South China Sea disputes were in a process of state building and identity formation in the postwar era. European colonial powers had declined, yielding room for local indigenous people to realize their pursuit and aspiration for independent state- and nationhood. In due course, territory had been deemed one quintessential element in their quest. For one thing, territory is one of four criteria for modern statehood, and has been enshrined in the 1923 Montevideo Convention.[29] A second reason is that territory has been elevated to be one parameter used to gauge national prowess with which corresponding international status is granted. Territorial acquisition thus becomes indispensable for the establishment of modern statehood, which in turn implies the monopolization of enjoyment of natural resources. Territorial right is also deemed a critical dimension of the realization and vindication of sovereignty of national government. In this context, territorial acquisition becomes one crucial dimension in the efforts of these Southeast Asian claimant countries in vindicating their South China Sea claims. This is where the trend of territorialization started.

Since the Law of the Sea convention (the Convention) was enacted in the 1980s, this territorialization trend has got further substantiated. On the one hand, a set of rules was established, so as to regulate the development of maritime resources in a more effective and efficient way. Creating a sui generis legal regime in maritime affairs, the Convention has premised its operation on either an intentional distance away from disputes of territorial/sovereign attribution, or as a deference paid to other international judicial organs in charge of these territorial disputes. With this presumption, to enjoy maritime interests generated under the aegis of the Convention necessarily entails occupations of these rocks, reefs and islands in the South China Sea.

Undoubtedly, this trend of territorialization has a profound impact in Southeast Asia and the South China Sea region. In short, a transformation as such may prolong the quest for a unified national identity of these countries. By territorializing previous boundaries established by these colonial administrations, also known as the *uti possiditus* principle, border policies of these newly independent countries are likely to be misdirected, by emphasizing on maintaining "border security" instead of "border control". The former implies an exclusive manner with which boundary demarcation and delimitation constitute one most crucial aspect of the policies. Safeguarding of these boundaries necessarily rely on varying degrees of use of force or violent means, albeit within the constitutional parameters of the country. This border security concept is a refraction of colonial regimes, viewing border lands as spheres of interest to which an oversimplistic linear line is drawn to make a separation of spheres falling into different colonial governments. A boundary line cannot explain the ethnic interconnection in these border lands, nor can it dismiss ethnic complexity that easily arouses conflicts between these peoples. Instead it requires a concept of "border control" to better vindicate management of these border areas and boundaries. This may be one major reason why ethnic issues have continued to plague the Southeast Asian countries.

Applying this logic to the South China Sea, it appears even clearer that a border security concept would not help solve the quarrels. These disputes have distinctive connotations. For countries such as China and Vietnam, these disputes are more of territorial in nature, with strong sovereign implications. In other words, China and Vietnam have deemed the South China Sea disputes constituting a crucial nexus in their identity-re-formation task. On the other hand, the Philippines [and Malaysia?] may have weighed these disputes more on the practical interests they entail. Fishery harvest and mineral potentials under the continental shelf may play a critical role in driving Manila and Kuala Lumpur to sustain their wrestling in the South China Sea. It is under this context that with varying aspects being emphasized by these claimants,[30] the intractableness of the South China Sea disputes is vividly demonstrated.

Paradoxically, all od these claimants share an emphasis on territorial rights over these rocks and islands. In other words, territorialization becomes a trend upheld unequivocally by these claimant countries, albeit with their different raison d'être and policy discourses.

IV Concluding remarks

At the turn of the twentieth century, neither China nor Southeast Asian countries were in a good shape to take seriously these rocks and islands, their potentials and implications in the South China Sea. The failed modernization and political reform had significantly debilitated the establishment of a modern navy in China. Meanwhile, Southeast Asian countries were under colonial rule and could not make such claims on their own behalf, in any sense. However, this line of argument also indicates one misunderstanding, seeing the South China Sea disputes as of a territorial characteristic in nature. From the beginning of the colonial era, colonial governments had enacted their border and boundary-making policies in Southeast Asia on the basis of maintaining "border security", but not one of exercising effective border control. To vindicate border security, a simplistic boundary-making approach was adopted, turning territorial line/boundary line into a conflicting zone that entails inevitably devastating impacts on local settings. The South China Sea had long been deemed a dangerous ground, and a zone of contact between the influence of various colonial powers. However, neither the concept of "border security" nor that of separation of "zone of influences" fits well into this South China Sea scenario. These Westphalian concepts only turn the South China Sea into a sea of conflict. This border and boundary concept, along with their implications on this region, will be elaborated further in Chapter 7.

In the early twentieth century, no colonial power had demonstrated a keen interest in claiming these barren land features. China had done so in 1909, via two southward expeditions, but was not able to sustain it in following decades. It was mainly the Japanese expansionism that had alerted these colonial powers. In a sense, the Japanese expansionist movement in the South China Sea constituted a critical step in its efforts for a modern national identity and deserved respects from its western counterparts. The South China Sea measures of Tokyo should be understood from this angle.

It was not until the postwar era that a trend of territorialization has developed in the South China Sea scenario. For different reasons, claimant countries go for the direction that further territorializes the nature of their claims. China and Vietnam may view the South China Sea disputes as an important nexus to their continuing quest for a modern national identity. However, Malaysia and the Philippines have concentrated more on the maritime interests that can be generated from these land features under the Law of the Sea convention framework. Yet both uphold the trend of territorialization. One inquiry remains: has this territorialization had a positive or negative impact on the development of the South China Sea disputes? Put differently, how has situations in the South China Sea turned out under this territorialization trend? More fragmented? Or with threads for dispute management and resolution in the bud?

Notes

1 Christine Vertente, Hsueh-chi Hsu, and Mi-cha Wu, *The Authentic Story of Taiwan: An Illustrated History, Based on Ancient Maps, Manuscripts, and Prints* (Knokke, Belgium and Taipei: Mappamundi Publishers and SMC Publishing Inc., 1991), 96–110, 127–130; Arthur Hummel (ed.), *Eminent Chinese of the Ching Period* (Washington, DC: U.S. Government Printing Office, 1943), 108–109, 653.
2 John E. Willis Jr., "The Seventeenth-Century Transformation: Taiwan under the Dutch and the Chen Regime", in *Taiwan: A New History*, Murray Rubinstein (ed.) (New York: M.E. Sharpe, 1999), 84–106; also, John R. Shepherd, "The Island Frontier of the Ching, 1684–1780", in *Taiwan: A New History*, Murray (ed.), 107–132.
3 Peter Perdue, "Boundaries, Maps and Movement: Chinese, Russian, and Mongolian Empires in Early Modern Central Eurasia", *The International History Review*, 20:2 (June 1998): 263–286.
4 In the 60s and 70s of the nineteenth century, two movements were conducted inside China, in responses to the increasingly rampant imperialist invasion, the Tongzhi Restoration (1862–74) and the Foreign Affairs Movement. Yet, scholars have been in disagreements regarding the outcome and implication of political measures thus conducted.
5 Kwang-Ching Liu and Richard Smith, "The Military Challenge: The North-West and the Coast", in *The Cambridge History of China*, vol. 11, Late Qing, 1890–1911, Part 2, John Fairbank and Kwang-Ching Liu (eds.) (Cambridge:

Cambridge University Press, 1980), 202–273; Ralph Powell, *The Rose of Chinese Military Power* (Princeton: Princeton University Press, 1955), 36–50; Benjamin A. Elman, "Naval Warfare and the Refraction of China's Self-Strengthening Reforms into Scientific and Technological Failure, 1865–1895", *Modern Asian Studies*, 38:2 (2004): 283–326.
6 Ibid. Also, Allen Fung, "Testing the Self-Strengthening: The Chinese Army in the Sino-Japanese War of 1894–95", *Modern Asian Studies*, 30:4 (1996): 1007–1031; Richard Smith, "Foreign Training and China's Self-Strengthening: The Case of Feng-huang-shan", *Modern Asian Studies*, 10:2 (1976): 195–223.
7 See, note 5. Also, see Mary Clabaugh Wright, *The Last Stand of Chinese Conservatism: The Tung-Chih Restoration, 1862–1874* (Stanford, CA: Stanford University Press, 1957), 59–66. The author provides the most-detailed description of the Sino-French War in 1884–1885.
8 It is argued that not until the Sino-Japanese war of 1895–95, when the Japanese Navy decisively defeated the Qing navy, did the alleged superiority of Japan in modern sciences had been recognized among the Chinese and Japanese intellectuals and patriots. At that time, the Arsenal in Shanghai and Shipyard in Fuzhou (Fujian province) had appeared superior in science and technology to the Yokosuka Dockyard in Japan.
9 Dong Wang, *China's Unequal Treaties: Narrating National History* (Oxford, UK: Lexington Books, 2005), Chapter 2, 37–53; Fang Gao, "The Development of Unequal Treaties in Contemporaneous China" [Jinxiandai zhongguo bupingdengtiaoyue de lailongqumai], *Social Sciences in Nanjing*, 2 (1992): 18–28. Also, see, John K. Fairbank and Kwang-Ching Liu (eds.), *The Cambridge History of China: Late Ch'ing, 1800–1911*, vol. 10 (1978) & 11 (1980) (Cambridge, UK: Cambridge University Press, 1978 & 1980); John K. Fairbank, Denis Twitchett and Albert Feuerwerker (eds.), *The Cambridge History of China: Republican China, 1912–1949*, vol. 12 (1983) & 13 (1986) (Cambridge, UK: Cambridge University Press, 1983 & 1986); Roderick MacFarquhar and John K. Fairbank (eds.), *The Cambridge History of China: The People's Republic, the Emergence of Revolutionary China, 1949–1965*, vol. 14 (1987) (Cambridge, UK: Cambridge University Press, 1987); Roderick MacFarquhar and John K. Fairbank (eds.), *The Cambridge History of China: The People's Republic, Revolutions within the Chinese Revolution, 1966–1982*, vol. 15 (1991) (Cambridge, UK: Cambridge University Press, 1991).
10 Several documents known as the "Treaty of Tien-tsin" were signed in Tianjin (Tientsin) in June 1858, ending the first part of the Second Opium War (1856–1860). France, United Kingdom, Russia and the United States were the parties. These unequal treaties opened more Chinese ports (after Treaty of Nanking in 1842) to the foreigners, permitted foreign legations in the Chinese capital Beijing, allowed Christian missionary activity, and legalized the import of opium. *The Diplomatic History of China* (Taipei: The Commercial Press, 1972), Section 8; "Signing of the Treaty of Tien-tsin on 27 June, 1858", *People. com.cn.*, www.people.com.cn/GB/historic/0627/2083.html, last visited 10 October, 2015.
11 "The Chinese Navy", in *Shanghai Defence Force and Volunteers*, James C. Mulvenon and Andrew N. D. Yang (eds.) (Shanghai: North China Daily Herald, 1929), 1302.
12 Jianming Shen, "China's Sovereignty Over the South China Sea Islands: A Historical Perspective", *The Chinese Journal of International Law*, 1:1 (2002): 94–157; Teh-Kuang Chang, "China's Claim of Sovereignty Over Spratly and Paracel Islands: A Historical and Legal Perspective", *Case Western Reserve Journal of International Law*, 23:3 (1991): 399–420. Also, Xin Hua

Beyond territorial disputes 35

News, "Historical Evidence of China's Sovereignty Over the South China Sea", 30 October, 2015, http://news.xinhuanet.com/english/photo/2015-10/30/c_134767912.htm.
13 A Dutch scholar Hugo Grotius (1583–1645) made this argument in his work Mare Liberum (1609). See, Hugo Grotius, *The Free Sea*, Richard Hakluyt (trans.) (Indianapolis: Liberty Funds, 2004); Peter Borschberg, "Hugo Grotius' Theory of Trans-Oceanic Trade Regulation: Revisiting Mare Liberum (1609)", *Itinerario*, 29:3 (2005): 31–53.
14 See Chapter 7 for more discussions of concepts of "boundary" and "border land".
15 The Kingdom of Siam was the only Southeast Asian country that had not been put under colonial administration in the age when European dominated the region. It also exercised a territory diplomacy by which the central traded border lands for the security and safety of the capital area. See Chapter 7 for more discussions.
16 Anthony Carty, "Issues of Legal and Historical Method & the South China Seas Islands Disputes", in *Cooperation and Development in the South China Sea*, vol. 1, Zhiguo Gao, Yu Jia, Haiwen Zhang and Jilu Wu (eds.) (Beijing: China Democracy and Legal System Publishing House, 2013), Section 8.
17 Ibid.
18 Supra, note 16.
19 These arguments are constructed on the observation that a nineteenth-century technological revolution shattered traditional trade, technology and political relationships and in their place laid the foundations for a new global civilization based on Western technology. See, K. McPherson, *The Indian Ocean, a History of People and the Sea* (New Delhi: Oxford University Press, 1993), 200, 240–241; D. Headrick, *Tools of Empire: Technology and European Imperialism in the Nineteenth Century* (Oxford: Oxford University Press, 1981), 177.
20 See, note 12.
21 Ibid.
22 Conference for the Conclusion and Signature of the Treaty of Peace with Japan, San Francisco, California, 4–8 September, 1951, Record of Proceedings, U.S. Department of State Publication, no. 4392, International Organization and Conference Series II, Far Eastern no. 3 (December 1951), 391–404. Treaty of Peace with Japan (also known as the San Francisco Peace Treaty), 8 September, 1951, 3 U.S.T. 3169, 136 U.N.T.S. 45.
23 The participant Asian countries were either placed under colonial regimes, or had rejected to join and sign the San Francisco Peace Treaty. Among several signing countries, Vietnam, Laos and Cambodia signed under the direction of the French colonial government, Ceylon and Pakistan had signed either under the construction of the British colonial government, or as a newly independent country under strong influence of its original metropole country. India and Burma (Myanmar) had refused to sign the treaty. Indonesia later signed a separate peace treaty with Japan in 1958. A detailed picture of these Asian signatories explains the legitimacy issue of SFPT. In short, inquiries remained. Under the context of the enactment and signing process of the treaty, to which countries holding great stakes in regional peace-making and peace-building had had no roles to play, how should SFPT be evaluated?
24 The Republic of China government in Taiwan (ROC) later sealed a peace treaty with Japan in April, 1952. "Peace Treaty between the Republic of China and Japan", United Nations Treaty Series, reg. no. 1858 (1952): 38–44. This document can be read on the Taiwan Document Project online, www.taiwandocuments.org/taipei01.htm, last visited 15 March, 2015.
25 See, note 21.

36 Beyond territorial disputes

26 Craig A. Lockard, *Southeast Asia: World History* (Oxford: Oxford University Press, 2009), Chapter 9 and 10; Amitav Acharya, *The Quest for Identity* (Singapore: Oxford University Press, 2000), Chapter 2 and 3.
27 See, note 23.
28 Ibid.
29 The Montevideo Convention lists four basic elements required for statehood: (1) a permanent population; (2) a defined territory; (3) government; and (4) capacity to enter into relations with other states. (Article 1) This definition is so oft-repeated that it is duplicated, nearly verbatim, in dozens of cases, treaties, and tomes. The Convention also states that although the "political existence of the state is independent of recognition by the other states," such recognition may be explicit or tacit. (Article 3 & 7). The Montevideo Convention on Rights and Duties of States art. 1, 26 December, 1933, 165 L.N.T.S. 19 (1933) [hereinafter Montevideo Convention]. In recent years, scholars have criticized the definition, arguing it is both under- and over-inclusive and lacks analytical room for developments over the past few decades, such as rising concerns regarding self-determination. See Thomas D. Grant, "Defining Statehood: The Montevideo Convention and Its Discontents", *Columbia Journal of Transnational Law*, 37 (1999): 403, 435, 437, 449; Nii Lante Wallace-Bruce, "Of Collapsed, Dysfunctional and Disoriented States: Challenges to International Law", *Netherlands International Law Review*, 47 (2000): 53–54; Christoph Schreuer, "The Waning of the Sovereign State: Towards a New Paradigm for International Law?", *European Journal of International Law*, 4 (1993): 447–471.
30 This also explains the overt emphasis of historical arguments in China and Vietnam's claims, but not in Malaysia and less in Philippine's.

3 A neglected dimension in South China Sea
Fishing

I Fishing in South China Sea: is it an issue?

As discussed, the South China Sea had been turned a sea of conflict, a place where colonial powers had wrestled to expand their influence and to obtain maritime interests. However, a dimension that had attracted less attention was fishing. In company with the advance of fishing technology and navigation capability, countries with great fishing capacity frequently go around the oceans worldwide for better harvests. The rise of distant-water fishing and presence of foreign vessels in littoral countries' offshore waters has led to the argument that fishing has become a critical dimension of the exercise of sovereign rights of littoral countries. Put differently, fishing has become "sovereignized", providing evidentiary effects to the sovereignty claim of the country.

Fishing has a long history in the coastal area in East and Southeast Asia. Fishing technology and the associated industry have also developed consistently through this history. Yet fishing, as a local and traditional practice of littoral communities, seemingly has long been a neglected dimension in the discussion of the South China Sea issue.

Fish now constitutes a significant portion of food supply to worldwide population. The Asia-Pacific region sees a rapid growth of human consumption of fishery product, accounting around 10 percent of global catch used for diet purposes.[1] Fishery products remain an important source of protein supplies in this region, as bordering economies have witnessed astonishing economic growth and have shared a deep rooted sea food culture. Around 22.3 percent of public diet is from fish protein in Asia, while the number worldwide is 16.1 percent.[2]

A brief sketch shows that fishing stocks in the South China Sea confront multiple challenges, when overcapacity and illicit fishing constitute two major threats that catalyse the depletion of fishery resources in this region. Yet the South China Sea seemingly has depicted a distinct picture compared to the other two seas bordering the Chinese coasts, the Yellow Sea and the East China Sea. Unlike the relatively active fishing and maritime culture farming/harvesting in east coasts of China, the South China Sea remains a remote sea that entails higher risks and uncertainties. Instead of frequent usage by littoral communities along the Chinese coast, fishermen from regional Southeast Asian and extra-regional countries converged, sailed through and stopped by in these great swathes of waters. In this context, had fishing been or ever become an issue in the South China Sea, in any sense ?

A "Fishing" in the historical context

China's fishing industry has achieved unprecedented accomplishments in past three decades. The success is reflected in its growing harvest numbers and the escalating proportion of marine production in agriculture GDP.[3] Along with a rising capacity of resource development, it is also discernible that how frequently a common fishing run-in can turn into a crisis that may bring an entire region to its knees.

What underlies this phenomenon is the competition for marine resources among coastal countries. In recent decades, marine resources, like fish, have been held in high esteem not only as a source of food, but also a national asset that carries weighing symbolic meanings of national proprietorship and sovereignty. In other words, fishing activities can be deemed as having evidentiary effects, which serve to fortify coastal countries' sovereign proclamations and effective administration in designated areas. Accordingly, fishing constitutes a crucial dimension of effective control over certain waters by the claiming country, as marine resources are devoted for its exclusive usage.

In a nutshell, the right to resource utilization has now been perceived as a quintessential dimension of sovereignty claims in the contested maritime area. Among all the cacophonies, the transformation and development of fishing, as a right and an interest, merit discussions. One quintessential dimension is the dynamism wrought by interactions between fishing, and "sovereignty".

The trend that fishing has become one focal point in the resource competition in China's bordering seas is vividly demonstrated. This trend also reifies the burgeoning intertwining of fishing and sovereignty claims, which can be construed from two distinguished yet related dimensions. For one thing, China has regarded fishing as a crucial constituent to its maritime sovereignty claim. China's contention largely dwells on the long-practised fishing activities that can be traced centuries back in its longue durée of history. Accordingly, fishing, under the categorization of the right to resource utilization, constitutes one major portion of China's historical claim.

While western scholars remain sceptical about whether historical claims are in line with contemporary international law, Chinese intellectuals tend to defend the validity and legality of China's historical claims.[4] Zou Keyuan, in particular, makes a convincing point. Since there remains open in regulating maritime historical claims in the Law of the Sea framework, China's historical claim cannot be deemed as a violation to relevant international legislation.[5] This line of argument is premised mainly on the openness, or deficiency, of international law regarding historical rights and interests in various maritime spaces. Nevertheless, it is indeed true that the lack of well-established legislation and legal principles in this scenario will also lead to a counter-argument that China cannot establish a historical claim absent due authorization and recognition.

Another example to support China's historical claims in the East China Sea is a fishery dispute between China and Japan from 1925 to 1935.[6] The wrestling aroused, due to resource competition over yellow croaker between China and Japan, in fishing grounds off the Zhoushan Archipelago off the coast of China's Jiangsu and Zhejiang provinces. The Chinese government intervened, after urging from the Chinese fishing industry, by claiming a three-mile territorial water zone along the coast.

Yet the decline of inshore stocks had already drawn Chinese fishing boats well beyond the three-mile limit, where Japanese boats did not come to fish either. Worse off, the unequal power relationship between China and Japan clearly gave Tokyo the clear upper hand in this fishery dispute. Chinese efforts to exclude Japanese harvest from the market had failed. As a result, both Chinese and Japanese fishing boats were engaging in aggressive pursuit of large and small yellow croaker, which ultimately led to the depletion of stocks by the mid-1930s.

Therefore, changes in the marine environment nowadays become more likely to trigger diplomatic conflict, when marine resources become a common parameter for the competing countries. These geopolitical struggles would intensify processes of environmental change, and hamper ecological efforts at various national and international levels.

Besides the transnational ecological characteristics, nation-centred perceptions towards marine resources and the environment largely shaped this dispute. Of significance is that both China and Japan had a profound understanding of how marine resources are one vital means to their national pursuit of wealth and power. With this development-oriented goal in mind, a fishing dispute was transformed into a geopolitical struggle when political means were heavily relied on in due course of dispute resolution.

B A changing pattern: illicit and illegal, unregulated and unreported fishing (IUU)

The term illicit fishing is used to cover a gamut of fishing practices that cause harm to the overall marine fishery. It includes practices not permitted within current frameworks under national, regional and international regulations. Illegal, unregulated and unreported fishing (IUU fishing hereafter) fall into this category. Three different categories are generally referred: illegal, unreported and unregulated fishing. However, misusage of the term "illegal fishing" to cross-refer to different kinds of activities is not uncommon. There is also a blurring when identifying different activities in accordance with these terms.

Further, throughout passage of time when technology development profoundly changes traditional ways of marine fishing, there emerge fishing practices challenging existing regulatory framework at national, regional and international levels. Challenges as such can be depicted in various forms. There are new practices that cannot be classified and regulated under current regulational framework. There are also those which take place in areas where regulations, at different levels, are yet to be completely established. A third possibility exists, in the sense that certain areas are enmeshed in highly politicized issues leading to dysfunction or mal-governance of regional fishery business.

In South China Sea, all troubles converge. Malpractices of fishing activities and incapable governance cause irreversible harms and exacerbate the depletion of marine fishery resources, which further accelerate resource competition among regional countries. To the extreme, rivalry as such would overshadow the stability of regional maritime order. Facing the deteriorating marine environment, bordering economies are greatly burdened in upgrading existing fishery management mechanism at national levels. Regional cooperation is also significantly affected, eyeing the vociferous opinions and interventions from extra-regional stakeholder countries. So far, the outcome of redressing these challenges, at both national and regional level, remains murky.

There are several explanations to current achievements, patchy at best, in fishery management in South China Sea. Instances include delayed regional cooperation; incomplete and anachronistic national measures; more environment-prone public awareness at an embryonic stage; heavy marine transport involving foreign vessels; and complicated commercial and legal practices. Yet, one pressing threat that can be clearly identified is illicit fishing practices, among which the IUU constitute a major portion. In short, the lack of an overall, effective fishery management and the prevalence of illicit fishing including mainly IUU activities, draw a chaotic picture of fishery management in the South China Sea.

II Clarifying the concept: illicit and illegal, unregulated and unreported fishing

IUU fishing as a major threat to global fishery

IUU has been a major threat to global fishery resources, and has greatly burdened up coastal countries in achieving effective marine resource management in recent years. The definition of IUU fishing is promulgated by the United Nations Food and Agriculture Organization, which is then adopted by the International Plan of Action to Prevent, Deter and Eliminate Illegal, Unreported and Unregulated Fishing (IPOA hereafter).[7] It is never the intention of the IPOA to focus attentions solely on fixing illegal fishing practices. Rather, efforts are directed at establishing a comprehensive management mechanism. That said, fishing practices harmful to the environment that also obstruct ultimate management goal are certainly a major, but never an exclusive target. Hence, to identify fishing activities that fall into prohibited categories would help clarify the concept, scope and derivatively, implications of illicit fishing practices. Relations between illicit and IUU fishing will also be clarified so that accurate assessment and future projection can be made with more efficaciousness.

Definition: illicit fishing v. IUU

IUU fishing contains illegal, unreported and unregulated fishing practices:

1   Illegal fishing is activity:
    - Conducted by national or foreign vessels in waters under the jurisdiction of a State, without the permission of that State, or in contravention of its laws and regulations;
    - Conducted by vessels flying the flag of States that are parties to a relevant regional fisheries management organization but operate in contravention of the conservation and management measures adopted by that organization and by which the States are bound, or relevant provisions of the applicable international law;
    - In violation of national laws or international obligations, including those undertaken by cooperating States to a relevant regional fisheries management organization.

2   Unreported fishing is activity:
    - Which have not been reported, or have been misreported, to the relevant national authority, in contravention of national laws and regulations;
    - Undertaken in the area of competence of a relevant regional fisheries management organization which have not been reported or have been misreported, in contravention of the reporting procedures of that organization.

3   Unregulated fishing is activity:
    - In the area of application of a relevant regional fisheries management organization that are conducted by vessels without nationality, or by those flying the flag of a State not party to that organization, or by a fishing entity, in a manner that is not consistent with or contravenes the conservation and management measures of that organization;
    - In areas or for fish stocks in relation to which there are no applicable conservation or management measures and where such fishing activities are conducted in a manner inconsistent with State responsibilities for the conservation of living marine resources under international law.

This definition is premised on two concepts: the compartmentation of marine spaces and the actors conducting fishing activities. The compartmentation is to spell out to whom the resource utilization rights attribute. For delineation of maritime zones and utilization of marine resources, United Nations Convention on the Law of the Sea (UNCLOS) comes into play. It has segmented the sea into those under national jurisdiction of a sovereign country and those as open areas. In areas under national jurisdictions of coastal countries, there exist different extents of state sovereign controls. In territorial waters, foreign vessels enjoy only innocent passage rights. Privileges to foreign citizens and vessels are extended further to marine scientific research activities and all such with peaceful purposes. These activities are nevertheless premised on coastal states' authorization obtained beforehand.

In areas designated as open areas, or High Seas, two variants are factored in: the existence of regional fishery management organizations (RFMOs) and rules, and the nationality of fishing vessels. RFMOs may promulgate rules, guidelines or general principles that are binding or generating hortatory effect upon coastal countries. When rules are legally binding, it is thinkable that illicit fishing which used to straddle in grey zones without clear indication of its encroachment upon law will largely be brought into due regulation. In other words, it is easier, from the perspective of efficient management, to tell which are breaking the rules.

Nationality of fishing vessels also set in uncertainty upon management results. It would largely improve management outcome if coastal and stakeholder countries join these RFMOs. A hidden concern is vessels with no nationality or flying flags of fishing entities whose participations and obligations in relevant RFMOs are yet to be clarified. These outsiders are inclined to free ride on the opportunity to conduct illegal fishing that nevertheless returns with rewarding harvests. Flowing from the logic, a figure helps clarify possible types of illicit and illegal fishing.

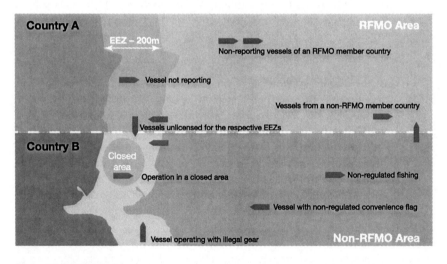

Figure 3.1 IUU Fishing

Source: The picture is from an online source, www.franciscoblaha.info/fisheries-comunication-and-extension/, last visited 6 June, 2016.

Source: Francisco Blaha, "EU Market Access & Eco-Labelling for Fishery and Aquaculture Products" (Osec publishing, Zurich: 2015), at 23. The document can be retrived from www.s-ge.com/sites/default/files/private_files/EU%20Market%20Access%20and%20Eco-Laberlling_0.pdf, last visited 21 July, 2016.

In sum, illegal fishing contains unauthorized activities in foreign EEZs, or in forbidden areas protected by relevant national laws. Other forms of illegality include fishing in contravention to gear/equipment requirements, without obtaining a license and the failure of fulfilling reporting obligations. Unreported fishing would also be considered as illegal, if national or regional fishery management authorities had mandated reporting as obligatory upon party members. In practice, illegal fishing generally will not be reported, leaving a great back figure when calculating total fish catch for purposes of enacting appropriate management measures.

Contrary to illegal and unreported fishing, unregulated activities appear to be relatively vague in terms of defining the scope, content and the actor involved. Vessels with no nationality, and those flying flags of States not party to RFMOs would be considered as fishing un-regulatedly in high seas when certain management measures are applicable therewith. Generally, these unregulated activities will not be reported either, as there exist no definite national and international authorities to which vessels should respond. Nevertheless, it goes without saying that these vessels would contravene international law obligations, provided that these rules and their legal bindingness are firmly recognized by the international community.

Having said such, the entanglement of the three concepts and illicit practices, in describing activities conducted could be charted as follows:

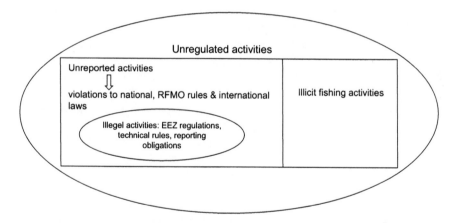

Figure 3.2 Conceptual Graphic of Illicit-IUU fishing
Sources: compiled by the author

The chart shows that despite illegal activities, there exists certain areas when management regulations are incomplete or yet to be established, leaving certain practices in obscurity in terms of its classification and corresponding management. The regulative vacuum can be one of the following: there exists no well-established regional fishery mechanism, let alone management regulation;

44 *A neglected dimension*

regional countries have not acceded into current regional and international fishery management regime; regional fishery mechanism cannot, for various reasons, effectively deal with IUU and devastating fishing (yet to be clear if it is also illegal) practiced by foreign vessels or ships with no nationality. Examples listed above are not exhaustive. For activities falling into these grey zones, they are termed "illicit fishing". It is yet to be clarified whether and to what extent these activities can be classified as illegal. Nevertheless, they have inflicted profound impacts upon the marine environment, ecology and the habitat in a negative way. The devastating effects thus generated are of little difference.

In following discussion, the term "illicit" will be used to refer to illegal fishing practices and those when regulatory parameters are yet to be well-established. In other words, the term is intended to cover as comprehensive as possible all types of IUU activities, and those with devastating effects world wide.

III Fishing in the South China Sea

Illicit fishing in the South China Sea

Fish landings are reported to reach 6 million tons, while considerable uncertainty continues to overshadow these reported numbers.[8] Marine fish constitutes an important protein source in East Asia, as an estimated 22 kg are consumed per person per year.[9] The comparative number for the world population is at an annual amount of 16 kg. The targeted fish are large, trophic spices such as tuna, billfish, mackerels and sharks, while reef fish, small coastal pelagic types and shrimps also make up significant percentages.

However, the status and future viability of fish stocks are not well understood. The biodiversity remained poorly studied. In early years, while some expeditions were indeed carried out by Chinese and Vietnamese scientists, the data were usually published in respective languages, or kept out of reach due to security and other miscellaneous concerns. Relevant UN bodies have made efforts to redress this deficiency when research projects and case studies are launched to familiarize the region and the international community with their common neighbour.[10]

Studies have shown that significant gaps exist in landing data which are not worth accreditation due to unidentified fishes, mostly due to illicit and IUU fishing. Yet, there are relatively few data that can accurately quantify and estimate the extent and costs of these activities. Up to the present, studies reported are generally based on subset topic of the region, such as spices and fisheries, economies or specific areas of water. In this sense, data show only piecemeal information that remains variable in terms of their credibility.

Bearing this in mind, a UNEP report indicates nevertheless provides some clues. It indicates that the steady increase from 600,000 tons in 1950s to over 6 million tons in 2004 is largely attributed to the landings of unidentified fish catch, constituting around two-thirds of the total landings in recent years.[11] It was concluded that there exists a high proportion of unidentified catch in landing statistics which sends wary signals of the deficiency of reporting system.

Despite the deficiency of data, reports point to Asia Pacific region as "hot spot" locations for illicit and IUU fishing, such as the Southeast Pacific, Northwest Pacific and Southeast Asia.[12] To further breakdown, the Sulawesi Sea, the east coast peninsular Malaysia, and the Southeast Asia in a general sense. In an effort to investigate the actuality of illicit and IUU fishing in the Asia-Pacific region, the APEC fisheries working group found that 80 percent of respondents (responses via questionnaires from Asia-Pacific region economies) replied that these controversial fishing activities took place in waters under their jurisdictions.[13] 66 percent of responses identify that migratory spices straddling through their waters and high seas are subject to these controversial activities.[14]

The region where illicit and IUU fishing occurs also varies. In the Southeast Asian waters where coastal countries' EEZ claims largely abut, a large portion of the illicit and IUU fishing falls within EEZ areas frequently involving foreign civilian and commercial vessels and local marine law enforcement agencies. In addition, a number of these boundaries overlap with each other. Clashes as such further increase the opportunity of illicit and IUU fishing in EEZ waters, but not in high seas.

As for the forms, illicit and IUU fishing occurs within EEZ areas by both domestic and foreign vessels. The most common form is with small-scale and industrial vessels. Yet, a range of illicit fishing practices can be identified:[15]

- use of prohibited gears and methods (dynamites, poisons, push nets...etc);
- unauthorized fishing in management zones;
- licence violations or unauthorized fishing violating moratorium;
- unreporting or misreporting of the catch;
- fishing unauthorized spices; landing in unauthorized ports.

Generally, countries have a better understanding of illicit and IUU fishing committed by domestic vessels. Regarding those involving foreign vessels, most of the reports and information available refers to illegal practices, rather than unreported and unregulated fishing. Yet, there are examples of these occurring. One sensible explanation may be that due to the largely abutting, even clashing, maritime boundaries in this region, it is less possible that fishing will take place in areas where, national or regional, rules and management measures can be applied. Thus, it is unlikely to see unregulated fishing happening in this area.

Despite the intricacy of the forms, the impacts are similarly devastating to the marine environment. A worrisome trend is the "fish-down" in the food web phenomenon as demonstrated also in the report.[16] As a prevailing situation in countries bordering the Sea, catch per unit effort in most fisheries has experienced a steady decline. A change in the major spices in the catch is clearly discernible. Further, loss of fisheries productivity has been identified as a trans-boundary issue, while most of the conventional species are on the edge of full and over-exploitation at the basin level.[17] The phenomenon thus described indicates severe exploitation, massive selective fishing pressure, and the loss of fishing productivity. Declining fish availability has led to destructive fishing practices by some fishermen in order to maintain incomes and food production in the short term. Fisheries trends suggest that production from capture fisheries will decline in coming years unless total fishing effort and capacity are reduced. The obvious problem in the reduction of fishing capacity is that most fisheries are small-scale with the majority of participants being highly dependent on fisheries for income, food and well-being.

IV Challenge ahead: fledgling regional efforts & disputed maritime boundary

Regional efforts in fishery resource management

Fish stocks in the Southeast Asian waters are threatened mainly from overfishing, illicit and IUU fishing. A deep seafood culture, along with developing economies and growing middle-class population, contribute to quick depletion of fishery resources in this region. For illicit and IUU fishing, it occurs mainly in the areas of the South China Sea, Sulu-Sulawesi Seas, and Arafura-Timor Seas.[18] Besides, even for legal fishing activities taken place in duly-designated areas, overfishing is prevailing. Generally, it occurs in offshore waters, where foreign EEZs areas are designated and maritime boundaries ye to be fully settled. Indeed, a high frequency of clashes in EEZ areas has been witnessed in this region. The phenomenon is reflecting the serious depletion of fish stocks in coastal waters which has become one common issue plaguing the region as a whole.

In this region, there are few examples of specific regional initiatives to address IUU fishing.

In May 2007, a voluntary instrument, the Regional Plan of Action to Promote Responsible Fishing Practices including Combating IUU Fishing in the Region (RPOA) was launched, and endorsed by Ministers from Australia, Brunei Darussalam, Cambodia, Indonesia, Malaysia, Papua New Guinea, The Philippines, Singapore, Thailand, Timor-Leste and Vietnam.[19] While the RPOA is not legally binding on these countries, it constitutes a platform to enhance conversations for better fishery resource management results in this region. A primer assessment is to identify information collection, and sharing and cooperation on Monitoring, Control and Surveillance systems as an initial priority.[20] Its target area is the South China Sea, Sulu-Sulawesi Seas and Arafura-Timor Seas. Australia and Indonesia also entered into a bilateral agreement for joint surveillance operations in the Arafura Sea in 2008.[21]

Other cooperation exists at a general level. The 40th meeting of the Southeast Asian Fisheries Development Centre (also known as SEAFDEC) in 2008, endorsed the establishment of a "Regional Advisory Committee for Fisheries

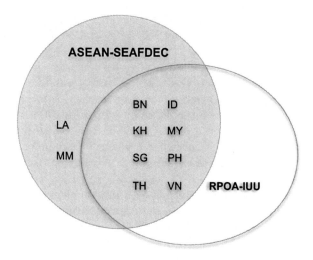

Figure 3.3 ASEAN countries and Regional fishery/IUU mechanism

* The blue circle refers to the mechanism of ASEAN – Southeast Asia Fisheries Development Center (ASEAN-SEAFDEC) Strategic Partnership. The white refers to the Regional Plan of Action to Promote Responsible Fishing Practices including Combating IUU Fishing in the Region (RPOA-IUU), which is a part of the international framework to combat Illegal, Unreported and Unregulated fishing. The alphabetical initials are member countries to these organizations.
* BN: Brunei; KH: Cambodia; SG: Singapore; TH: Thailand; VN: Vietnam; LA: Lao; MM: Myanmar; ID: Indonesia; MY: Malaysia; PH: Philippines. China is not in any of the three initiatives.
* The figure is modified by the author, from the information provided in Mery J. Williams, "Will New Multilateral Arrangements Help Southeast Asian States Solve Illegal Fishing?", *Contemporary Southeast Asia*, 35:2(August, 2014): 258–283, at 267.

Management in Southeast Asia (RAC) as a subsidiary body of the SEAFDEC Council.[22] The committee will assist SEAFDEC members to achieve sustainable utilization of fisheries resources through improved fisheries management for food security, sustainable livelihoods of the people, as well as economic development and integration in Southeast Asia. Its advisory opinions will be conveyed to the Association of Southeast Asian Nations (ASEAN) through the ASEAN Sectoral Working Group on Fisheries as well as other relevant agencies including the Coordination Committee of the RPOA.

Another example is an agreement at a more general level, a Sustainable Development Strategy for the Seas of East Asia, that includes a wide range of members, from ASEAN countries, to those in Northeast Asia, such as Japan and North Korea.[23] Among the plethora of issues, "equitable and sustainable fisheries and conservation of fish stocks" constitutes an important element to the overall strategy. Members had agreed upon various measures.[24] This action highlights the need for better and more integrated domestic fisheries management, greater cooperation with immediate neighbours and the development of alternative livelihoods for fishers displaced by more effective and sustainable management of marine resources.

It is telling that members in Southeast Asia have managed to pace up their efforts to address the common challenge of fishery resources management. ASEAN remains the centrality in more general agreements, despite many bilateral arrangements also exist between specific countries. As for China that possesses largest fleets and most powerful fishing capability, its role in this scenario is certainly not comparable to its overall overwhelming economic lures to the region. China has been consistently upheld the position that supports further ASEAN integration.[25]

In due course, the Chinese role would be with a supplementary idiosyncrasy when the centrality and focus falls on the ASEAN community itself. Chinese participation can be meaningfully implemented via joint activities with ASEAN, as in the case of the RPOA and the Sustainable Development Strategy for the Seas of East Asia. Another way is to vindicate Chinese contribution via bilateral agreements entered by China and ASEAN countries. The Chinese-Vietnamese agreement in managing maritime incidents serves exemplary effect.[26] It is believed that external patronization can be mostly appreciated and welcomed by ASEAN community, when resource competition and relevant tension have consistently escalated in recent years.

Despite the fruitful, albeit slow-paced, regional efforts, another issue that requires closer attention is the still brewing maritime sovereignty and delimitation disputes. The spats have been enmeshed in a malicious cycle, when all involved are now inclined to more hawkish positions without positive signs of compromise anytime soon in the future. The implication casts an ominous outlook for efforts in fishery resource management and marine environmental protection. In this aspect, China is the factor with second-to-none leverages. Its every move and interaction holds great momentum in not only the political scenario, which influences also the progress in environmental agenda.

Maritime boundary: a malicious cycle

Southeast Asia also witnesses a hike of maritime clashes in recent years, due to disputed and un-delimited maritime boundaries, unsettled sovereignty of islands and rocks, and unclarified maritime zoning by coastal countries.

Island sovereignty is of relevant importance to maritime delimitation, when current international Law of the Sea still prioritizes land-related entitlements. In other words, whoever wins sovereignty over islands will have the rights to utilize maritime zones and to block marine resources for their exclusive use.[27] Last but not least, the concept of utilization of maritime zone is far from complete settlement. Whether usages in relation to military-oriented or intelligence-related purposes are also at coastal countries' disposal remains a thorn in the flesh. A cleavage of the view can be clearly discernible in the international community.

The South China Sea serves an exemplary case study. The area is witnessing all three issues and the implication when these issues intermingle altogether. In short, disputed sovereignty attribution over certain islands and rocks impedes delimitation of maritime zones, which in turn confuses the limits for legal/ authorized fishing activities. The disputants are yet to make substantial progress in settling their discords on neither islands sovereignty, nor allowable activities in designated marine zones. Table 2 provides a snapshot view of how illicit and IUU fishing has tumbled up regional maritime order.

Table 3.1 Major Conflicts involving Chinese fishermen in the South China Sea 2008–2012

Date	Event
November 2008	A Chinese fishing vessel was hijacked by pirates armed with grenade launchers and automatic weapons off the coast of Kenya, which aroused strong indignation in China.
September 2010	The arrest of the captain of a Chinese trawler by Japan after a collision dramatically increased tensions between China and Japan over Diaoyu Island.
December 2011	A Chinese fishing boat captain stabbed two South Korean coast guards, killing one, which triggered intense tension between China and South Korea.
March 2012	One Chinese fisherman, believed to be fishing illegally off the Pacific island nation, was killed by Republic of Palau police officers and another 25 Chinese fishermen were detained.
April 2012	A fishing dispute involving Chinese fishermen who were accused of illegally fishing in the disputed area led to a serious maritime standoff between Chinese and Philippine vessels.
July 2012	36 Chinese fishermen were detained and two ships were seized after being fired upon by the Russian coast guard for entering an exclusive economic zone in its far eastern Primorsky region.
April 2013	The Philippines has charged 12 Chinese fishermen with poaching after their boat ran aground a protected coral reef in Tubbataha reef park, a UNESCO World Heritage site. The boat is the seventh Chinese fishing vessel caught in the area since 2002, according to a statement from the Tubbataha reef park.
May 2013	A Taiwanese fisherman was shot to death by the Philippines Coast Guard Police in an area where Taiwan and the Philippines laid overlapping EEZ claims. The dispute has extended on, when investigations are now conducted by the disputants in a cooperative manner.

(*Continued*)

Table 3.1 (Continued)

Date	Event
June, 2014	Chinese ships were accused of chasing and later sinking a Vietnamese fishing boat which was smaller in size.
	In May, 2014, Vietnamese and Chinese ships have been in a stand-off for a month after a Chinese owned oil rig, called Haiyang 981, was moved into waters claimed by both countries.
August, 2015	Indonesia sinks 34 foreign boats to curb illegal fishing. These vessels are from Vietnam, Philippines, Thailand, and Malaysia.

Source: edited by the author.

Accordingly, pending the final resolutions of the territorial spat, countries, including China, have promulgated relevant legislations regulating fishing activities and resource management issues. Despite the bona fide intention for better marine resources management, the existing inter-state mechanism is still fledgling and not ready to jump in to accommodate conflicting national laws and management measures. To mitigate the frequent confrontations between civilian vessels and national law enforcement agencies would be too demanding a requirement for inter-state agencies when they are still struggling for obtaining nominal legitimacy and practical enforcement resources. That said, territorial disputes catalyse the unilateralism of national behaviours in environmental protection and resource management, an unhealthy practice that may further exacerbate the depletion of marine resources in the area.

Fishing in the South China Sea has profound security implications. In a general sense, spillover effect on food security is devastating. The region would need to re-examine its current policies, and focus on securing the safety of fishermen, while insuring that their fishing methods would be in line with relevant international fishing regulations. In this aspect, knowledge of relevant international rules and prevailing customary laws, along with fishery legislation of coastal countries, would greatly ensure more satisfactory implementation outcomes.

In other words, due respect and attention not to commit egregious violations would be a sine qua non for the safety and legitimacy of fishing in the South China Sea. The depletion of fishery resource in the South China Sea is acute and irreparable. The problem is better dealt with before it becomes a reality. The area would need to start off cooperation on management of marine resources and environmental protection, before common assets being turned into common debts to the region and the mankind.

Notes

1 Will Rogers, "The Role of Natural Resources in the South China Sea", in *Cooperation from Strength: The United States, China and the South China Sea*, Patrick Cronin (ed.) (Washington, DC: Centre for A New American Security publication, 2012), 85–97.

A neglected dimension 51

2 Ibid., 90.
3 Ministry of Agriculture Bureau of Fisheries. *China Fishery Statistics Yearbook* 2011.
4 Keyuan Zou, "China and Maritime Boundary Delimitation: Past, Present and Future", in *Conflict Management and Dispute Settlement in East Asia*, Ramses Amer and Keyuan Zou (eds.) (Farnham, UK: Ashgate, 2013), 149–169; Nong Hong, *UNCLOS and Ocean Dispute Settlement: Law and Politics in the South China Sea* (Abingdon: Routledge, 2012), 73.
5 Hong, *UNCLOS and Ocean Dispute Settlement*, 70–71.
6 Micah Muscolino, "The Yellow Croaker War: Fishery Disputes between China and Japan, 1925–1935", *Environmental History* 13 (April 2008): 305–324.
7 Frank Meere and Mary Lack (eds.), 2008. *Assessment of Impacts of Illegal, Unreported and Unregulated (IUU) Fishing in the Asia-Pacific*, Sustainable Fisheries Management, Asia-Pacific Economic Cooperation Fisheries Working Group, 5.
8 K. Sherman and G. Hempel (eds.), 2009. *The UNEP Large Marine Ecosystem Report: A Perspective on Changing Conditions in LMEs of the World's Regional Seas*, UNEP Regional Seas Report and Studies No. 182 United Nations Environmental Programme. Nairobi, Kenya, 300.
9 Rogers, "The Role of Natural Resources in the South China Sea", 90; Ralf Emmers, "Resource Management in the South China Sea: An Unlikely Scenario" (paper presented at the conference of "Recent Development of the South China Sea Dispute and Prospects of Joint Development Regimes", Haikou, China, 6–7 December, 2012).
10 There are certain exemplary studies: C. Paterson and J. Perenttà (eds.), 2008. *Integrating Fisheries and Habitat Management: Fisheries Refugia in the South China Sea*, Reversing Environmental Degradation Trends in the South China Sea and Gulf of Thailand, GEF 885/UNEDP 248, 22 May, 2009. The report can be retrieved from www.unep.org/eou/Portals/52/Reports/South%20 China%20Sea%20Report.pdf, last visited 31 December, 2015.
11 Sherman and Hempel (eds.), *The UNEP Large Marine Ecosystem Report*, 300.
12 Meere and Lack (eds.), *Assessment of Impacts of Illegal, Unreported and Unregulated (IUU) Fishing in the Asia-Pacific*, 14.
13 Ibid., 15.
14 Ibid.
15 Ibid., 16.
16 Sherman and Hempel (eds.), *The UNEP Large Marine Ecosystem Report*, 301.
17 Ibid., 302.
18 Prospectus of FAO/APFIC Regional Workshop to Support The Implementation of The 2009 FAO Port State Measures Agreement, Food and Agriculture Organization of the United Nations, Fisheries and Aquaculture Department, 23–27 April, 2012. Bangkok, Thailand, 3.
19 Meere and Lack (eds.), *Assessment of Impacts of Illegal, Unreported and Unregulated (IUU) Fishing in the Asia-Pacific*, 64.
20 Ibid.
21 Ibid., 65.
22 Ibid.
23 Ibid., 66. Members are Brunei Darussalam, Cambodia, China, Indonesia, Japan, Malaysia, North Korea, the Philippines, Singapore, Korea, Thailand and Viet Nam.
24 Ibid.
25 "China's Ambition in an Ocean Era: Wang Yi Comments on South China Sea Disputes", *Duowei News*, 5 August, 2013. Among four points proposed by Wang, Foreign Affairs Ministry of China, the importance of reaching a common consensus is reiterated. In other words, China is suggesting that all members'

opinions, including the ASEAN, should be paid with high regards. Mark Valencia, 'Little hope for a code of conduct in South China Sea', *South China Morning Post*, 30 June, 2014. Available at: www.scmp.com/comment/insight-opinion/article/1541782/littlehope-code-conduct-south-china-sea, last visited 30 August, 2016.
26 "China Vietnam Agreed upon Guidelines of Management of Maritime Clashes", in Press by Foreign Affairs Ministry of People's Republic of China on Incidents of Attacks to Chinese Fishermen, *Huanqiu News*, 12 October, 2011.
27 Article 121 in the United Nations Convention on the Law of the Sea mandates this logic: islands sovereignty, maritime zoning and utilization of marine resources.

4 From the centre

The dash-line claim as a historical imaginarium or a quest for new course?

I The dash-line claim

A *The origin and early history*

In the South China Sea dispute, the most controversial is the Chinese contention of a dash-line claim, which was announced in 1947, after studies and preparation by relevant governmental divisions. The Chiang Kai-shek's Republican government drew the "eleven-dash line" on Chinese maps of the South China Sea,[1] enclosing the Spratly Islands and other chains, demonstrating that the ruling Nationalist Party (also dubbed as Kuomintang, KMT) had declared the reclamation of these land features. This dash-line claim contained twin messages. These land features were re-claimed and now under Chinese sovereignty. China's sovereignty had been restored, indicating that it was an extension from the past, and would continue, suggesting that this sovereignty would be sustained and practiced in the future. Cartographers of the Republican Chiang regime drew the U-shape of eleven dashes in an attempt to enlarge China's "living space" in the South China Sea. Following the victory of the Chinese Communist Party in the civil war in 1949, the People's Republic of China (PRC) adopted this cartographic claim, but had revised it into a "nine-dash line" after erasing two dashes in the Gulf of Tonkin in 1953.[2]

However, as an original authority of this dash-line claim, the Republic of China (the ROC, Taiwan) has long been a quiet claimant. The Chiang administration retreated to the island, after failing the civil to Mao's Chinese Communist Party in 1949. On one hand, Taiwan stayed in rivalry with Mao's China. On the other, however, Chiang and his predecessor adopted a proposition upholding claims over the South China Sea similar to Beijing. Due to the pending issue of the status of Taiwan and the Republic of China government, Taiwan (ROC)'s claim have long been marginalized, with voices of the people unheard.[3]

The dash line, also dubbed as u-shaped line, has claimed around 90 percent of the South China Sea, without specifying whether the area constitutes one part of its territorial waters, or as maritime spaces which brought along economic interests. In actuality, Taiwan (ROC) has not acceded into the United Nations

Convention of Law of the Sea, despite that it passed relevant domestic legislations zoning its coastal and adjacent waters around its home and outcropping islands in both East and South China Seas.[4]

During the two generations of the Chiang administration (Chiang Kai-Shek, from 1949 to 1975; Chiang Ching-Kuo, from 1978 to 1988), despite the drawn-out hostility across the Taiwan Strait, the two sides had seemingly reached a tacit understanding over the South China Sea issues.[5] In short, both sides would not protest against the other's territorial claims over the disputed waters.[6] Rather, in certain occasions, they would manage to reaffirm the dash-line and territorial claim as well.

The South China Sea issues caught the public's attention when the Filipino navy boarded and claimed to discover an island in the Spratly in 1956.[7] Both Beijing and Taipei staged formal protests to Manila. Due to the event, Taiwan (ROC) had thus formally stationed on the Itu Aba in the Spratly from 1956. In the late 90s, the troops were then replaced by the Coast Guard Agency till present days.

II Evolving maritime order: an essence of freedom in the Asian theatre

Tensions have simmered and gradually escalated after rounds of wrestling in political, diplomatic dimensions and now, at international arbitral forum. Despite the hortation for a Code of Conduct among all claimants and stakeholders for decades, its fruition has been delayed in the wake of an exacerbating resource competition and a race-up of construction process upon land features in the South China Sea. Leaving aside the dynamism wrought by contextual challenges, what remains unsettled and has continued to unnerve all those interested in the South China Sea dispute are China (People's Republic of China, PRC)'s approach by upholding the dash-line claim in the South China Sea, to which international lawyers and legal scholars, ingrained much with the Westphalia perspectives of what an international legal order should be, cannot fully understand. Among the lengthy and seemingly archaic historical arguments, the most confusing may be, contents of the dash-line claim, which require more elaborations of the historical political context of not only then regional order in this part of Asia, but also its interaction with western countries under the framework of the western imperialist international law. Indeed, from the western perspective, the seemingly most beguiling characteristic lies in China (PRC)'s additional introduction of obscure arguments about historic title in the South China Sea region.

A Regional-international order in Southeast Asia before the age of colonialization

Maritime order in Asia before the arrival of western imperial powers was under the helm of different value sets operating respectively in various parts in this region. The intrinsic developments and the ensuing dynamism, had interweaved into forming different stories of how maritime order had been construed, practiced and maintained in Asia before the age of colonialization.

Pre-colonial Southeast Asian countries were far from peaceful and stable. Fierce competition for survival and domination had characterized the balance of powers politics throughout the pre-colonial era. Till present, regarding the perspective to examine and evaluate then regional-international relations, opinions vary. Some have regarded pre-colonial Southeast Asian countries as vassal components to the Chinese dynasties, by which then regional-international relations were studied in the China-centred tributary system. Others argue instead that then regional-international relations were characterized more by Hinduism-ist and Islam-ist civilizations, which had formed complex political structures with Mandala-style characteristics. Amid these ongoing debates, one point nevertheless has been reaffirmed, that the Southeast Asia has become the converging point of different civilizations, whose confluence would reasonably creep up on regional maritime order in the South China Sea in this pre-colonial era.

An overview shows that maritime order in pre-colonial era in the South China Sea had largely been under control, for two reasons. For one thing, under the aegis of the Chinese tributary system, trade was largely controlled by certain ruling groups in the polities in Southeast Asia.[8] Private trade, on the contrary, was not encouraged. Without burgeoning commercial activities that generated human and commodities flow, maritime spaces in the South China Sea were largely at the helm of these state-sponsored fleets, which sailed northwards to the Chinese continent on a frequency of biannual or triannual time spans.[9] This, thus, had left the great swathes of waters in the South China Sea relatively calm and peaceful. Nevertheless, private trade thrived when China was weakened. The Chinese decline would be accompanied with the fading of credentials and prowess wrought by this tributary system, which in turn would have attenuated its influences upon maritime order in the South China Sea. Yet, even with the declining of the Chinese influence, maritime order in this region had not lapsed into chaos either. With a Chinese power vacuum looming from time to time, there exist other stabilizing factors, or, *explanans* (the explanation of that phenomenon). In this sense, different conceptions over maritime spaces in the Chinese/Han and Nusantara/Malay culture fill in this gap. Meanwhile, this dimension, by taking into account local customs and maritime practices in ancient periods, also helps in sorting out the incongruence embedded in deep memetic level, in littoral communities in the Sinic (China, Taiwan, Singapore and, to some extent, Thailand) and Nusantara/Malay (Brunei, Indonesia, Malaysia and the Philippines) block.[10] A clarification as such helps dismiss the entailing misunderstandings, and consequently, prevent policy mis-judgment.

Different conceptions of "spaces"

Briefly put, in the South China Sea region, there exists a conflux of different conception of spaces informed mainly by two civilizations, one from the North, and another, the South. The Northern Chinese tend to show a bounded conception of space, while the Southern Malay define their conceptions of spaces, terrestrial and maritime, along with their Mandala-featured understanding of governance and realm of authority.

The Chinese hold a bounded conception of spaces. After frequent usage and regular presence on certain land pieces, a sense of ownership developed. The Chinese intended to show clearly defined boundaries, marking the limits of territories with a wall and relevant defensive constructions laid in an ideal pattern.[11] There are two messages implied from this description. For one, the Chinese/Han civilization is originated in the Chinese continent. This origin has spoken much for itself the characteristics, such as "land-oriented" and "land-dominated". This is the raison d'être, together with the rather unique China-centred view of world order (regional order in its real sense) that guided people's concepts of and actions on the sea. The sense of ownership got developed first towards these land features. For the great swaths of maritime spaces, this proprietorship implication was boosted logically subsequent thereto, and reasonably a consequential outcome to the one upon land features.

Contrary to the Chinese perspective of the "maritime domain", the Malay/Nusantara culture holds a relatively more dis-integrated conception towards spaces. A primary assessment is that the Malay tends to understand the space, based on how they define the displaying of authorities. In this sense, the "Mandala principle of governance" plays a significant role.

The Mandala rule says that power is ritually and actually concentrated in the person of the sultan and his ruling location.[12] With the increase of the distance, the influences of the authority dwindle and become rather limited. The realm of sultanates thus becomes diluted the farther away from the ritual centre of the state. One understandable outcome is that this power-rippling structure may lead to a rather fussy border area with overlapping suzerainty in the most remote, peripheral regions. In this sense, the South China Sea falls into this category.

Another characteristic featuring this Malay/Nusantara conception towards "spaces" is that it is not shaped/construed as a structured/organized hierarchy framework, shaped by the interactions between the ruling and ruled. Rather, it is a single-actor system, centring solely on the ruling sultan, whose palace was surrounded by those serving palace duties, but not his people or even, urban citizens in present terms.[13] Further, each sultanate's realm and the display of its authority would be presented not as a complete and organized unit. Instead, a chequered pattern of authority better features how this Malay/Nusantara view of their surrounding geo-spatial domains was laid out.

Generally, the Malay villages consist of houses and groupings without clearly demarcated boundaries. Along with it, there exists no conception of "urban" space, even none for a clear delineation of the realm of each sultanate. Rather, villages or groupings, which owe allegiance to different sultans, may sit next to each other, which constitute a chequered pattern of different authorities, rather than a bounded space paying allegiance to a sole dominating authority. In this sense, a sultanate, once exiting from the central area where the sultan situated, would be composed of villages scattering on the continent. Sitting in a sporadically scattered manner, village A may pay loyalty to a sultan different from its immediate neighbour, village B. Yet B's neighbour and rival C may belong to the same sultanate realm as A. In a nutshell, even if senses of rivalry between A and B may not be necessary, alliance between C and A is naturally and reasonable, which also reflects the projection generated and implied by a scattered pattern of authorities presented under the aegis of the Mandala principle of governance.

As a result, for the Malay/Nusantara culture, it generates quite a different projection of "sovereignty" and of "territorial rights" upon their geo-spatial domains. For land features in particular at the most remote and peripheral area, there exist fussy borders and areas where influences overlap. Different sultanates exert limited authorities, whereas no one has a dominated control. It is in this sense that the Malay had focused their activities, terrestrial and maritime, more in their neighbouring areas.

As shown, the Malay has a relatively weaker sense of terrestrial proprietorship and a rather loose, or dis-integrated, view in terms of the displaying of authorities on land continents. How had this terrestrial spatial conception shaped up its understanding towards the sea?

Seeing maritime spaces as free and undefined, this rather open conception towards the sea had not nourished much Malay's aspiration to explore and conquer farther maritime areas. Rather, out of technology limitation, shortage of knowledge to the great potentials of the sea other than a source of diet supply and the guidance of the Mandala principle of governance, the Malay's understanding of maritime spaces had focused mainly on neighbouring waters. Adjacent seas, such as the Sulu Sea, Sulawesi Sea and Java Sea, had recorded most of their footprints. Viewing together the terrestrial and maritime dimensions, the Malay has construed spaces as formed by entities, divided and joined by seas, rivers and short land passages.[14] The location of their capitals at the estuary of a major river is more a reflection of an ocean-friendly, open-ended space conception,[15] but not a sense of territorial exclusiveness applied upon these maritime spaces.

Although the Chinese conception of "maritime spaces" is indeed contrary to the Malay, it is not necessarily closed, exclusive and aggressive. Because of the land-based characteristic, some scholars opine that the ancient Chinese always had a complex psychic relation to the vast ocean, longing, but disdaining.[16] It is also held that traditional Chinese coastal defence concept is featured with "alongshore defence", indicating a passive, but not strategic offense projection with the safeguarding of land territories centering in this thinking.[17] It is in this context that when the Chinese appear to view the South China Sea as a part of, however peripheral, bounded territories under their aegis, Malays, instead, view the sea as a free and undefined space, where everyone could go conducting fishing and other maritime activities freely.

With these two different conceptions of spaces, the inherent limitation wrought by a fluid "sea domain" brings in further uncertainty. For one thing, limitations, in and of itself, of a marine domain, mandate that a different set of perspective and measures were required. With certain land features drifting on the sea where only a small portion of them were able to accommodate populations at some scales, these land features were intrinsically limited to facilitate sustainable human economic activities. It thus appeared rather difficult to identify concrete evidence for governmental administration. Second, both the Chinese/Han and Malay/Nusantara cultures are not characterized with a strident desire of territorial acquisition, which prefers exclusive usages of that conquered land pieces. This would be even more attenuated in a most remote and peripheral region, in and of the sea, such as the South China Sea.

Yet, it is fair to say that the Chinese/Han influences are relatively more powerful. Nevertheless, the South China Sea area remains a rather free space, where control and administration was rather loose, sporadically-spotted, and waxed and waned in the wake of the vicissitude of the Chinese dynasties. It is thus justified and reasonable if the ancient/inherent maritime order in East/Southeast Asia is examined mainly from a Chinese/Han cultural perspective, as a border, but not hinterland, where regular governance measures that deliver strong sovereignty implications could not be identified easily.[18] This further de-mystifies the lack of relevant governance evidences, when viewing from a Westphalian perspective of international law and order.

B The South China Sea: a territory with an open-ended boundary

Generally, regional maritime order shares an intricate and intrinsic connection with the Chinese tributary system. Regional maritime order appeared to be relatively calm and stable when the tributary trade peaked, often in early and prosperous days of a Chinese dynasty. Private trade was not encouraged, and even outflow of human migration was banned from time to time. Leaving, for whatever pursuit, but not returning had been a loathsome idea in the Chinese culture. In particular, at a time when the Southeast coast had been haunted persistently by sea robberies and raiding by groups of gangster, sea ban policy was imposed to restrict human outflow from the Chinese continent. It is in this sense that even viewing the South China Sea as a part of its territory, the Chinese Emperor would be less likely to employ strict regulations and to shut down seaborne transportation, however few, for the purpose of border control or collection of levies.

In this sense, the Chinese management dwelled more on a basis of personal jurisdiction, *ratione personae*, and less on its spatial, and impliedly absolute, characteristics.[19] Management measures had been imposed upon human objects, but not on a spatial basis, even viewing the South China Sea as a part of its territory. This attests to the prescription that the Chinese dynasty had seen the South China Sea a territorial region, albeit with an open-ended boundary. Resultingly, regulations and inspections were imposed on persons moving across the South China Sea, mostly the Chinese people, and on people from foreign lands entering the Chinese continent for business purposes. It thus reaffirmed the contestation that the Chinese jurisdiction in the South China Sea region is featured with two characteristics, a spatial jurisdiction focused mainly on "security" issue, and one on persons who move across the region towards the Chinese continent.[20]

In this sense, the South China Sea appeared more an open and loosely controlled domain. This "territorial water with an open-ended boundary", on which a "jurisdiction right upon objects travelling thereupon" had been implied, together constituted a concept rather different from the one developed in the Westphalian international law, under which a sort of maritime zonings are established.

An opposite perspective also concurs with this description that the South China Sea was regarded a territory-like maritime space, albeit with an indeterminate boundary, under the leverage of the Chinese dynasties. It is a rather different mindset in the Nusantara/Malay culture, seeing the maritime domain as a free space and in the outer circle of the dynastic influences that largely had not developed a consciousness of delimiting clear boundaries in either a physical term or a conceptual sense. It is also due to the rather fragmented, and centre-oriented characteristic of the Nusantara/Malay civilization, that these littoral communities in the Southeast Asia had not projected for more advanced maritime development in their histories.

In terms of the maritime domain, the South China Sea was not one major ocean space for regional maritime activities. One reason may be that the Nusantara/Malay culture is informed with an emphasis on a centre as the seat of vitality and power, and a layering when power radiates therefrom would later become diminished with distance. In this sense, these Nusantara/Malay polities would tend to focus on near-shore waters but not farther areas, such as the South China Sea. Moreover, due to this perspective with Mandala features of power radiation, there had not developed a vision among these littoral communities to sail farther, or to envisage great potentials from the sea. Indeed, lack of development in maritime domains, in a relative sense, is not unique and can be seen in many areas.[21] To some extent, situating at a converging location where two civilizations meet has generated advantages and also, disadvantages.

On one hand, the location has brought in a conflux of impacts from different civilizations which have nourished cultural diversity and vitality.[22] On the other, the downside is that, there may emerge a power vacuum and a cultural complex in the South China Sea, when sitting on the fringe of both the Chinese/Han and Nusantara/Malay civilization. This may be one explanation for the toils haunted upon the efforts to understand maritime history in this region. Indeed, even been described as the Mediterranean Sea in Asia, the South China Sea remains unified only in name. In actuality, it never became a culturally integrated Mediterranean. The Chinese appears to be more land-based, whose influence together had shaped the Thais and Vietnamese to look inward more to their vast hinterland. The Malay remains highly fragmented, as these polities tended to concentrate on their own Mediterranean Seas, such as the Sulu, Sulawesi and

60 *The dash-line claim*

Java seas and the Straits of Malacca. Even after western colonial expansion, the South China Sea remains much more a denomination with more geographic characteristics, denoting a sea south of China.

III The dash-line claim in contemporary international maritime legal order

Both China(s) – the People's Republic of China (PRC) and the Republic of China, Taiwan (ROC) – have laid sovereign claims over the South China Sea.[23] Leaving aside thorny issues, such as Taiwan (ROC)'s legal status and the battle of Chinese representativeness between Beijing and Taipei,[24] one common point shared in China (PRC)'s both Taiwan (ROC) and claims is, however peculiar to their counterpart claimants, the dash-line claim.[25] A primary assessment is that the 11-dash line, originated by Taiwan (ROC), and the nine-dash line, later adjusted by China (PRC), are two sides of the same coin, which covers considerable parts of the South China Sea waters.

Since 2009, the South China Sea issue has been brought back to the front burner, when Vietnam and Malaysia submitted their Note Verbales concerning the outer limit of their continental shelf to the Commission of the Limit of Continental Shelf.[26] China's responses trigger a row of reactions from its ASEAN counter-claimants,[27] whose focus unequivocally fell on the nine-dash line map that has covered up to 70 percent of the South China Sea waters. Whether the dash-line claim has fallen outside UNCLOS framework remains a contested issue. Both China(s) has yet to come up with a clear interpretation of its scope and content, let alone its legal implications on the two China(s)' South China Sea positions.

A *Three dimensions of China (PRC)'s South-China-Sea claims*

Absent an official elaboration, voluminous official statements, relevant domestic legislations and scholarly papers nevertheless provide some insightful guidance.[28] China (PRC)'s claim in the South China Sea could be construed as containing three dimensions, which have informed one another mutually and interchangeably. To begin with, the dash-line claim indicates that China (PRC) claims sovereignty upon all land features, islands or rocks, located within this line.[29] Subsequently comes the delimitation of the exclusive economic zone (EEZ) and continental shelf. China has expressed in various occasions its willingness to enter into bilateral negotiations with interested countries regarding the delimitation issue.[30] Further, pending the ultimate delimitation of maritime boundary, China (PRC) has proposed the concept "joint development" to encourage regional cooperation. For these two aspects, China (PRC) has enacted corresponding domestic legislations, codifying these positions at the most minimal expenses of its compliance with UNCLOS system.[31]

Then, the third dimension is the dash-line claim, by which China (PRC) asserts sovereign rights and jurisdiction upon waters, the seabed and subsoil thereof within this dash line.[32] China (PRC) has stopped short of further deliberation of the "sovereign right" and "jurisdiction" upon the waters, seabed and subsoil. Yet, as explained by an incumbent Chinese judge in the International Tribunal for the Law of the Sea, Gao, and a law professor in Faculty of Law in Qinghua University, Jia, this dash line, which is informed by abundant historical evidences that predating UNCLOS, is nevertheless conditioned upon prescribed rules in UNCLOS, and is entailing multiple possibilities that could refer to sovereignty upon land features, and upon maritime spaces as a potential maritime boundary line.[33] This scholarly position lends supports to the argument that there exists the third dimension, the dash line, which is distinctive but not in isolation from the previous two propositions.

Rather, this nine-dash line claim should be viewed, from a perspective implying one possible scenario, the sovereign rights/jurisdiction rights over maritime spaces.[34] Under this category, this dash-line claim is claiming sovereign/jurisdiction rights upon maritime spaces, which ought to be construed under the context and by taking into account regional customs in times before western imperial invasions and also the 1940s, when World War II was wrapped up after resilient resistance of the Chinese people.

As also indicated by Gao and Jia, China (PRC) has held UNCLOS in high esteems and would not seek to vindicate its rights and interests in the South China Sea at the expense of impairing and jeopardizing rights and obligations prescribed in UNCLOS. Instead, China (PRC) seems to seek preferential privileges in either maritime zoning or resource utilization in the South China Sea. From China (PRC)'s perspective, these privileges are well justified out of its centuries-long practices of being a regional power that delivered security guarantees, and a magnet of cultural and economic prowess.

B Understanding the dash-line claim: the inherent uniqueness and intra-built conflicts

When categorizing China (PRC)'s claim into three dimensions, several issues attract attention. Without doubt, the relations between this concept of "sovereign/jurisdiction rights upon maritime spaces" and the dash-line claim, and how this concept is to be elaborated, constitutes one blatant controversy. For the former, this "sovereign/jurisdiction rights upon maritime spaces" provides one perspective to understand the dash-line claim, which has its root embedded on an underbed of civilization and local customs. In other words, the dash-line claim may be reflecting a long-exercised, yet unchallenged regional practice until the age of imperial invasion by western countries in nineteenth century. Nevertheless, its materialization and development has not been realized until the dawn of the twentieth century,[35] when China had taken initiatives to demonstrate, via a row of measures, its sovereign rights in the South China Sea. This string of measures is driven by defensive requirements and

62 The dash-line claim

aspirations for an independent statehood to secure respects from the international community.

Another hot point harbingering controversies is if there exist inherent conflicts between the dash-line claim and the one of maritime zoning, which largely has observed the Law of the Sea prescription. In other words, what is the role and function of the dash-line claim? The answer would shed decisive light on a subsequent inquiry, how this dash-line claim interacts with China's other claims, in particular, the maritime zoning prescribed in the Convention as what China consistently paid respects thereto.

i The uniqueness: a claim on island-attribution

One perspective is to view this dash-line claim as a boundary by which China (PRC) claims sovereignty upon all land features within this limit. In other words, it is a line denoting sovereignty attribution of all land features situating inside. This position was proposed by Taiwan (the Republic of China, ROC) in the early 1990s and has been upheld ever since. China (PRC) also shares this point, which it asserted that its sovereignty upon all these land features are indisputable.[36]

This perspective has its historical roots, and concerns out of strategic calculations and contextual considerations, where foreign invasions took place in the 1920s, and again during the Second World War. It is also from these incidents that the argument had been re-affirmed, that the dash line is of a defensive nature, and that the dash line is not to intervene in regular and civil navigation activities, but more as a military/invasion deterrence.

In the 1930s, the French had set foot on the nine small features in the South China Sea, which had triggered diplomatic wrestling between the French and British government over the legality and legitimacy of the French occupation.[37] The French occupation also greatly unnerved Japan, which issued official protests, and had prepared its own claim to the Spratly Island.[38] Japan had based its claim on its possession of Taiwan. Japan's opposition and strategic move to propose its own claims had paved the way for its ambition for southward conquest which was later realized step by step along with the festering of Japan's invasion encroachment into East and Southeast Asia. During the Second World War, in particular, from early 1942 to January 1945, the Japanese southern conquest had turned the South China Sea a "Japanese lake". All these incidents indicated that this maritime domain was of great strategic values, to whoever bordering it, and whoever desiring to set their feet into this region. In particular, these land features had become one focal/fortifying point to vindicate their aggressive aspirations. Interestingly, Chiang Kai-shek's Chinese government, or the Government of Guangdong Province, allegedly, had protested to the French occupation. The French Foreign Ministry, nevertheless, did not register any such protest.[39]

These historical and eventful incidents show one assured dimension of the dash-line claim, its denotation of China (PRC)'s sovereignty upon all land features located within its limit. In other words, this dash-line is to assert that all land features, be they islands, rocks, shoals or reefs, belong to China (PRC).

The dash-line claim 63

In this sense, this line serves one function of maritime delimitation, with regard to land features sporadically scattering on the great swathes of waters. Judging that all land features lying thereupon had been perceived to be Chinese, a sovereignty implication could be presumed that sovereign attribution of this great swathes of waters has rested also upon China (PRC) since ancient times. It is in this context that the dash-line claim serves the function of first, sovereignty attribution of all land features, and of a subsequent one that refers to the sovereign rights of great swathes of waters. Viewed together, this dash-line claim demonstrates not only maritime delimitation regarding all land features, but also maritime spaces in the South China Sea.

Nevertheless, even with sovereignty contestation over lands and references over waters, and even with its defensive nature from its commencement, this dash-line claim should not be deemed as predatory and exclusive in nature. Yet, there indeed remain concerns on the consistency between the dash-line claim and contemporary Law of the Sea regime. Of relevant importance is the standard in the Convention in generating maritime zones, such as the territorial sea, exclusive economic zone and continental shelf. Put frankly, the issue lies on if the dash-line claim could be recognized as a means to generate maritime limits, and would not conflict with the system established in the Convention.

That said, the dash-line claim is not a static conception, but a developing process. More efforts are indeed required for its elaboration. In a sense, the dash-line claim serves a unique role of bridging the eventful past in this region, and contemporary law and order infused with the Westphalian characteristics. Clearly, the dash-line claim has its roots set in the history, has evolved in the wake of the changing regional context and has possessed the potential to project a resolution to the South China Sea dispute with effectiveness, efficiency and expediency.

Consequently, issues for contestation are clear. What is the goal and function of the dash-line claim? If the dash line serves, or at least is evolving, as a boundary line, will it be compatible with contemporary Law of the Sea regime? Is it serving as a standard for generating maritime limits? Or is it developing to be a line of maritime delimitation in the South China Sea? With a positive answer, how should rights and interests of maritime spaces within this dash line be prescribed? In short, it is the congruence issue between the maritime-zoning standard established in the Convention and the dash-line claim that merit studies. This doubt reflects an intra-built contradiction in this dash-line claim, in both its essence and practices.

ii The intra-built contradiction: maritime limits and delimitation

I THE BLURRING BETWEEN "MARITIME LIMITS" AND "MARITIME DELIMITATION"

Leaving aside contentions dwelling upon extra-legal dimensions, such as economic, cultural, sociological and environmental phases, one illuminating alternative is to examine this dash-line claim from the perspective of "maritime limits" and "maritime delimitation", which are two closely intertwined, but intricately nuanced concepts and practices.

Maritime delimitation and maritime limits

These two intricately interwoven, yet different concepts, easily generate confusions. There is a world of difference between "maritime delimitation" and "maritime limits".[40] The former is to describe a "process of establishing lines separating the spatial ambit of coastal State jurisdiction over maritime space", which in due course may involve another state with overlapping legal titles. Therefore, "maritime delimitation" is an operation to be effected between two or more states, because it aims at clarifying title attribution in areas where legal titles by different sovereigns compete and each claimant tends to exercise jurisdiction over same maritime spaces. One essential characteristic of "maritime delimitation" is its international character. As denoted by the Chamber of the International Court of Justice in the Gulf of Maine case, "No maritime delimitation between states with opposite or adjacent coasts may be affected by one of those states".[41] In this sense, maritime delimitation is not a unilateral act, but must be effected between a plurality of states. In the ongoing arbitration between the Philippines and China (PRC), China (PRC)'s contention holds credentials, asserting that "subject matter (referring to territorial sovereignty as perceived by China (PRC) the essence of this arbitration) would constitute an integral part of maritime delimitation between the two countries. . .".[42]

Further, maritime delimitation displays unusual technical complexity and political relevance. It is a combination of legal, political, technical, historical, environmental and economic elements, thus studied not only by jurists, but hydrographers, geographers, cartographers and other experts. In this sense, disputes on maritime delimitation usually are replete with a complex of legal and extra-legal factors. Yet, case law suggests that the adjudicating body tends to treat geographical parameters as paramount, leaving neglected or only with limited weight to arguments based on population, socioeconomic and security considerations.

On the other hand, "maritime limits" denote the establishment that consists of drawing lines that define maritime spaces of a single state, which generally refers to, by its nature, a unilateral act.

In contemporary Law of the Sea Convention (also known as UNCLOS) establishes a standard for generating "maritime limits", by dividing maritime spaces into various categories upon their distance from the coast. The first category includes internal waters, Archipelagic waters (Part IV), the territorial sea (Part II), straits sued for international navigation (Part III) and buffer zone (known as the Contiguous Zone, Part VI). Farther away, the Exclusive Economic Zone (EEZ, Part V) and Continental Shelf (Part VI) constitute spaces under sovereign rights to marine resources of coastal states. The exclusive usage of marine resources in these areas is monopolized solely to coastal countries. Going beyond EEZ and Continental Shelf lie the High Sea and deep sea bed. For the High Sea (Part VII) and deep seabed (known as the Area, Part XI), these are under the compass of common heritage of mankind, on which coordinated management is mandated under an institutionalized mechanism established in the Convention.[43] In these three zones, thematic rules and management measures vary. Yet of particular, if not paramount, relevance, is the territorial water domain, which may be deemed as heralding the zoning of spaces falling in the second and third categories.

Nevertheless, there is no denying that "maritime limits" and "maritime delimitation" may constitute in a subsequent lineal order when an arbitration is initiated on a maritime dispute. In a world where the approximately 60 percent of maritime boundaries are still to be defined, international adjudication has experienced a burgeoning of relevant cases, leading to a process of progressive definition in several ways in maritime delimitation disputes.

II THE DUAL FUNCTIONS OF THE DASH-LINE CLAIM

This intricate distinction between maritime limits and maritime delimitation easily generates confusions. To some extent, developments of the dash-line claim vividly attest to, whether intentionally or not, this confusion. A primary assessment is that the dash-line claim, under the context of the Chinese approach, serves a dual function of both generating a "maritime boundary", and a standard to measure "maritime limits". In other words, the dash line, in China (PRC)'s words and deeds, indicates that it serves as a way for maritime zoning, and is, of itself, a maritime zone.

This observation is not totally out of expectations, and should not be regarded as an absolute wrong in and of itself. Rather, this ostensibly contradicting result sheds light on two prospective directions. First, it reconfirms the observation that the dash line is both a historical incident generated from the past, and a legal construction projected into the future. As a result, it is a progressive evolution, but not allegations that China is to revive an anachronistic China-centred regional order. Second, this developing process to flesh out the dash-line claim shows that regional customs/traditions may set in to remould contemporary regional maritime order, particularly when the dominating legal discourse appears to be of no avail. In a sense, what remains in the memetic deep would be revived, when it comes to a critical moment, when all possible rules and constraints have lapsed into ineffectiveness. This is thus a resuscitation of how Asians attest to/realize a right to survival, which they had been practiced and relied upon for generations since ancient times.

The dash line as a maritime boundary line

Ever since the submission of the dash-line map as an integral part to China (PRC)'s claim on the South China Sea to the CLCS in 2009, there develops a trend that China (PRC) has intended to evolve this dash-line claim to one serving the role as a maritime boundary. Several incidents help reify this observation.

For one thing, China (PRC) has reiterated on several occasions two critical elements in its claim. China (It contends that it has had sovereignty upon all land features lying within the dash line. Subsequently, its claim of

66 *The dash-line claim*

"sovereign rights in the waters and seabed" within the dash-line limit is justified. Accordingly, patrols and law-enforcement actions conducted by the Chinese Marine Police are well justified as a vindication of its rights and interests in said area. These contentions have implied/connoted the Chinese aspirations to the dash-line claim, however implicitly, that this dash line serves as a boundary line regarding all land features lying inside, and also functions as a maritime boundary by which all waters inside are under the sovereign right of China (PRC).

Reflecting/echoing this aspiration, burgeoning scholarly efforts try to provide reasoned deliberations of the dash-line claim to demonstrate that it would not defy the Convention regime, while serving China (PRC)'s interests. This intellectual brainstorming has attested to an observation that the dash-line claim is/ should be regarded as an outcome of a developing process, which aims at explaining and managing regional and customary maritime practices.[44] Without doubt, Chinese scholars have embarked on this mission.

Third, the ongoing arbitration initiated by the Republic of the Philippines against the People's Republic of China in January, 2013, on certain issues in the South China Sea,[45] further place this issue in peak of contentions, to which the Chinese approach shows a clear lineage to deem the dash-line claim as one of maritime delimitation.

In this ongoing arbitration, the distinction between "maritime delimitation" and "maritime limits" is of such complexity that it leads to two totally different interpretations of involving disputants. For China (PRC), the essence of the subject matter of the arbitration is the territorial sovereignty over several maritime features in the South China Sea.[46] China (PRC) contends, accordingly, that the tribunal does not have jurisdiction, since an issue of territorial sovereignty over maritime features would fall beyond the scope of interpretation or application of the Convention.[47] For the Philippines, it seeks from the tribunal explanations of what a submerged feature, low-tide elevation can generate in terms of its entailed maritime interests, and clarification upon what China (PRC)'s dash-line claim can generate regarding its effect on maritime interest and limits.[48]

The interpretations held by China (PRC) and the Philippines towards, on the surface, the dash-line claim, and in the essence, the standard of generating "maritime limits and interests", are vividly demonstrated. For China (PRC), this is an issue of "maritime delimitation", to which a precondition of territorial sovereignty over land features should be dealt with. On the contrary, for the Philippines, it is an issue of re-confirmation of the standard of "maritime limits and interests" established in the Convention, and of evaluation if the dash-line claim fell into any of this category. What further muddies the water are the words put out by the official statement of the Chinese government, when they uphold simultaneously the dash-line claim, the EEZ maritime limits, and their respects to the Law of the Sea as a whole.[49]

In this context, the dash line serves dual functions, as it denotes a way to confirm a maritime boundary, so that the Chinese sovereignty laid over any feature, and arguably, waters situated within should not be questioned. This dash line also can be regarded, along with its function in delimiting a maritime boundary in the South China Sea, as a Chinese interpretation of a method of generating "maritime limits". However, a subsequent inquiry would be, should China (PRC) intend to uphold this dash-line method as a method of generating maritime limits solely applicable in the South China Sea, as a regional custom? Or an alternative means more inflicted with historical characteristics and can be widely applicable should conditions being met? Further, this dash-line claim may conflict with the zoning standard established in the Convention, in particular the EEZ system. In this case, how should the dash-line claim be construed so as not to contradict China (PRC)'s one frequently held position that it is to respect the Law of the Sea regime?

This dash-line claim with these dual functions has provoked criticism among claimants and stakeholder countries. For one thing, it may make blurring the distinction between the concept of "maritime delimitation" and "maritime limits". Further, this dual function would increase/deepen the suspicion of other claimants that China (PRC) is, not with any possibility, to solve the dispute under the aegis of the Convention and general international law. This menace or threats, however perceived, would further fester deep-seated hostility among other claimants against China (PRC), which may easily spoil inter- and intra-state relations in this region. In this regard, it is one challenging, while not totally impossible, mission for China (PRC) to generate a modern attestation of the dash-line claim, not in defiance of the established Law of the Sea regime and general international law.

IV Concluding observation

- The dash line as an alternative approach in ocean management

Elaboration of the dash-line claim has triggered waves of criticism upon, on the one hand, China (PRC)'s continuing resistance in clarifying its content, while on the other, its allegedly increasing presence in the South China Sea in various aspects. In this sense, benefits of doubts are further attenuated by the impression that China (PRC)'s forceful presence marks its intention to deviate from the track of international law. Yet, in the longue dureé of history, the operation of multiple political hierarchies and frameworks in different parts of this region, along with maritime practices in littoral communities have created a unique cultural atmosphere, connoting that extra-legal factors should also be taken into considerations. A brief, but not exclusive, list contains, the practice of the Chinese tributary system, the Mandala principled governance in Southeast Asian polities and the different conception towards territorial domains and maritime spaces.

Also, the South China Sea is a converging point where the Chinese/Han civilization had spread southwards from the north and the Nusantara/Malay culture had extended to the shore in this region. In other words, the sea is, if not a clear-cut demarcation, a conflux that incorporates two different sets of culture and values. In the light of their convergence and interaction, different conceptions towards spaces and patterns of authority help explain the status of the South China Sea, and a monumental land mark, such as the dash-line claim.

It is out of this historical legacy that besides contemporary legal concepts, China (PRC), by delineating a dash-line claim, has deemed the South China Sea as part of its territorial waters, but one with an open boundary, with which no stringent border controls would be implemented in the fore points. Yet, as a part of its territorial water, China (PRC) will be crowned with one privilege, to exercise "sovereign/jurisdiction right upon maritime spaces". There exist two lines of arguments that lend supports to this extra, but not necessarily a defiant and redundant jurisdiction right upon maritime spaces.

For one thing, China (PRC) has, for generations, been a dominating power in the South China Sea, which then had been a peripheral border land marking the farthest reach of its cultural, commercial and political impacts. Even with intrinsic limitations wrought from a maritime domain, the Chinese/Han civilization, as compared to the Nusantara/Malay culture, by and large appeared more likely to have a concept of bounded territorial domain, which had been laid upon the great swathes of waters in the South China Sea. Yet, its concept and management of this territory-like maritime space was not exclusive in nature. Instead, the Chinese governance appeared to be fluctuating, contextual and dependent upon the wax and wane of its own national prowess.

Second, the dash-line claim and an open-ended territorial water can also be examined from a perspective, focusing on the potential incongruence between them and the set standard of maritime limits in the Convention. In other words, the Chinese claim has been informed with the suspicion of incompatibility between the dash-line claim and maritime zoning in the Convention, in particular the EEZ system. Among sorts of maritime zoning in the Convention, of particular relevance is the exclusive economic zone. Put bluntly, what the dash-line claim more egregiously confronts in the South China Sea is the claim of exclusive economic zone held by other claimants. It is in light of this incongruence that the duality of China (PRC)'s dash-line claim is mostly demonstrated.

As a result, suspicions are rife, on following two aspects: if the dash-line claim by serving the role of primarily, sovereignty attribution, and of derivative implication in maritime delimitation, in the South China Sea constitutes defiance to contemporary maritime legal order established in the Convention. In this sense, the fear that China (PRC) intends to establish a self-centered regional order, sharing certain if not all similarities with the ancient tributary system, has been greatly felt in ASEAN capitals. Even self-exaggerating, speculations as such would inevitably overshadow maritime order in the South China Sea.

The Chinese academics have embarked on the mission of fleshing out the dash-line claim under the context of the Law of the Sea regime in the Westphalian system. The mission is undoubtedly challenging, and suspicions on its deference to contemporary Law of the Sea regime are rife. Prediction of the outcome, of any sort, has its intrinsic limits and entails some inherent risks.

Yet some advices are well justified, in the light of possible externalities of the outcome, which would overwhelm, without discrimination, everyone in this region.

This evolving process should include maritime practices generated from past incidents, and establish a system/set of calibration parameters capable of providing guidance to future activities. Nuances and variances rooted from cultural and social contexts, however trivial, should be factored in due course of the deliberation. Meanwhile, the Law of the Sea regime, along its contribution and institutional influences, should not be overlooked and thus, defied. Further, some balancing mechanism should be contemplated, for the sake of common interests to the community, even recognizing the realistic and paramount consideration of its own national interests of every actor. In short, the dash-line claim in the modern context should be built on a combination of historical legacies and of future expectations. It is only in this sense that this dash-line claim could make positive contributions, serving as the bridge between the past and the future, and the once suppressed and the oppressing.

Notes

1 Jinming Li and Dexia Li, "The Dotted Line on the Chinese Map of the South China Sea: A Note", *Ocean Development & International Law*, 34 (2003): 287–295.
2 Teshu Singh, "South China Sea: Emerging Security Architecture", the Institute of Peace and Conflict Studies Special Report 132 (August 2012). Online available at www.ipcs.org/pdf_file/issue/SR132-SEARP-Teshu.pdf, last visited 28 November, 2013.
3 Upholding, still, the age-old dash line claim, Taipei regarded the great swathes of waters in the South China Sea as its historical waters, including the Spratly, the Paracel and the Pratas Islands, and the Macclesfield Bank. Such claim was based on "history, geography and international law". Raymond C.E. Sung, "Chinese Claims in the South China Sea: With a Reference to Historical Arguments" (paper presented at the annual meeting for the "Chinese (Taiwan) Society of International Law", Taipei, Taiwan, 8 December, 2012).
4 Taiwan passed laws regarding territorial seas, contiguous and exclusive economic zones and continental shelves in 1998. Absent the membership to the Law of the Sea regime, the laws largely conforms to the principles, endowing similar rights and interests to Taipei in utilizing adjacent maritime spaces to the island. However large its maritime territorial claims over the South China Sea, Taiwan's actual control is restricted to the Pratas Islands in the North, and the Taiping Island or Itu Aba, the largest in the Spratly. "Law on the Territorial Sea and the Contiguous Zones of the Republic of China", Law and Regulation Database, http://law.moj.gov.tw/Eng/LawClass/LawAll.aspx?PCode=A0000009, last visited 28 March, 2013; "Law on the Exclusive Economic Zone and Continental Shelf of the Republic of China", Law and Regulation Database, http://law.moj.gov.tw/Eng/LawClass/LawAll.aspx?PCode=A0000010, last visited 28 March, 2013.
5 Liang Feng, Wei Wang and Yimin Zhou, "Liangan Nanhai Xiefang Lishi" [The History of Cross-Strait Cooperation in the South China Sea], *Forums of World Economics and Politics*, 4 (2010): 2–4; Lianglong Mu, "Nanhai: Liangan Xiefang Hezuo Shifou Kexing" [The South China Sea: A Feasible Assessment of Cross-Strait Cooperation], *Shijiezhishi* [World Knowledge], 11 (2012): 1–3.

70 *The dash-line claim*

6 It should be noted that both sides would be refrained from launching protests or objections to the other's claims. However, no explicit endorsement or approval would be expected either.
7 Kuncheng Fu, *Nanhai de Zhuquan yu Quangcang: Lishi yu Falv* [Sovereign Rights and Mineral Resources of the South China Sea: A Historical and Legal Perspective] (Taipei: Youth Press, 1980), 59–60; Zhengwen Tsai and Wencheng Lin, *Duiwoguo Nanhai Qingshi Fanzhan Guojia Anquan he Waijiaoguanxi de Yingxiang* [Developments of the South China Sea Disputes and the Implications to National Security and Foreign Relations of the Republic of China], National Policy Foundation Policy Research Report RDEC-RES-089-033(30 November, 2001), 20; Chengyi Lin and Yanhui Song, *Nanhai Qingshi yu Woguo Yingyou de Waijiaoguofang Zhanlue* [Developments of the South China Sea and the Corresponding Foreign Policy and National Security Policies], Research, Development and Evaluation Commission Policy Research Report (October 2006), 43.
8 Min Shu, "Balancing in A Hierarchical System: Pre-Colonial Southeast Asia and the Tribute System", *Waseda Global Forum*, 8 (2011): 227–256; Bruno Hellendorff, "Hiding behind the Tribute: Status, Symbol, and Power in Sino-Southeast Asian Relations, Past and Present", in *Interpreting China as a Regional and Global Power: Nationalism and Historical Consciousness in World Politics*, Bart Dessein (ed.) (Houndmills: Palgrave & Macmillan, 2014), pp. 142–168; Peng Er Lam and Victor Teo, *Southeast Asia between China and Japan* (Newcastle, UK: Cambridge Scholars Publishing, 2012).
9 China had designed different time spans for vassal states to come to pay their tributes, depending on their relations with the Chinese court. There were some enjoying a rather close relation with China, such as the ancient Ryukyu and Joeson Kingdom, and Annam, which came to pay tributes every one or two years. There were also some that came on a three-or-five-year time frame, such as Southeast Asian polities/dynasties and Myanmar. Geoffrey Gunn, *History without Borders: The Making of an Asian World Region, 1000–1800* (Hong Kong: Hong Kong University Press, 2011); Min Shu, "Hegemon and Instability: Pre-Colonial Southeast Asia under the Tribute System", *Waseda Institute for Advanced Studies Research Bulletin*, 4 (March 2012): 45–62. For more discussions of the Chinese tributary system, see Fangyin Zhou, "Equilibrium Analysis of the Tributary System", *Chinese Journal of International Politics*, 4:2 (2011): 147–178; Yongjin Zhang and Barry Buzan, "The Tributary System as International Society in Theory and Practice", *Chinese Journal of International Politics*, 5:1 (Spring 2012): 3–36; Feng Zhang, "Rethinking the 'Tribute System': Broadening the Conceptual Horizon of Historical East Asian Politics", *Chinese Journal of International Politics*, 2 (2009): 545–574.
10 In terms of conception of space, there exist opinions that Thailand forms a distinctly different culture area, distinguished from the Sinic and Nusantara block. However, the distinctions are not clear-cut. All these countries have a multiethnic population, in which politically dominant ethnic groups would have determined long-term political processes. Hans Dieter-Evers, "Understanding the South China Sea: An Explorative Cultural Analysis", *International Journal of Asia Pacific Studies*, 10:1 (January 2014): 77–93.
11 Dieter-Evers, "Understanding the South China Sea", 85–89.
12 Pandu Utama Manggala, "The Mandala Culture of Anarchy: The Pre-Colonial Southeast Asian International Society", *Journal of ASEAN Studies*, 1:1 (2013): 1–13; Siska Lund, "A Mandala for the Southeast Asian International System", *The Bulletin of the Centre for East-West Cultural and Economic Studies*, 6:1 (2003), Article 2, 1–12.

13 For more sociological and historical studies of Southeast Asia, see Amitav Acharya, *Civilizations in Embrace: The Spread of Ideas and the Transformation of Power; India and Southeast Asia in the Classical Age* (Singapore: Institute of Southeast Asian Studies, 2012); Amitav Acharya and Barry Buzan, *Non-Western International Relations Theory: Perspectives on and Beyond Asia* (Abingdon: Routledge, 2010); Patrick Ziltener and Daniel Kunzler, "Impact of Colonialism: A Research Survey", *Journal of World Systems Research*, 19:2 (2013): 290–311; Amitav Acharya, *The Making of Southeast Asia: International Relations of a Region* (Singapore: Institute of Southeast Asian Studies, 2012).

14 Kenneth Hall, *A History of Early Southeast Asia: Maritime Trade and Societal Development, 100–1500* (Lanham: Rowman & Littlefield Publishers, 2010); Leonard Andaya, "A History of Trade in the Sea of Melayu", *Itinerario*, 24 (2000): 87–110.

15 Victor King, "What Is Brunei Society? Reflections on a Conceptual and Ethnographic Issue", *Southeast Asia Research*, 2 (1994): 176–198.

16 Lixin Sun, "Chinese Maritime Concepts", *Asia Europe Journal*, 8:3 (2010): 327–338; Angela Schottenhammer and Roderich Ptak (eds.), *The Perception of Maritime Space in Traditional Chinese Sources* (Wiesbaden: Harrassowitz Verlag, 2009).

17 Sun, "Chinese Maritime Concepts", 334.

18 Taxation and military conscription/stationing feature two symbolic sovereign measures in border management policy. Dazheng Ma, "Border Policy and Management of Ancient China" [Zhongguo gudai de bianjiang zhengce yu bianjiang zhili], *Studies of Western Territories* [Xiyu Yanjiu], 4 (2002): 1–15.

19 The Chinese concept towards "space" is featured with "boundedness", along with certain markers erected for boundary delimitation. This had been a prevalent practice on land territories. However, on maritime domain such as the South China Sea, this boundary-marking practice was not as discernible and identifiable. Yet, the Chinese authority imposed regulations upon the Chinese people who travelled to the Southeast Asia, and collected levies upon their returning. Nevertheless, the Chinese authority had not inflicted strict measures to curb maritime trade during Yuang and Ming Dynasty. One major concern that impeded this maritime freedom and security concerned the sea pirates that raided the southeast coast of Chinese continent. However, some considered that the trade activities of these pirates (also dubbed as extra-national pirate traders), ostensibly an egregious security threat to the Chinese Empire, had advanced maritime trade in East and Southeast Asia. Rigen Wang, "Maritime Policy of the Yuan-Ming-Qing Dynasties and the Vicissitude of Port Cities in Southeast Coast Area" [Yuanmingqing zhnegfu Haiyang zhengce yu dongnan yanhaigangshi de xingshuai shanbian pianlun], *The Journal of Chinese Social and Economic History* [Zhongguo shehui jingjishi yanjiu], 2 (2000): 1–7; John Chaffee, "Song China and the Multi-State and Commercial World of East Asia", *Crossroads*, 1:2 (2010), this article can be retrieved from www.eacrh.net/ojs/index.php/crossroads/article/view/4/Vol1_Chaffee_html, last visited 10 April, 2015; Roderich Ptak, "Ming Maritime Trade to Southeast Asia, 1368–1567: Visions of A System", in *From the Mediterranean to the China Sea: Miscellaneous Notes*, C. Guillot, Denys Lombard and Roderich Ptak (eds.) (Wiesbaden: Otto Harrassowitz Verlag, 1998), 157–193; Geoff Wade, "Ming China and Southeast Asia in the 15th Century: A Reappraisal", ARI Working Paper, No. 28, July, 20014, www.ari.nus.edu.sg/pub/wps.htm.

20 This concept of jurisdiction right on maritime space will be studied further in Chapter 6.

21 Despite the inherent restrictions, such as features posing navigation hazards, the perception that the sea is a free and open space prevails. The general public draw

a clear line between the "open sea" and the highly differentiated land area. Yet human history shows that maritime potentials and consciousness have got belated development, as compared to terrestrial one. Generally speaking, for one thing, mankind civilization emerged and thrived in the hinterland of continents where there were easily accessible water sources. Therefore, societies were established in great land masses where the central authority tended to be more terrestrial-oriented. Secondly, even when the population spread and set foot in coastal areas, these littoral societies, due to unique geographical characteristics and limitations, have more in common with other littoral societies than their inland neighbours. Tensions are inevitably developing between these inland and littoral societies, pulling the polities (states in modern context) into either a maritime or terrestrial direction. Even not necessarily in day-to-day politics, in the long run, as measured in the concept of the "long duree" of history by Fernand Braudel, incongruence is, not surprisingly, rife.

22 A consensus was reached among scholars that in pre-colonial Southeast Asia, the inter-principalities system could be termed as the mandala system. Several characteristics featured its operation, such as overlapping sovereignty, patrimonial authority and vaguely definable and continuously shifting territorial boundaries. See further, Amitav Acharya, "Imaging Southeast Asia", in his *The Making of Southeast Asia: International Relations of a Region* (Ithaca: Cornell University Press, 2013), 51–104; Lam and Teo, *Southeast Asia between China and Japan*; Manggala, "The Mandala Culture of Anarchy", 1–13; Lund, "A Mandala for the Southeast Asian International System", Article 2, 1–12.

23 Ministry of Foreign Affairs(Republic of China (ROC), Taiwan), "Ministry of Foreign Affairs of the Republic of China (Taiwan) Reiterates Its Position on the South China Sea", 11 August, 2011, www.mofa.gov.tw/News_Content.aspx?n =604CBAA3DB3DDA11&sms=69594088D2AB9C50&s=0FF97EBBDDD0 A0B6, last visited 20 November, 2014.

24 Despite the prevailing political recognition that the only China, including Taiwan, in the world refers to the People's Republic of China (PRC) government in Beijing, the battle lingers on in some scenarios under the table, as the Republic of China (ROC) government continues to exist in Taipei (Taiwan). The ROC government receives formal recognition from not more than 25 countries in the world. Nevertheless, Taiwan (ROC) remains a political entity that enjoys limited international legal personality in the international community.

25 The term "dash-line claim" is used in this article, for the purpose of convenience for discussions. The Republic of Taiwan asserted an 11-dash line claim which was drawn in 1947. The People's Republic of China (the mainland, PRC) upheld a nine-dash line claim, which succeeded and had substituted, as it asserted, the ROC's dash-line claim. Yet, the ROC has maintained its 11-dash line claim till present, despite it has not given rooms in either negotiation or arbitration forum.

26 Pursuant to a Decision adopted by the Meeting of States Parties (SPLOS/72), a State for which UNCLOS entered into force before 13 May, 1999, the date of commencement of the 10-year time limit for making submissions is 13 May, 1999. Submissions, through the Secretary-General of the United Nations, to the Commission on the Limits of the Continental Shelf, pursuant to article 76, paragraph 8, of the United Nations Convention on the Law of the Sea of 10 December, 1982, Division for Ocean Affairs and the Law of the Sea, United Nations, www.un.org/depts/los/clcs_new/commission_submissions.htm, last visited 20 November, 2014.

27 On 6 May, 2009 Malaysia and Vietnam made a joint submission to the CLCS for a portion of the continental shelf of the two States into the South China Sea. On 7 May, 2009 Vietnam made a Submission to the CLCS in the area north of its joint submission with Malaysia. On 4 August, 2009 the Philippines

submitted separate Notes Verbale to the UN Secretary-General in response to the Joint Submission of Malaysia and Vietnam and on the Submission of Vietnam. On 7 May, 2009 China submitted a Note to the UN Secretary-General concerning the Joint Submission of Malaysia and Vietnam. See Commission on the Limits to the Continental Shelf (CLCS) website available at www.un.org/Depts/los/clcs_new/issues_ten_years.htm.

28 There are plenty of scholarly research, official statements and position papers about China's position in the South China Sea issues. Yet the most authoritative article is co-authored by a Chinese judge currently serving in the International Tribunal for the Law of the Sea (ITLOS) and a law professor in Qinghua University in Beijing, China, and published in American Journal of International Law in 2013. Zhiguo Gao and Bingbing Jia, "The Nine-Dash Line in the South China Sea: History, Status, and Implications", *The American Journal of International Law*, 107:1 (January 2013): 98–124. Also, for official statements, the statement of the spokesperson of Foreign Affairs Ministry in the People's Republic of China, in a press conference held on 29 February 2012, could be of particular importance. In that statement, the spokesperson clearly considered that China, neither any other claimant, is not seeking sovereignty upon waters included within the nine-dash line. He nevertheless reaffirmed that sovereignty of all land features within this line has belonged to China since ancient times. See, Foreign Ministry Spokesperson Hong Lei's Regular Press Conference on 29 February, 2012, the statement can be retrieved from www.fmcoprc.gov.mo/eng/gsxwfb/fyrth/t910855.htm, last visited 20 November, 2014.

29 China (PRC) has reiterated repetitively that all land features located within this nine-dash line constitute an inherent part of its territory. Its sovereignty thereupon is indisputable. See, for example, Foreign Ministry Spokesperson Hong Lei's Regular Press Conference on 29 February, 2012.

30 One demonstrating statement is made by incumbent Foreign Affairs Minister, Wang Yi. See "Foreign Minister Wang Yi on Process of 'Code of Conduct in the South China Sea'", Ministry of Foreign Affairs of the People's Republic of China, 5 August, 2013. www.fmprc.gov.cn/eng/zxxx/t1064869.shtml, last visited 20 November, 2014.

31 Law of the People's Republic of China Concerning the Territorial Sea and the Contiguous Zone, adopted by the Seventh National People's Congress on 25 February, 1992, effective on the same date; Law of the People's Republic of China on the Exclusive Economic Zone and the Continental Shelf, adopted by the Ninth National People's Congress on 26 June 1998, effective on the same date.

32 The document submitted by the Permanent Mission of the People's Republic of China to the United Nations. Note of China, CML/18/2009, 7 May, 2009. The document is available at the Commission of the Limit of Continental Shelf website, at www.un.org/Depts/los/clcs_new/submissions_files/mysvnm33_09/chn_2009re_mys_vnm_e.pdf.

33 Gao and Jia, "The Nine-Dash Line in the South China Sea".

34 This concept is an attempt, however audacious, for conflict management in the South China Sea area. It is based on the Chinese dash-line claim, taking into account historical rights and local practices, and is not in a position to defy contemporary Law of the Sea regime. Rather, it is to be further developed to help accomplish current shortages in the Law of the Sea regime, which is egregiously witnessed in the stalemate in the South China Sea. This concept will be discussed later in Chapter 6.

35 The Chinese concept towards maritime domain management has undergone certain transformation, in particular, beginning in the second half in the nineteenth century, when western imperial encroachment was intensified. In 1907,

74 The dash-line claim

the Qing government sent troops to patrol the Dongsha Islands (Pratas) and held a ceremony to erect a monument of sovereignty on the Islands. The Qing's sovereignty demonstration was an interaction to the Japanese attempts for natural resources development in the Dongsha Islands. Shicun Wu, *Solving Disputes for Regional Cooperation and Development in the South China Sea: A Chinese Perspective* (Oxford, UK: Elsevier, 2013), 65–69.

36 China (PRC) has reiterated repetitively that all land features located within this nine-dash line constitute an inherent part of its territory. Its sovereignty thereupon is indisputable. See, for example, Foreign Ministry Spokesperson Hong Lei's Regular Press Conference on 29 February, 2012 China (PRC) has reiterated repetitively that all land features located within this nine-dash line constitute an inherent part of its territory. Its sovereignty thereupon is indisputable. One latest example is the position paper of China regarding the ongoing arbitration initiated by the Philippines, "Position Paper of the Government of the People's Republic of China on the matter of Jurisdiction in the South China Sea Arbitration Initiated by the Republic of the Philippines". The document is available at the Foreign Affairs Ministry of the People's Republic of China website, www.fmprc.gov.cn/mfa_eng/zxxx_662805/t1217147.shtml, last visited 10 April, 2015.

37 Wu, "Solving Disputes for Regional Cooperation and Development in the South China Sea", 72–74; Stein Tønnesson, "The South China Sea in the Age of European Decline", *Modern Asian Studies*, 40:1 (2006): 1–57. Mohan Malik, "Historical Fiction: China's South China Sea Claims", *World Affairs Journal* (May/June 2013). This article can be retrieved from www.worldaffairsjournal.org/article/historical-fiction-china%E2%80%99s-south-china-sea-claims, last visited 10 April, 2015.

38 Tønnesson, "The South China Sea in the Age of European Decline", 9–20; Malik, "Historical Fiction".

39 Tønnesson, "The South China Sea in the Age of European Decline", 7.

40 Yoshifumi Tanaka, *The International Law of the Sea* (Cambridge: Cambridge University Press, 2012), 87.

41 Gulf of Maine case (United States v. Canada), 1984 International Court of Justice Reports, paragraph 112(1).

42 The Position Paper of the Government of the People's republic of China on the Matter of Jurisdiction in the South China Sea Arbitration Initiated by the Republic of the Philippines, Section III., paragraph 57–75, 7 December, 2014. This document can be retrieved from Foreign Affairs Ministry of the People's Republic of China, www.fmprc.gov.cn/mfa_eng/zxxx_662805/t1217147.shtml, last visited 10 April, 2015.

43 United Nations Convention on the Law of the Sea, 10 December, 1982 1833 U.N.T.S. 397.

44 There have been quite many scholarly discussions in the Chinese approach in the South China Sea dispute. See, for example, Junwu Pan, *Towards a New Framework for Peaceful Settlement of China's Territorial and Boundary Dispute* (The Netherlands: Martinus Nijhoff Publishers, 2009); Keyuan Zou, "Historic Rights in International Law and in China's Practice", *Ocean Development and International Law*, 32:2 (2001): 149–168.

45 The arbitration is registered with the Permanent Court of Arbitration. More information can be found in the website of Permanent Court of Arbitration, "The Republic of the Philippines v. The People's Republic of China", www.pca-cpa.org/showpage.asp?pag_id=1529, last visited 10 April, 2015.

46 See the Chinese position paper, The Position Paper of the Government of the People's republic of China on the Matter of Jurisdiction in the South China Sea Arbitration Initiated by the Republic of the Philippines, paragraph 3.

47 Ibid.
48 The Republic of the Philippines, Notification and Statement of Claim, 22 January, 2013. See also, International Tribunal for the Law of the Sea, Press Release, 25 April, 2013.
49 The Chinese government has repeated in various occasions that it upholds the Law of the Sea Convention and the regime. See for example, Foreign Ministry Spokesperson Hong Lei's Regular Press Conference on 29 February, 2012.

5 From the centre

A proposal of jurisdiction right upon maritime spaces

I A brief review of the evolution of maritime order

A Maritime order in the Westphalian system

For hundreds of years the concept *mare liberum* had dominated international maritime order. This term refers to, in *Merriam-Webster* and *Encyclopedia Britannica*, freedom of the seas.[1] Literally speaking, it means the sea [that] is open to all nations.

This concept depicts how the marine order had been re-moulded in early days when international maritime order began to see multi-polarized developments. The diversification was presented in the proliferation of actors, the discovery of new lands, the fierce competition between countries in trades with these new areas, and the confrontation between countries with unbalanced maritime forces. Developed by a prospective young counsellor representing Holland, this idea had not been regarded of great weight, as with intellectual values, in the beginning.[2]

Some explanations help shed light on this early neglect. On the one hand, this idea was proposed under certain circumstances for specific objectives: to prevent Holland, a new comer in maritime trade in the Indian Ocean and with most areas in the West Coast of Africa, from acceding to the exclusive claims of its adversaries, Spain and Portugal, over the above said areas.[3] On the other, this concept was acting to vindicate the conduct by his countrymen by an inexperienced youth in his early twenties filled with high ideals. In other words, Grotius set out to do so by formulating and promulgating a new theory of the freedom of the seas, under which Holland would be legally justified in carrying on trade with the East Indies. Accordingly, the promotion of a free sea open to everyone is a strategic counterbalance proposed by a new-comer nation state, with relatively weak naval fleets, which wanted to join the game of trades with newly discovered lands in the Far East.

Another issue is that this *mare liberum* concept was acting more like a special custom, prevailing in the community of Christendom, and those converted thereto.[4] For most parts in the Far East, and the continent of Africa, no obligations as mandated by international law were owed to these heretics who defied the European political and religious authority. That said, this concept lent a helping hand, far from championing peace and the freedom of navigation on the high seas, but on advancing Dutch colonial rule in Asia in early days.[5]

Accordingly, this Grotian idea is not well received when measured by its knowledge and method. Rather, as a commentator pointed out, "it had the incontestable merit of having proclaimed the freedom of the seas and of having entered directly into the spirit of modern civilization".[6] Gradually, this Grotian idea set its foot sound and clear in modern navigation practices, and engaged in the development of the Law of the Sea regime.

Developments have been meteoric in the modern era. In short, practices are rife and discernible. Except being barred from a narrow strip of waters under the purview of territorial waters of coastal states, the oceans are meant to open for all users for all peaceful purposes.[7] Any claims or application of domestic legislation over oceanic spaces would be an encroachment on freedom of use of and navigation on the sea. This traditional logic has undergone some changes after the Second World War II when international law-making activity regarding territorial seas, contiguous zones, continental shelf and later exclusive economic zone was taking place in the late 1950s. Highlighting a shift from unlimited freedom on the sea to a premise featuring sovereign privileges over certain oceanic spaces, international maritime legislation manages to balance between the pre-eminence of *mare liberum* and the emerging distinction of inclusive and exclusive utilization of oceanic spaces. This shift has portended an overemphasis on sovereignty over marine affairs since then.

B The Law of the Sea Convention (UNCLOS): maritime order on a Grotian ideal

Until recently, the traditional view of the ocean was that its vastness had rendered it impossible for humans to overexploit its living and non-living resources.[8] The world's oceans had been viewed as common grounds, which any nation could navigate and utilize. As a result, most maritime zones are previously portioned as parts of the High Sea, and a result of the process of expansion, yet circumscribed, of the coastal state's rights. Some therefore describes that the first and utmost task of the Law of the Sea Convention (the Convention, UNCLOS) has been to establish a network of spatial property rules for areas of ocean spaces to be held privately, publicly, in common, or not at all.[9] Accomplishment and completion of this task remains a focus of contestation till present days.

In the Law of the Sea regime, maritime zoning will be settled following attribution of land features. This principle, also dubbed as "the land dominates the sea", has been re-affirmed by a long line of cases.[10] Zoning great swathes of maritime spaces constitutes the initial step in delineating rights of those acting thereon, and their incurred responsibilities. In a sense, this zoning system can be deemed as a response to tackle the downside entailed in seeing the ocean as an unlimited free domain, the common pool issue.[11] Generally, exploitation of a common pool, or common resource, is likely to create critical negative externalities. Different types of these externalities, all relating to the exploitation of the resource, can be identified.[12] Inter alia, the kind that leads to excessive consumption of resources and dissipation of social surplus from such is often categorized as over-exploitation. Another related type leads to excessive investment or a massive overtly pooling of resources at the stage of search and identification. This latter one can also be dubbed as, excessive search.

The zoning system provides one balanced resolution to tackle this "common pool resource" dilemma. In the essence of this zoning system, it is the managing, coastal countries, and the spatio-geographical jurisdiction bestowed thereto. Coastal countries can exercise management of maritime affairs in a most economically efficient and effective way. As a result, it is bestowed with a spatio-geographical jurisdiction right, with certain nuances, in adjacent maritime zones up to 200 nautical miles from the coast. This centrality of managing the ocean from a spatio-geographical perspective is supplemented by identifying the subject actor, with whom all kinds of maritime activities are conducted and resources, developed. Accordingly, jurisdiction *ratione personae* is granted to flag-state countries, whose responsibilities to regulate its nationals' activities in foreign EEZ constitute an important, but supplementary role.

In the wake of advances in maritime technology, control over larger portions of the ocean has become possible. The sea is thus, to be managed as land territories, under which a bounded confinement applied in land territories is not unrealistic and practically feasible. However, the downside is that with the extension and monopolization of regulatory authority upon certain maritime domains to mostly, one single coastal country, there emerge issues of policy coordination in a variety of aspects, such as in marine environmental protection, maritime safety, and those regarding trans-boundary marine resource management. In particular, population growth, technological change and economic development have increased demand for the ocean's resources to the extent that overexploitation and congestion have become serious problems. Accordingly, this relatively nascent legal regime has been developed in a course of trial and, if not errors, corrections.

It is in this sense that inquiries are raised, on whether the Convention and its zoning system can deliver effectively the outcome intended in marine resources management. Fish swim around, and oil and gas often straddles abutting zones. Fishermen chased after their harvests and would easily trespass beyond these artificial boundaries. Nevertheless, the design of international cooperation and collegiality in responsibilities-sharing in the Convention is aimed to redress this shortcoming. Yet, this design sees a structural flaw of a free-riding problem among party states, which is pacified further under the disguise of inviolable sovereignty.

II Why is the Law of the Sea unable to solve current stalemate in the South China Sea?

One critical concept underlying the Law of the Sea regime is the zoning of maritime spaces as a reflection of territorial delimitation on the continental landmass, as what has been dubbed "the land dominates the sea". In light of this zoning system, issues of the legality of countries' behaviour in areas with abutting and overlapping maritime zoning inevitably arise. When maritime delimitation is yet to be fully settled, the boundary between behaviours to strengthen sovereignty claims, and those that would jeopardize and hamper the achievement of final agreements of maritime zoning is thus blurred. This inevitably leads to the following situation. When behaviours fall into the category of state acts out of sovereignty claim over maritime spaces, should these acts then be balanced or circumvented by their alleged impacts upon the pending maritime delimitation (for exclusive economic zone or continental shelf) agreement?

Conflicts, between sovereign acts upon maritime spaces and those circumscribed under the Convention as in EEZs or continental shelf, constitute a paradox. In other words, sovereignty over maritime spaces and sovereign rights defined by this "land-dominating zoning" rule under certain conditions, may have caused contradicting effects against each other, running the risk of diminishing the intended regulatory goal. In the context of the South China Sea dispute, the Exclusive Economic Zone (EEZ) is one of unique relativity to current stalemate, in which this paradoxical dilemma is vividly demonstrated.

A The paradox of exclusive economic zoning and delimitation

Exclusive Economic Zone is an area falling under the aegis of sovereign rights of coastal countries over the exploitation and development of marine resources. The EEZ design is described as one significant invention in the development of maritime management in the Convention. Despite all loftiness in the goal and rule prescription in the Convention, the EEZ system hits a stalemate in an area like the South China Sea, which is replete with historical legacies and regional traditions. This area is also informed with characteristics that may bring challenges to the Westphalian system of international order.

To begin with, the blurring and overlapping of territorial sea and EEZ claims contributes to simmering tensions in the South China Sea. In past decades, claimants and China (PRC) as well, have made all possible efforts and necessary measures to solidify their contestation in the South China Sea, in whatever manifestation. Yet the difficulty lies in their overlapping claims, which integrate not only conflicting EEZ claims, but also rivalry between EEZ and territorial seas. Simply put, there exists the dilemma, when claims of EEZ and of territorial sea overlap, out of the reason that it would be extremely difficult to generate a parameter to calibrate the "reasonableness" of claimants' contending activities.

The Convention has not laid out clear definitions and boundary, of and between reasonable state acts aimed at strengthening claimants' maritime sovereignty propositions, and limitations that these state acts are to be observed so as not to jeopardize and hamper the final solution of maritime delimitation.[13]

Under this modern concept – namely that "the land dominates the sea" – states are thus more likely to incur into international responsibilities by breaching primary rules relating to action *within* disputed maritime spaces, but rarely those regarding ascertaining their respective sovereign claims. For activities within disputed areas that breach rules in the Convention, examples include unauthorized exploratory drilling for oil in the continental shelf, and fishing in foreign EEZs. For the latter, it is relatively more difficult to frame exemplary acts. Yet demonstrating acts may be the promulgation of domestic legislations and unilateral enforcement by one claiming country. When states' sovereignty claims overlap, a duplication of such entitlement which enables states' exercises of exclusive right in said areas may lead to unilateral acts by the states involved.

The dilemma seemingly is more troublesome, in EEZ zoning, instead of zoning of territorial waters which takes place only after the decision of sovereignty attribution of land features. To some extent, the EEZ zoning is even thornier, as it contains not only a decision of the calibration of the "zoning", but also a decision between rivalry claims on whose is duly proved, more justified and more "reasonable".

Two provisions in the Convention envisage this difficulty, when delimitation of the boundary of EEZs and continental shelf is pending. This is one dilemma that has long plagued the South China Sea, and one reflective of the hidden intricacy of conflicts between claims of territorial sea and of EEZ. Article 74(3) concerns situations pending final delimitations of EEZs,[14] while Article 83(3), the continental shelf.[15] Viewing together, these two provisions impose two obligations on states, when final delimitation agreement is beyond their immediate reach.[16] On the one hand, states should make every effort to enter into provisional agreements of a practical nature, should conflicts arise in delimiting EEZs and continental shelf between them. On the other, states should also spare no efforts not to engage in activities that would prejudice the final settlement of the dispute. Yet, this latter requirement imposes realistic difficulties in an area where territorial and EEZ claims have overlapped, and may have conflicted against each other, in particular, regarding activities implemented to demonstrate one country's territorial claim, exclusive in nature, where other disputants may deem it as their EEZs, which is relatively more inclusive in and of itself. This is what characterizes the South China Sea.

In short, this two-dimensional obligation stipulated in Articles 74(3) and 83(3), certifies again the vacuum in UNCLOS of what constitutes a "reasonable" behaviour by a claimant state to assert its sovereignty proposition, which are not only admissible, but also necessary in order not to lose entitlement to a contested maritime area.

Question thus arises. How can we identify acts and legal responsibilities thus incurred, which would be legal if carried out on a maritime area appertaining undisputedly to the acting state, but whose legality may be challenged in the case in a non-delimited maritime area? Put differently, has UNCLOS established the concept of "reasonable claim", defining the limit of claimant states' enforcement activities that can be carried out in contested maritime areas?

B State responsibilities and enforcement actions

A related issue of the effectiveness and efficiency of the EEZ system is the lack of secondary rules in international law defining state responsibilities, should violations of their Convention obligations, or those in general international law scenario, occur. In this aspect, the Convention has specified in Article 293 that applicable laws to tribunals would cover both the Convention and all relevant international law.[17] Further, decision of a case *ex aequo et bono* is also possible, should parties so agree.[18] Yet, this provision seems to provide little guidance to the structural vacuum and conflict between maritime sovereignty and zoning claims. Further jurisprudential efforts or legislative law-making would be required.

Put simply, there lacks a standard in the Convention to calibrate member countries' enforcement action, so that the attribution of responsibilities could be more effectively determined. Accordingly, a more clarified responsibilities-sharing rule set would help facilitate the ensuing reparation work entailed in these damages.

Despite this structural deficiency, some provisions may shed some lights. The Law of the Sea regime provides only a set of rules concerning enforcement by the coastal states in the scenario of protection of the marine environment in Part XII (protection and reservation of the marine environment), Section 6 (enforcement).[19] Besides, a number of provisions also indicate the connection, however weak, between enforcement actions and states' responsibilities thus incurred. Article 27 stipulates the criminal jurisdiction on board a foreign ship that exercises the right of innocent passage through the territorial sea.[20] Article 74 provides enforcement, along with some requirements by coastal states of its laws and regulations concerning the conservation and exploitation of marine living resources in EEZ.[21] Article 224 to 227, in Part XII (protection and reservation of the marine environment), section 7 (safeguards), concerns the exercise and limitations of enforcement with respect to pollution of the marine environment,[22] while Article 232 provides for the liability of states arising from enforcement measure in the field of protection of the marine environment.[23]

Despite rather sporadic provisions in the Convention, states indeed incur into international responsibility by taking enforcement that may violate rules, general or specific, in international law. In the case of enforcement action, there exist limitations from general and specific regimes. In the former, the Tribunal in the *Guyana/Suriname* case considers if action undertaken by Suriname against a country licensed by Guyana, so as to conduct exploratory drilling in the contested area, constituted a "threat of the use of force".[24] The Tribunal in the final award adopted the position that this said drilling could be deemed not only as a "threat of the use of force", but also an act hampering or jeopardizing the final settlement of EEZ and continental shelf delimitation.[25] To deem the unlicensed exploratory drilling in the continental shelf as a threat of the use of force denotes a violation of Article 2(4) in the United Nations Charter. However, in a contested area when both assert competing/overlapping sovereignty claims, to view the contested drilling as a threat of the use of force amounts to a prohibition in absolute terms of a state, whose activities intend to impose its domestic legislation and legal activities thus authorized as a manifestation of its sovereignty proposition. The Tribunal's effort to balance between the interests of disputant states seemingly does not sustain.

States' enforcement may also generate responsibilities prescribed in specific regimes. In this case, the law regarding state responsibilities comes into play, defining states' responsibilities for unlawful acts, even in contested maritime spaces. The first result will be the obligation to cease the unlawful conduct, while offering of appropriate assurances and guarantees of no-repetition.[26] In a situation when maritime sovereignty claims are contested by many claimants, states could be liable to several violations of their obligations against various disputants. States also remain under a continued duty to comply with the requirements of these provisions. Also, responsible states may be required to make full reparation for the injury caused.[27] This obligation includes all forms of reparation, including satisfaction, restitution and compensation. Yet, practices in the international adjudication show that money damages payments even for corrective purposes are very rarely awarded or quantified for injury to state interests.[28] Even if money claims by individuals before international tribunals tend to be more frequent, they are almost invariably decided on a corrective justice basis, apart from occasional small symbolic monetary awards.

It is indeed of considerable credits that, arguing by Grotius, law reaching beyond a single state (*civitas*) should aspire to achieve corrective justice, but not distributive justice.[29] The supreme value of Westphalian sovereignty of every state is thus upheld, and their independence as a polity to choose preferred political and legal systems, respected. However, ocean affairs and marine management is largely of a collaborated character. Inter-state cooperation would be a sine qua non for its eventual success and sustainable development. By continuing the corrective justice practice, which s to identify the wrongdoer and may thus generate name-calling effect and blatant resistance from the blamed party, grandeur objectives requiring responsibilities sharing and collegiality among all parties in the Law of the Sea regime would not be effectively observed. Under this context, the chaotic situation in the South China Sea, along with the controversial dash-line claim, actually, has launched serious challenges, nevertheless, a new direction to carve a way out of the jungle.

C Ratione materiae and personae jurisdiction in exclusive economic zone

i Ratione materiae jurisdiction on a spatial basis

One most significant contribution of the Law of the Sea regime is to establish a system of maritime zoning, separating maritime spaces into various domains to which rights and obligations affiliated vary. This zoning system reflects the long upheld tradition in international law, which sought to maintain order by dividing the world and assigning exclusive or quasi-exclusive regulatory authority over areas to states. To some extent, the Convention represents a broadly sensible response to a wide range of externality problems that arise when nations prioritize national interests to common goods, and have acted non-cooperatively, or ineffectively, to manage the sea. Regulatory jurisdiction is for the most part allocated to the nations that value it the most and can exercise it most cheaply.[30] In the Convention, constraints on designated jurisdiction respond to externalities that arise when regulators tend to ignore the welfare of other countries. Further, in the scenario where national regulation alone would fail or is inadequate, international cooperation on regulatory efficiency and harmony is encouraged and systemically facilitated.

In this zoning system, coastal states are granted sovereignty over internal waters and territorial seas. For waters beyond territorial seas, coastal states are given sovereign rights over marine resources and all relevant issues. Resources in near-shore areas are comparatively cheap to exploit for nearby actors. This allocation of regulatory authority over waters lying within 200 nautical miles from the coast covers approximately 142 million square kilometres, an area almost as large as the land surface and 40 percent of the world's ocean.[31] This area contains 90 percent of marine resources. Accordingly, the guiding principle is the proximity of the resources to the claimant country. Put differently, property rights over maritime spaces are awarded to those who are close, and easy to patrol. Indeed, allocation of authority over near shore waters to the coastal states is not only the most efficient option, but also most likely a stable arrangement if international cooperation is to be realized and sustained. It is in this sense that the geographical proximity, together with the subject matter, such as fishery or mineral resources in the sea, that serve the rule of thumb in this maritime compartmentalization system.[32]

Obeying such guidance, it can be summarized that jurisdiction of coastal states in near-shore waters rests mainly upon sovereignty in territorial waters, and a limited spatial jurisdiction in Exclusive Economic Zones (EEZ). The former is relatively clearly defined, as this small band of coastal sea is deemed as a part of coastal state's territory. The latter, on the contrary, is innovative and ambitious. This limited spatial jurisdiction in EEZ is characterized by its sovereign-like authority, but only in maritime resources and relevant issues. In this sense, the limitation is twofold. On one hand, this authority is confined in the EEZ area. On the other, its exercise is subject to certain limited rights of other states,[33] and on only designated subject matters, in this case, marine resource and its relevant issues.

TWO INCIDENTS LEND REIFYING SUPPORTS
TO THIS PRESCRIPTION

For one thing, the *ratione materiae* jurisdiction on marine resources has been re-affirmed in the Law of the Sea jurisprudence. In the *M/V "Virginia G"* case, the International Tribunal for the Law of the Sea concluded that "it is apparent from the list in Article 62 (*utilization of the living resources [in EEZ]*), paragraph 4, of the Convention that for all activities that may be regulated by a coastal state, there must be a direct connection to fishing."[34] Fishery resource is one critical constituent to the conservation and management of living resources in the EEZ.

Other articles also lend support. Article 56 provides coastal states with sovereign rights to explore and exploit living or non-living natural resources, along with conserving and managing responsibilities.[35] Subsequent provisions, Articles 61 and 62 require coastal states to study and determine allow catch of the living resources in its EEZ, and to grant access to other states the surplus of the allowable catch.[36] In order to realize this purpose, coastal states may take necessary measures, as prescribed in Article 62, paragraph 4 and Article 73, paragraph 1, to ensure the compliance of foreign vessels.[37] Accordingly, the *ratione materiae* jurisdiction of coastal states in marine resources in a designated area, its EEZ, has been well established under the Convention framework.

Secondly, the spatial characteristic of coastal states' jurisdiction is reaffirmed, when coastal states grant fishing access to vessels from distant waters. This is common practice, which earns coastal states considerable revenues, in situations when foreign, but not coastal states, have larger vessel capacity and fishing capability (and may even have depleted fishing resources in their own EEZs). Articles 61 and 62 provide the legal basis for these fishery arrangements between coastal countries and those from far distance.[38] An example is the European Union, which has entered into twenty bilateral fishing agreements with, largely, developing countries in Africa, and can fish in these foreign EEZs.[39] Under these arrangements, fishing access is given to EU, while coastal countries play as an environment steward over these areas.[40] Countries procuring fishing access are subject to the stewardship duties of coastal countries. These fishing arrangements provide foreign nationals an access to coastal states' EEZ, albeit with certain limits. In other words, these foreign vessels would need to either obey coastal states' designated requirements in the EEZ, or to obtain licenses, when conducting fishing. It is in this sense that coastal states' spatial jurisdiction with a *ratione materiae* limit has been mostly demonstrated.

This explains why jurisdiction in EEZ is on a spatial basis, but with limited focus. Put lucidly, in EEZ, coastal states are given jurisdiction *ratione materiae* on a spatial basis, which is confined to focus on marine resource issues in an area that extends up to 200 nautical miles from the coast.

ii The Ratione personae jurisdiction

All rationale and stakes aside, the prescription that jurisdiction in EEZ is one of a spatial characteristic and with limited *ratione materiae* focus, nevertheless, conveys a paradoxical message. This spatial jurisdiction with a designated subject matter reveals one downside, the relatively neglected *ratione personae* jurisdiction in EEZs. In particular, when fishing arrangements are made between coastal and distant-water countries, vessels flying flags of coastal and foreign countries can fish in the EEZ. Nevertheless, they are mainly under different jurisdiction, should conflicts arise. For foreign vessels, they not only have to observe those designed by coastal countries, but also they are placed under the aegis of personae jurisdiction of the countries on which their nationalities are determined.

The Law of the Sea regime has seemingly attached more emphasis on jurisdiction and authority given to coastal states which is on a spatial basis, and fewer attentions on the authority and responsibility of flag states of foreign vessels which is on a personal basis. In other words, in particular concerning the EEZ management, coastal countries have been playing a major role. The flag state responsibility, comparatively, has fallen out of public views. Also, this logic is reflected in the Convention. The Convention has specified clearly that the primary responsibility for taking the necessary measures to prevent, deter and eliminate illegal fishing rests with coastal states.[41]

Yet, advances in maritime technology have made possible the sailing into farther and foreign waters, and the control over larger portions of the ocean. The greater mobility the ship has, the larger burdens would be imposed on coastal country's maritime management. In the light of these terms, the effectiveness and efficiency of this zoning system which is based on spatio-geographical proximity may be further attenuated. These dangers are not totally unrealistic, but developing quickly and becoming imminently. Nevertheless, they are not totally unstoppable either. A way to redress this shortcoming of contemporary maritime legal order is to revitalize the role and importance of flag state in maritime management. This is also an alternative perspective to view China's dash-line claim, regarding if new elements can be added to re-furnish current Law of the Sea regime.

THE FLAG STATE: A LONG QUIET ROLE

While accepting that the primary responsibility of conserving and managing natural resources in EEZ have been vested mainly on coastal countries, it is argued that other states, in particular those with great stakes, are not released from their obligations.

General and specific obligations of flag states are stipulated in the Convention for the conservation and management of marine living resources. In Articles 91 and 92, the nationality and status of ships, also dubbed as the determination of flag states, are fixed.[42] Further in Article 94, duties of flag states, in particular fishing activities, are stipulated.[43] In fulfilment of its responsibility to exercise effective jurisdiction and control in administrative matters, flag states must adopt necessary administrative measures to ensure that its flag states do not engage in conducts that will undermine its responsibilities in respect of the conservation and management duties stipulated in the Convention. If violations occur and are reported by other states, flag states are obliged to investigate and take necessary measures to redress the wrongdoing. Further, two subsequent provisions provide fortifying supports to this flag-state duty regime, Articles 192 and 193.[44] These two provisions impose on all parties duties and obligations to protect and preserve the marine environment, to which fishery conservation and management is one critical element. The *Southern Bluefin Tuna* Cases reifies this observation. The Tribunal opined that ". . .conservation of the living resources of the sea is an element in the protection and preservation of the marine environment".[45]

Specific obligations are mandated in Articles 58 and 62.[46] Viewing together, these two provisions provide that flag states are obliged to take necessary measures to ensure the compliance of their nationals and vessels with the conservation measures, laws and regulations set by coastal states in EEZs. Taking it a step further, flag states are invested with obligations to ensure that their nationals and vessels are not engaged in activities, including illegal fishing, that will undermine their conservation, protection and management duties.

It is with these designs that flag states are given, even if not primary, but equivalently weighing responsibilities to vindicate the goal of sustainable resources development of the Convention. In this regard, the flag state is said to have a genuine link with the vessel so that the nationality can be bestowed thereupon appropriately.[47]

As suggested by the ordinary meaning, the context and object and purpose of the Convention, a "genuine link" between a ship and the flag state must be a real and not an artificial or tenuous one.[48] A subsequent condition is that the flag state must be able to exercise effective control and jurisdiction over ships to which it has granted its nationality. International jurisprudence has up to now lent limited support to the clarification of this "genuine link" requirement. In *M/V Saiga (No.2)* case (*St. Vincent and the Grenadines v. Guinea*),[49] the Tribunal did not deal with the contention by Guinea upon a genuine link existed between St Vincent and the Grenadines and the ship. Rather, the Tribunal dismissed Guinea's contention by the lack of sufficient legal basis in Guinea's claim.[50] Although it is not clear what factor the Tribunal regards as relevant to the existence or otherwise of a genuine link, it seems to suggest that, on the consequences of the absence of a genuine link, effective exercise of flag state administration is a central element in the existence of a genuine link.[51]

It is thus logical to observe that the flag state is bestowed with weighing responsibilities in constraining vessels flying its flag not to engage in conducts undermining the object and purpose of the Convention in EEZs of coastal states. It is also a fair observation that Article 91, identical to Article 5 in the 1958 High Seas Convention, has provided a *ratione personae* jurisdiction of flag states upon vessels flying their flags. An effective control requirement of the flag state is laid out in Article 94 paragraph 1 in the Convention, which is later supplemented by a list of duties of flag state which fill out the general obligation in paragraph 1. This list is indicative, but not exhaustive.

As prescribed in the preamble, the Convention has aimed at establishing a legal order for the seas and oceans which promotes, inter alia, the equitable and efficient utilization and conservation for and of resources, and the study, protection and preservation of the marine environment.[52] The zoning system is designed so as to better deliver the aspired outcome, by assigning regulatory authority in certain spaces to one single actor, coastal state.

However, in the South China Sea where sovereignty attribution over land features from which territorial rights can be claimed upon maritime spaces are yet to be settled, claimant countries easily incur responsibilities when they make all possible efforts to substantialize or reify their respective sovereignty/territorial claims. For example, claimant countries may launch efforts to construct and enlarge small islets so as to pave the way for or to better facilitate their maritime claims.[53] In the Convention, Article 60 provides for such a right for coastal countries in their EEZs.[54] Yet what remains intriguing is the unsettled status of the South China Sea waters, thus leaving room for claimant countries to vindicate their claims respectively by pursuing unilateral measures. Before final agreement, it can hardly blame these acting countries for the law breaking of their activities. Rather, it is the inappropriateness and illegitimacy of these activities that have inflicted upon these countries moral stains. A similar instance can be drawn to fishing activities, and the danger of burgeoning fishing run-ins, when territorial and EEZ boundaries remain unsettled.[55]

Clearly, in an area where territorial attribution remains disputed, the design in the Convention accordingly would doom the settlement of EEZ delimitation. Without a clearly demarcated line, fishermen are confronted with greater risks when fishing in the South China Sea. Similarly, conservation and management measures, with national divergence and contradiction, would be easily shrugged off. Their intended goal and impacts therefore are to be seriously attenuated. It is in this sense that the flag state may/would need to take a larger role, greater than what is designated in the Convention. By strengthening constraints on their own nationals, claimant countries would be easier to bring under control escalating tensions, and eventually, pacify the simmering rivalry among all stake holders.

In the Convention, the mechanism has accorded, respectively, coastal and flag countries their responsibilities. Yet, as demonstrated in the South China Sea stalemate, certain flexibility is required in the apportioning of these duties so that regional and local situations could be better facilitated. This adjustment may be realized via various existing platforms and channels, judicial and non-judicial. In the South China Sea context, the dash-line claim may provide a thread out of this current stalemate, as one good start for regional conciliation and dispute resolution.

D Recontemplating exclusive economic zoning

In this aspect, some reconsiderations are worth the efforts before proposals being attempted.

The EEZ regime is an invention by the Convention in bringing in line diversifying practices in marine resource utilization. The contribution lies, in terms that by the single attribution of the right for resource development into one coastal country would better realize the goal of conservation and development in the marine environment. Also, wrestling toiled among coastal and sea power countries in due course of the negotiation further materializes the fact that the EEZ system is a quid prod quo, or at least compromises, so that the territorial water is confined within a scope of 12 nm from the coast.[56] However sublime the intended goal for marine environmental protection is, the single-country management system which is coupled with a spatial jurisdiction in the EEZ is not as productive as what is purposively intended.

On the contrary, this single-country management system has been stymied in delivering the much-awaited outcome of successful marine resource conservation, whose paralysis further leads to anarchical competition for marine resource among countries. One example of blatant evidentiary effect is the request for an advisory opinion of the International Tribunal for the Law of the Sea by a Sub-Regional Fisheries Commission,[57] concerning the relatively inefficient EEZ management, by launching a request to clarify responsibilities of flag states and fishery organization that issue fishing authorization in the EEZ of its member countries.[58]

One sensible explanation to this single-country management system which enables coastal countries to enjoy sovereign rights over marine resources, is rooted from the Westphalian concept towards the international order. In a sense, one way to calibrate national prowess in the Westphalian system is via acquisition of land territories and restriction of access to resources, which may be achieved by formal agreements, extra-treaty actions and violence. Restriction of access to resources could be traced all the way back to the colonial era when not all polities were allowed to join in the international political hierarchy, let alone to partaking in resource sharing and development.[59] In the new iteration of the Westphalian international order, this legacy nevertheless has lingered. Yet, its impact is cushioned off by a United Nations institution, under which the throat-cutting competition to resource is less likely to take place. All things equal, this race-to-the-bottom competition is most likely to occur when international law does not render a helpful hand in conflict management, dispute resolution or is in itself the raison d'etre of the problem. In this sense, international law is functioning as one last means to keep the lid on wild aspirations of every country to external competition in a state of lawlessness.

The South China Sea has to some extent fallen into this category, when international law seemingly does not render helping hands to dispute resolution. Under a vacuum of legal authority, power politics fills in the gap, as can be seen for past decades. This helps explains the escalation of recent rounds of tensions, and their consistent focus on resource competition which is also coupled with fears of revived imperialist conquest over territories and monopolization of resource access. As such, whether there exists an alternative other than this law-of-the-sea system, is worth contemplation. The Chinese approach, by contending a dash-line claim, may provide a breakthrough, or as attempts for intellectual brainstorming and deployment for future actions.

Having identified the EEZ complex and its potential inappropriateness in solving the South China Sea issue, the dash-line claim held by China (PRC) steps in as one denoting a context that makes the application of the Convention inappropriate and unfeasible. In other words, even if China (PRC)'s activities in contending its EEZ-relevant claims are seemingly inappropriate and beyond what is widely recognized as "reasonable", the dash-line claim may help justifying that these great swathes of waters fall within this dash-line limit and have been under the aegis of China (PRC)'s influences, in whatever manifestation, thus mitigating the alleged illegitimacy and accountability of the Chinese activities.

This concerns, in the wake of the gradual "territorialization" of the South China Sea waters by China (PRC), may be further solidified. Accordingly, inquiries are raised. Is the EEZ system the only option available for maritime zoning in an area like the South China Sea? How would the dash-line claim, apparently in the middle of a progress of development and materialization, contribute to bring in peace on to this region that would benefit all?

III The dash-line claim and jurisdiction right upon maritime spaces

A *Jurisdictions upon maritime spaces*

The trend that China (PRC) has marched towards further "territorialize" the waters lying within the dash-line claim confirms one observation that contemporary Law of the Sea regime may be short of providing appropriate instruments in an area replete with historical legacies, in particular, when these past memories are revived in company with a change/shift of power balances in the regional sphere. From a contextual point of view, China (PRC)'s development has to a large extent helped push through the revival of these historical legacies.

One critical issue overshadowing China (PRC)'s effort is whether this "territorialization" would defy contemporary Law of the Sea regime, which would shatter the established consensus in the international community regarding the unimpeded navigation freedom in, generally, all maritime spaces for peaceful and regular purposes. These worries are not totally unrealistic, and have been greatly felt in capitals of ASEAN and other stakeholder countries. In the light of such and the potential destructiveness, China (PRC) would need to bear on the challenges to generate more elaborations to flesh out the dash-line claim.

90 A proposal of jurisdiction

In this sense, the concept "jurisdiction right upon maritime spaces" may shed light on the Chinese effort for carving out a new course.

i The jurisdiction right upon maritime spaces

The dilemma of current Law of the Sea regime in the South China Sea is rooted on, briefly speaking, two different zoning systems, between an ancient conception towards maritime spaces, China (PRC)'s dash-line claim, and a contemporary compartmentalization standard, maritime zoning standard in the Convention. In other words, China's clinch to the dash-line claim is reflecting, and will inevitably entail conflicts between traditional maritime practices and concepts rooted in Asia, and those being developed and dominating around globe in near past Western centuries.

The dash-line claim denotes a concept of "jurisdiction upon maritime spaces" (or maritime-space jurisdiction), which requires serious considerations. It lends explanatory supports to clarify what this concept means and constructive effects to substantialize what this concept can offer for the resolution of the South China Sea dispute.

I THE GOAL: ORDER-MAINTENANCE, CONFLICT-MANAGEMENT AND NAVIGATION FREEDOM

One thing requires clarification is that by upholding this dash-line claim under which a maritime-space-jurisdiction concept is proposed does not, by any means, to defy contemporary Law of the Sea regime. Rather, this maritime-space-jurisdiction is to be developed on this well-established maritime legal basis, by filling what has been unclear or missing in this system. In other words, this concept serves a short-term and long-term goal. For the former, it hopes to make a contribution to solve the South China Sea dilemma, mostly under the manifestation of order maintenance and conflict management. From a long-term perspective, it is to explore the possibilities to facilitate Asian values in contemporary international political and legal system.

Firstly, this maritime-space jurisdiction concept aims at "order maintenance" and "conflict management", while seaborne activities can be guaranteed of non-interruption and of persistent peaceful utilization for all stakeholder countries. In this sense, measures thus entailed would concern mainly security maintenance and conflict prevention and management. Also, it would be practised on a spatial basis, by which the waters lying within this dash line are deemed as a part of China (PRC)'s territory. Yet, this territorial-like zones is distinguished from regular territorial waters in one aspect, this zone is marked by an open-ended boundary. In other words, China (PRC) would be given a spatial jurisdiction by this dash-line zoning, which would be marked by an open-end boundary, and to deliver its effect by exercising a *ratione-materiae* jurisdiction on "security". This would help realize its aspiration to the goals of "order maintenance" and "conflict management".

Yet, current dilemma in the South China Sea sends an alarming message of how current Law of the Sea regime, with a focus tilting on the spatial jurisdiction of coastal countries with a limit of a *ratione-materiae* focus, may fall into stalemate. In light of this, China (PRC)'s maritime-space jurisdiction would not be fully functional, if a *ratione-personae* jurisdiction of flag states was not receiving equivalent role. Put lucidly, regional maritime security could most efficiently be maintained if the flag state responsibilities over vessels flying its flag be emphasized along with China (PRC)'s spatial jurisdiction.

Another thorn in the flesh that requires contemplation is the resource development and utilization. Current Law of the Sea regime has assigned this regulatory authority, in particular in EEZs, to coastal country, subject to certain limits to safeguard peaceful and regular non-resource relevant utilization of other countries.[60] By imposing a maritime-space jurisdiction, this current resource-developing and sharing mechanism in the Convention[61] should be respected. Further, inter-state negotiations, bilateral or multilateral, could be employed, should thornier issues arise, while the concept of "joint development" would be of instrumental and pragmatic assistance.

Two reasons lend supports to this proposal

For one thing, this maritime-space jurisdiction has had a security focus, and has been defensive in nature. A brief review of historical incidents would reify this contention. In the South China Sea, this concept has long served a stabilizing function, as Chinese influences had rarely disturbed, impeded or forbidden regional seaborne activities. Generally, it is from early Ming dynasty that the "sea ban" policy was applied against threats from pirates and bandits.[62] In other words, it is a defence-oriented approach, and to address more on regulating its nationals and the enhancement of coastal defence.[63] In the Qing dynasty, this defence-oriented mentality held great sway in the maritime security concept and coastal planning of the government, and local elites.[64] Even after the limitation of foreign trade to one harbour, Guangzhou, in mid-Qing period (1757), the approach remains inward-looking.[65]

In this sense, it is hardly convincing to say that "jurisdiction right upon maritime spaces" long-practised in pre-nineteenth century Asia was eyeing on the monopolization of marine resources and of an aggressive nature, which would make egregious encroachment to regional and littoral countries' interests. The persistently thriving seaborne trade and human mobility (emigrants and overseas Chinese business communities), except the sea-ban policy intermittently implemented by emperors in Ming and Qing dynasties, supported this observation.

The second raison d'être is that China (PRC) would be able to live up its words, as demonstrated in several occasions, that it has benefited from current international legal order, and would respect this system. In the South China Sea, what comes to egregious confrontation with China (PRC)'s maritime-space jurisdiction would be the EEZ zoning system, and the affiliated rights and interests. However, due exercise of this maritime-space jurisdiction would show that these concerns are far-fetched.

As explained, this jurisdiction is exercised on a spatial basis, with two limits, a ratione-materiae focus on mainly "security" matters and an open-ended boundary. Resource development and sharing would not fall into this "security" jurisdiction, and should be regulated under current EEZ zoning and management system in the Convention. Not only has China (PRC)'s repeated statements endorse the resource developing and sharing system in the Convention, but also the historical practices which would not hinder regular seaborne activities, be them sailing, fishing or others. Further, out of population growth, technological change and the surging demand of marine resources, the cooperation and management mechanism established in the Convention provides a reliable platform to deal with these resource depletion issues and to effectively curb externality evils, such as free-rider problem, and the common pool dilemma.[66]

In short, this maritime-space jurisdiction would be exercised with a spatial characteristic, upon waters falling within the dash line. This water is marked by an open-ended boundary line (the dash line), with a *ratione-materiae* focus on "security" matters. To better achieve the aspired maritime security and order maintenance, flag state responsibilities over vessels flying its flag should be emphasized too. Further, this jurisdiction would not be used as to monopolize resource development and utilization. Rather, the EEZ system and resource development rules would be deferred and observed. In this regard, should thorny issues arise, they should be resolved via negotiations, with the concept "joint development" serving pragmatic assistance to dispute resolution.

IV Conclusion

In the Convention, maritime zoning is following attribution of land features. Zoning great swathes of maritime spaces constitutes the initial step in delineating rights of those acting thereon, and their incurred responsibilities. Yet, this centrality of managing the ocean from a spatio-geographical perspective is supplemented by identifying the subject actor, with whom all kinds of maritime activities are conducted and resources, developed. Following this line, contemporary maritime legal order is founded, mainly, on the granting of a spatio-geographical jurisdiction to coastal countries. This spatial jurisdiction is vividly reflected in the zoning system in the Convention. When going beyond a small band of coastal sea into the EEZs, this jurisdiction right is subject to a *ratione-materiae* focus, the development and conservation of maritime resource. Meanwhile, the Convention also bestow flag state due responsibilities to constrain its nationals and vessels. This *ratione-personae* jurisdiction functions to replenish the possible regulatory vacuum in maritime affairs being infused with burgeoning diversity and complexity.

Put in another way, it is spaces and people – the *managing*, subject actors whose activities are classified in different zones – by which the regulatory framework is designed and established. Marine species and environmental issues – *the managed*, which do not obey/observe this zoning and has moved around freely – are subject to this zoning and jurisdiction system. Some therefore describes that the first and utmost task of UNCLOS has been to establish a network of spatial property rules for areas of ocean spaces to be held privately, publicly, in common, or not at all.[67] Accomplishment and completion of this task remains a focus of contestation till present days.

However, this regulatory system has been confronted with challenges, in particular, in areas such as the South China Sea. Put briefly, the dilemma in the South China Sea is first, the blurring between maritime limits and maritime boundary, and subsequently, conflicts between two measures for generating maritime limits. It also explains why the zoning system established in the Convention cannot effectively solve the South China Sea dispute.

Re-contemplations of this zoning system, in particular the EEZ compartmentalization, do not necessarily lead to a full-scale defiance of contemporary maritime legal order. A review of incidents in the South China Sea reveals that there may exist, a concept of "jurisdiction upon maritime space", which has its origin rooted in past practices in East/Southeast Asia and would help thaw the South china Sea stalemate. This jurisdiction right is characterized with its *ratione-materiae* focus on "security" matters, and is marked by China (PRC)'s dash-line claim, a open-ended boundary line. "Maintenance of maritime order" and "peaceful utilization of resources" are two pillars, and goals as well, fortifying this jurisdiction. To carry out these projections, China (PRC) and other stakeholder countries would need to negotiate on strengthening the role of the *ratione-personae* jurisdiction of a flag state upon its nationals and vessels. This jurisdiction should not be deemed as an instrument for resource monopoly. Rather, resource development and sharing should observe the rules established in the Convention, to which inter-state negotiation and the concept of "joint development" should exercise as of supplementary, but equivalently important assistance.

The South China Sea dispute, while seemingly posing considerable threats in the security dimension, should be deemed as a window of opportunity to have a serious look of how memetic incongruence embedded in the cultural and conceptual breeding could structurally shatter a well-received international legal and regulatory framework. The South China Sea dilemma also indicates that expedient adjustment, in particular in some doctrinal areas, may turn out to be necessary. It is why this "jurisdiction right upon maritime space" should not be easily overlooked, and deserves appraisals.

This concept of "jurisdiction right upon maritime spaces" is discernible in areas under the influences of regional great power, and may refer, much likely, to a collective right to survival of littoral communities in this region. While the manifestation of its implementation may be varied, two characteristics could be found informing its practice, "the management of regional maritime order" and "peaceful utilization of marine resources by all those acting upon". Yet it is to be borne in mind that "utilization of marine resources" at that time would mainly concern fishing and marine harvest activities. Oil and ore under deep seabed remain far beyond the reach of mankind, out of the fact that the required technology remained at an embryonic stage, while knowledge towards petroleum resources, yet to be enlightened. In this aspect, the concept "joint development" should be upheld, and seriously contemplated.

Strictly speaking, this concept is not an innovation, but a retrospect for regional actors to look into their traditional and cultural soils where their vital interests on the sea are embedded and best explained. The resuscitation of this concept is, also, not to unseat contemporary Law of the Sea, or to defy anyhow the established regulatory framework in the Law of the Sea scenario. Rather, this concept of "jurisdiction rights upon maritime spaces" may serve to address the structural dilemma in the Law of the Sea regime.

Yet, to bring it to the field and apply it in the real world could best testify if this concept could and should be upheld. In the next two chapters, application of this concept would be attempted in selected cases.

Notes

1 Merriam-Webster Dictionary, "mare liberum", www.merriam-webster.com/dictionary/mare%20liberum, last visited 15 July, 2014; Encyclopedia Britannica, "mare liberum", www.britannica.com/EBchecked/topic/218563/Mare-Liberum, last visited 15 July, 2014.
2 Alison Reppy, "The Grotian Doctrine of the Freedom of the Seas Reappraised", *Fordhalm Law Review*, 19:3 (1950): 243–285, 256–257; Peter Borschberg, "Grotius' Theory of Trans-Oceanic Trade Regulation: Revisiting Mare Liberum (1609)", IILJ Working Paper 2005/14 Revised August 2006, this paper can be retrieved from www.iilj.org, last visited 30 July, 2014; Benedict Kingsbury, "A Grotian Tradition of Theory and Practice?: Grotius, Law and Moral Skepticism in the Thought of Hedley Bull", *Quinnipic Law Review*, 17:3 (1997): 1–33.
3 Reppy, "The Grotian Doctrine of the Freedom of the Seas Reappraised"; Borschberg, "Grotius' Theory of Trans-Oceanic Trade Regulation".
4 Anthony Anghie, "Finding the Peripheries: Sovereignty and Colonialism in Nineteenth-Century International Law", *Harvard International Law Journal*, 40:1 (Winter 1999): 1–71; Anghie, *Imperialism, Sovereignty and the Making of International Law* (Cambridge, UK: Cambridge University Press, 2005); Arnulf Becker Lorca, "Universal International Law: Nineteenth-Century Histories of Imposition and Appropriation", *Harvard International Law Journal*, 51:2 (Summer 2010): 475–552; Benedict Stuchtey, "Colonialism and Imperialism: 1450–1950", *European History Online*, 24 November, 2011, http://ieg-ego.eu., last visited 30 July, 2014.
5 During the first two decades of the seventeenth century, *Mare Liberum* is essentially a propagandistic treatise and had argued for Holland's merchants to freely access emporia in Asia by unimpeded navigation across the high seas. In this sense, this concept should be regarded a subset to the overarching arguments on the freedom of access and trade. During the first two decades of the seventeenth century, Grotius lent a helping hand in the process of forging political

and commercial treaties between the United Netherlands' East India Company and Asian rulers.
6 Reppy, "The Grotian Doctrine of the Freedom of the Seas Reappraised", 264–266, 272.
7 Bernard Oxman, "The Rule of Law and the United Nations Convention on the Law of the Sea", *European Journal of International Law*, 7 (1996): 353–371.
8 For example, the reproductive capacities of fishes, were thought to exceed the quantity of those that were commercially harvested. Also see, Robin Craig, "Sustaining the Unknown Seas: Changes in U.S. Ocean Policy and Regulation since Rio 92", *Environmental Law Reporter*, 32 (February 2002): 10190–10218; Harry Scheiber, "Ocean Governance and the Marine Fisheries Crisis: Two Decades of Innovation and Frustration", *Virginia Journal of Natural Resources Law*, 20 (2001): 119–137.
9 William Wertenbaker, "The Law of the Sea – I", *The New Yorker*, 15 August, 1983.
10 For example, North Sea Continental Shelf Cases (Federal Republic of Germany v. Denmark; Federal Republic of Germany v. Netherlands), International Court of Justice Report. 3 (1969); Maritime Delimitation and Territorial Questions between Qatar and Bharain (Qatar v. Bahrain), Merits, Judgment, International Court of Justice Report. (2001). Also, see Barbara Kaiatkowska, *Decisions of the World Court Relevant to the UN Convention on the Law of the Sea: A Reference Guide* (Hague: Kluwer Law International, 2002), 2–3; Yoshifumi Tanaka, *Predictability and Flexibility in the Law of Maritime Delimitation* (Portland: Hart Publishing, 2006), 121–122, 151–160.
11 It is not until recently that a country, or a single actor, could assert dominion or, at least, to exploit and develop marine resources at considerable scales. This kind of resource is deemed as a common property, also dubbed as "common pool resource". Generally, two characteristics can be identified: no single actor has established controls over the resource; the consumption of this common pool resource is to some extent rivalrous. When one consumes the resource, its quantity or quality will be diminished, harming the potentiality for other consumers. See more discussions in, Thrainn Eggertsson, *Economic Behaviours and Institutions* (Cambridge: Cambridge University Press, 1990). The electronic file of chapters in this book are available at the website of Cambridge University Press, http://ebooks.cambridge.org/ebook.jsf?bid=CBO9780511609404, last visited 20 April, 2015.
12 Eric A. Posner and Alan O. Sykes, "Economic Foundations of the Law of the Sea", *American Journal of International Law*, 104: 4(2010): 569–596.
13 UNCLOS in several provisions stipulate that before final maritime delimitation agreements are reached, states are to make every effort to enter into provision arrangements, while being restrained from activities that may jeopardize and impair the reaching of an ultimate delimitation. These obligations are inherently conflictual, See detailed discussions will be unfolded in Part II, section I)-I, on sovereignty of the sea. United Nations Convention on the Law of the Sea, 10 December, 1982, 1833 U.N.T.S. 397 [hereinafter the Convention].
14 Article 74, paragraph 3, "Pending agreement as provided for in paragraph 1, the States concerned, in a spirit of understanding and cooperation, shall make every effort to enter into provisional arrangements of a practical nature and, during this transitional period, not to jeopardize or hamper the reaching of the final agreement. Such arrangements shall be without prejudice to the final delimitation."

96 *A proposal of jurisdiction*

15 Article 83, paragraph 3, "Pending agreement as provided for in paragraph 1, the States concerned, in a spirit of understanding and cooperation, shall make every effort to enter into provisional arrangements of a practical nature and, during this transitional period, not to jeopardize or hamper the reaching of the final agreement. Such arrangements shall be without prejudice to the final delimitation."

16 See the Convention, Article 74(Delimitation of the exclusive economic zone between States with opposite or adjacent coasts), paragraph 3, in Part V(Exclusive Economic Zone) and 83(Delimitation of the continental shelf between States with opposite or adjacent coasts), paragraph 3, in Part VI (Continental Shelf).

17 See the Convention, Article 293(Applicable Law), paragraph 1, in Part XV(Settlement of Disputes), Section 2(Compulsory Procedures Entailing Binding Decisions).

18 See the Convention, Article 293(Applicable Law), paragraph 2, in Part XV(Settlement of Disputes), Section 2(Compulsory Procedures Entailing Binding Decisions).

19 See the Convention, Part XII (Protection and Reservation of the Marine Environment), Section 6 (Enforcement), Article 213 to 222.

20 See the Convention, Article 27 (Criminal Jurisdiction on Board a Foreign Ship), in Part II(Territorial Sea and Contiguous Zone), Section 3(Innocent Passage in the Territorial Sea), Subsection B(Rules Applicable to Merchant Ships and Government Ships Operated for Commercial Purposes).

21 See the Convention, Article 74(Delimitation of the Exclusive Economic Zone between States with Opposite or Adjacent Coasts), paragraph 3, in Part V(Exclusive Economic Zone).

22 See the Convention, Article 224 to 227, in Part XII(Protection and Reservation of the Marine Environment), Section 7 (Safeguards).

23 See the Convention, Article 232(Liability of States arising from Enforcement Measures), in Part XII(Protection and Reservation of the Marine Environment), Section 7 (Safeguards).

24 Arbitral Tribunal Constituted pursuant to Article 287, and in accordance with Annex VII of the United Nations Convention on the Law of the Sea in the Matter of an Arbitration between Guyana and Suriname (Guyana v. Suriname), Award of 17 September, 2007. See Final Award, paragraph 445. The Award and pleadings are available at www.pca-cpa.org.

25 The Tribunal does not draw a distinction between use of force against another State and use of limited force in the case of enforcement activities. The use of force in urgency to prevent infringement of a State's rights constitutes another scenario. This approach raises doubts, in the sense that use of force, of limited force and in case of urgency to prevent infringement of states' rights should have been distinguished. Conditions for a legitimate use of force in these occasions also vary.

26 Responsibility of States for Internationally Wrongful Acts, *Yearbook of the International Law Commission*, 2001, vol. 2, Part 2. The text can be retrieved from http://legal.un.org/ilc/texts/instruments/english/draft%20articles/9_6_2001.pdf, last visited 20 November, 2014. Text reproduced as it appears in the annex to General Assembly resolution 56/83 of 12 December, 2001, and corrected by document A/56/49(Vol. I)/Corr.4. See Article 30.

27 See Responsibility of States for Internationally Wrongful Acts, Article 31.

28 The Corfu Channel case, concerning Albania's responsibility for mining of British warships was exceptional. The Corfu Chanel Case (United Kingdom v. Albania),

International Court of Justice Decision, 9 April, 1949 [1949] International Court of Justice Report, 4.
29 Benedict Kingsbury, "International Courts: Uneven Judicialization in Global Order" (2011). New York University Public Law and Legal Theory Working Papers. Paper 259. http://lsr.nellco.org/nyu_plltwp/259.
30 For discussions on general economic problems that justify international regulation, see Alan O. Sykes, "The Economics of Public International Law", in *Handbook of Law and Economics*, A. Mitchell Polinsky and Steven Shavell (eds.) (Elsevier, 2007), 757–822; for international regulation of the oceans, see Robert Friedheim, "A Proper Order for the Oceans: An Agenda for the New Century", in *Order for the Oceans at the Turn of the Century*, Davor Vidas and Willy Ostreng (eds.) (Hague: Kluwer International, 1999), 537–539; Eric A. Posner and Alan O. Sykes (eds.), "The Law of the Sea", in *Economic Foundations of International Law* (Cambridge, MA: Harvard University Press, 2013), Chapter IV-17.
31 Jan Stel, "Ocean Space", in *Encyclopedia of Global Environmental Governance and Politics*, Philipp H. Pattberg and Fariborz Zelli (eds.) (Cheltenham, UK: Edward Elgar Publishing, 2015), 388–397.
32 Geographic proximity plays a weighing role in contemporary maritime jurisprudence in the international judiciary bodies. Generally, jurisprudence has consistently attached coastal geographical parameters with paramount importance in maritime boundary delimitation. Factors, such as the length and configuration of the relevant coasts and coastlines, proportionality, islands and its distance to the coast, receive weighing considerations. Others, such as socioeconomic, security and cultural arguments, tend to be ignored or viewed only with limited evidentiary weights.
33 Several provisions in Part V (Exclusive Economic Zone) provide guidance of the right and interest of other states in the coastal state's EEZ. For example, Article 58, 59, 63, 69, 70 and 74.
34 M/V "Virginia G" (Panama/Guinea-Bissau), Judgment of 14 April, 2014, paragraph 215.
35 See the Convention, Article 56, provides rights, jurisdiction and duties of the coastal State in the exclusive economic zone.
36 See the Convention, Article 61 and 62, about the conservation and utilization of the living resources.
37 See, the Convention, Article 62, paragraph 4, regarding the utilization of the living resources, and the compliance to coastal states' regulation in EEZ by other nationals. Article 73, paragraph 1, about the enforcement of laws and regulations of the coastal State.
38 See the Convention, Article 61 and 62, about the conservation and utilization of the living resources.
39 Margaret A. Young, *Trading Fish, Saving Fish: The Interaction between Regimes in International Law* (Cambridge: Cambridge University Press, 2011), 35–38. Also, for a list of bilateral agreements between EU and outside countries, see European Commission, "Bilateral Agreements with Countries Outside the EU", http://ec.europa.eu/fisheries/cfp/international/agreements/index_en.htm, last visited 20 April, 2015.
40 There exist controversies about these fishery arrangements and the ecological impacts on the local marine environment. See Emma Witbooi, "The Infusion of Sustainability into Bilateral Fisheries Agreements with Developing Countries: The European Union Example", *Marine Policy*, 32 (2008): 669–679; Darren Calley, *Market Denial and International Fisheries Regulation: The Targeted and*

98 A proposal of jurisdiction

Effective Use of Trade Measures Against the Flag of Convenience Fishing Industry (Amsterdam: Martinus Nijhoff Publishers, 2011), 161–207; Melanie King, "Coastal Communities and the International Fishery Framework", *Sea Grant Law and Policy Journal*, 1:2 (December 2008): 15–39.

41 In light of the special rights and responsibilities given to the coastal states in EEZs, the primary responsibility to curb illegal, unregulated and unreported fishing has rested on coastal states. See Article 55 and 56, paragraph 1, Article 62, paragraph 1 to 4, and Article 73.
42 See, the Convention, Articles 91 and 92, about the nationality and status of ships.
43 See, the Convention, Article 94, about duties of the flag state.
44 See, the Convention, Part XII, Protection and Preservation of the Marine Environment, about general obligations and sovereign right of states to exploit their natural resources.
45 Southern Bluefin Tuna (New Zealand v. Japan; Australia v. Japan), Provisional Measures, Order of 27 August, 1999, International Tribunal for the Law of the Sea (ITLOS) Reports 1999, p. 259, paragraph 70.
46 See, the Convention, Article 58, Rights and duties of other States in the exclusive economic zone, paragraph 3 and Article 62, Utilization of the living resources, paragraph 4.
47 See, the Convention, Article 91, about nationality of ships.
48 See, the Vienna Convention on the Law of Treaties, in Article 31 and 32, for treaty interpretation. For more discussions in Vienna Convention, see Ian Sinclair, *The Vienna Convention on the Law of Treaties* (Manchester, UK: Manchester University Press, 1984); Anthony Aust, *Modern Treaty Law and Practice* (Cambridge: Cambridge University Press, 2000).
49 The M/V 'SAIGA' (No. 2), Saint Vincent and the Grenadines v Guinea, Merits, Judgment, ITLOS Case No. 2, ICGJ 336 (ITLOS 1999) (OUP reference), read on Oxford Public International Law, http://opil.ouplaw.com/view/10.1093/law:icgj/336itlos99.case.1/law-icgj-336itlos99, last visited 20 April, 2015.
50 The Tribunal held, by 18 votes to 2, there is no legal basis for the claim of Guinea that it can refuse to recognize the right of the Saiga to fly the flag of St Vincent and the Grenadines on the ground that there was no genuine link between the ship and St. Vincent and the Grenadines." Judgment, paragraph 86.
51 See, The M/V 'SAIGA' (No. 2) (ITLOS 1999), Judgment, paragraph 83.
52 See, The Convention, Preamble.
53 For these past years, ASEAN claimants and China have engaged in construction works to enlarge the land features under their occupation. There exist two structural problems that make these construction works controversial and questionable, legally and morally: the status and conditions of an island and rock (Article 121), and the EEZ delimitation (Article 55–75) in the South China Sea. Both lack a clear definition in the Convention.
54 See, the Convention, Article 60, about artificial islands, installations and structures in the exclusive economic zone.
55 Unsettled territorial lines and EEZ delimitation are two major raison d'êtres for these fishing spark-up in the South China Sea. For one thing, fishermen are in an inherent disadvantageous position to get to know various legislations of claimant countries. Further, fish do not observe these unilateral or tentative lines, leading fishermen to chase around in the South China Sea, with increasing risks that they easily break up national legislations of coastal countries.
56 R.R. Churchill and A.V. Lowe, *The Law of the Sea*, 3rd ed. (Manchester, UK: Manchester University Press, 1999); Donald R. Rothwell and Tim Stephens, *The International Law of the Sea* (Oxford, UK: Hart Publishing, 2010); Tommy Koh and Shanmugam Jayakumar, "The Negotiating Process of the Third United Nations Conference on the Law of the Sea" in *United Nations*

Convention on the Law of the Sea 1982: A Commentary, vol. 1, Myron Nordquist (ed.) (Dordrecht: Martinus Nijhoff Publishers), pp. 29–134; ; also, see Robert Beckman and Tara Davenport, "The EEZ Regime: Reflections after 30 Years" (papers from the "Law of the Sea Institute, UC Berkeley–Korea Institute of Ocean Science and Technology Conference", held in Seoul, Korea, May 2012).
57 Request for Advisory Opinion Submitted by the Sub-Regional Fisheries Commission, Advisory Opinion, 2 April, 2015, ITLOS Reports 2015, to be published. For more information, International Tribunal for the law of the Sea, "Request for an Advisory Opinion Submitted by the Sub-Regional Fisheries Commission (SRFC)", No. 21, 2 April, 2015, www.itlos.org/cases/list-of-cases/case-no-21/#c2272, last visited 20 April, 2015.
58 Four questions are posted to the Tribunal. They are: the obligations of the flag state in cases where IUU fishing activities are conducted within the EEZ of third-party states; to what extent shall the flag state be held liable for IUU fishing activities conducted by vessels flying its flag; where a fishing licence is issued to a vessel within the framework of an international agreement with the flag state or with an international agency, shall the state or international agency be held liable for the violation of the fisheries legislation of the coastal state by the vessel in question; and the rights and obligations of the coastal state in ensuring the sustainable management of shared stocks and stocks of common interest, especially the small pelagic species and tuna.
59 Prasenjit Duara, *The Global and Regional in China's Nation-Formation* (Abingdon, UK: Routledge, 2008), 186–188; Peter Nolan, *Re-Balancing China: Essays on the Global Financial Crisis, Industrial Policy and International Relations* (London: Anthem Press, 2015), 177–199.
60 See The Convention, Part V, Article 55–75.
61 The resource-sharing and development mechanism in the Convention has both domestic and external dimensions. The regulatory authority is bestowed mainly on coastal countries. The Convention has required these coastal countries to bring in line their domestic legislation with the Convention regime. The external dimension mainly addresses the peaceful utilization of maritime spaces by non-coastal countries, and international cooperation on scenarios where effort of single country could hardly deliver substantial outcomes. Examples are like the Area and High Seas.
62 Tian Xiu-juan, "A Brief Analysis of the Coast Defence Slack and Japanese Invaders Rampancy in the Late Ming Dynasty", *Journal of Liaoning Educational Administration Institute*, 25:11 (2008): 46–48; Rigen Wang, "Maritime Policy and the Vicissitude of Port Cities in Southeast Coast in the Yuan-Ming-Qing Period" [Yuan-Ming-Qing zhengfu Haiyang zhengce yu dongnan yanhai gangshi de xiangshuai shanbian pianlun], *The Journal of Chinese Social and Economic History*, 2 (2000): 1–7; Dahpon David Ho, "Sealords Live in Vain: Fujian and the Making of a Maritime Frontier in Seventeenth-Century China" (Ph.D. Dissertation, University of California, San Diego, 2011); Hugh R. Clark, "Frontier Discourse and China's Maritime Frontier: China's Frontiers and the Encounter with the Sea through Early Imperial History", *Journal of World History*, 20:1(2009): 1–33.
63 It is argued that by imposing strict seaban policy on the Southeast coast in China, peoples in the coastal communities were plagued with difficult living conditions, turning these coastal areas into barren landscapes. The Seaban laws of the Ming Dynasty had laid the basis for revolt effectively criminalizing the coastal population of Fujian.
64 Gongzhong Li and Xia Li, "The Memory of Sea Bandit (Wokou) and Development of Maritime Power in China" [Wokou jiyi yu zhongguo haiquan guannian

de yanjin], *Jianghai Academic Journal*, 3 (2007): 150–155; Yue Gao, "An Analytical View of the Development of Maritime Power in Contemporary China" [Jindai zhongguo haiquan sixiang qianxi], *Zhejian Academic Journal*, 6 (2013): 5–12.
65 Yu He, "An Inquiry to the Ideological Root of the Coastal Areas and Territorial Seas Policy in the Qing Dynasty" [Qingdai haijiang zhengce de sixiang tanyuan], *Studies in Qing History*, 2 (1998): 77–89.
66 Eric A. Posner and Alan O. Sykes (eds.), "The Law of the Sea", in *Economic Foundations of International Law* (Cambridge, MA: Harvard University Press, 2013), Chapter IV-17; and Sykes, "The Economics of Public International Law"; Friedheim, "A Proper Order for the Oceans".
67 Wertenbaker, *The Law of the Sea – I*, 39–40.

6 From the periphery

The South China Sea as a frontier and application of the maritime space jurisdiction right

I Boundary, frontier and the South China Sea

A A sketch of the evolution of boundary concept in Southeast Asia

The evolution of boundaries in Southeast Asia has not followed the classical model of an international boundary. It is observed that due to the political discontinuity created by the intervention of European colonial powers, the evolution of boundaries in Southeast Asia has seen a discursive development.[1] Generally, the four stages—namely, allocation or definition, delimitation, demarcation and administration[2]-are not conducted in a linear order. Instead, the map, if not physically connoted, has been more like a patchwork piece, which is imbued with boundary disputes and conflicts being festered at different stages. Unfortunately, before regional countries can once and for all dismiss the chaos in Southeast Asian continent, rough and tumble appears to creep to the great swathes of South China Sea waters that several of Southeast Asian countries have bordered. To some extent, the increasing involvement of Southeast Asian countries in the scuffle in the South China Sea is once assimilated as what had been happening in the pre-colonial era of old kingdoms,[3] when they keenly looked into the sea as a source of wealth and revenue of royal and dynastic authorities.

Before the arrival of the Europeans and the imposition of more systemic and depredatory colonial administration, the concept and practice of borderlands and boundaries in Southeast Asia were rather alien to these western invaders. In short, the ebb and flow of conflicts between coastal people and upland tribes had rendered unstable and undetermined boundaries in Southeast Asia mainland. Boundaries between local kingdoms and dynasties were not stable, non-delimited and non-demarcated. Further, within the region, zones of contact,[4] and in some cases, of separation[5] and intermittent positional warfare, serve the functional equivalent of borders. Accordingly, the "sovereign" extension of these kingdoms, dynasties and principalities were determined by a power relationship that was always subject to change.[6] Despite the conceptual variance of "boundary" and "boundary-making", technical underdevelopment also explains this Southeast

Asian political map without borders. The legal and cartographic instruments of border definition and identification were absent. Under the realist context that the central authority had dwindled while administration could barely reach into remote territories, whose inhabitants were used to this neglect by the alleged central authority and hardly would identify themselves with the lowland political authority. These pre-colonial concepts and practices of boundaries, territory and sovereignty nevertheless had been traceable among these Southeast Asian polities in both colonial eras and present days. As what are to be discussed in later discussions, the strategies, policies and perspectives of Southeast Asian countries towards the South China Sea disputes, are actually reflective of these ancient culturally-informed thoughts and understandings. Thus, while the essence of sovereignty was of great importance, the territorial aspect of sovereignty was in fact negotiable.

The European encounter with Southeast Asian kingdoms, dynasties and principalities had inflicted upon the region profound changes. In terms of the development of concepts of sovereign nation states and territoriality, also termed as an outcome of western impositions, colonial ruling had left behind, both implicit and explicit, political and legal legacies that continue to shape the Southeast Asian geographical and political map. In the maritime domain, the idea that the sea unites rather than segregates territories and regions, through the linkages created by maritime networks, has been present in various parts of the world.[7] This, also applies to Southeast Asia, and the great swathes of waters in the South China Sea. But things, to some extents, may have festered, as this modern South China Sea issue has seen not only politicization of corresponding actions and reactions of involving countries, but also legalized rules mandating clear limits like 12-mile territorial sea and 200-mile economic zone. Under this context, challenges appear harsher. Changes to be wrought about by this still developing South China Sea issue is not just the units of seas, as what had been facing the indigenous Southeast Asian polities in ancient times, or just land units during the colonial period. Rather, challenges today are a combination of both. In other words, in company with the development of the South China Sea issue and further integration in the mainland Southeast Asia, it is a fair observation that political units from today onwards will be one of land and seas. Further, in some cases, the units of seas will be much larger than the political units on land. In this sense, history is paradoxically yet to come one full circle.

B Frontiers in the contemporary context and the South China Sea

A frontier and a zone of contact

Since the prevalence and heightening of European colonialism and mercantilist administration in Southeast Asia in the nineteenth century, both the ruling and ruled encountered difficulties wrought by clashes of different sets of values and orders stemmed from distinctive cultural, political and legal backgrounds.

It was expected that the European colonialists would thrust upon these newly acquired colonial territories an administrative apparatus, to which draconian governance and severe laws were two constituents of the foremost importance. Law and order would not precede but follow from a certain general agreement as to the desired legal order. As long as such a consensus remained wanting, politics were necessarily posited in a more primary, pre-rule of law stage. Yet, these encounters had generated roughs and tumbles in the metropole and the colonial Southeast Asia. The imposition of clearly defined boundaries, which to certain degrees had obfuscated local realities and customs, served one example. This boundary obfuscation, with which a territorialization effect had been assumed, could also be deemed as one critical factor that has since enmeshed scholars, policy-makers and the public in the South China Sea conundrum.

Nevertheless, the main focus here should not boil down to moral debates that have put European colonialism in Southeast Asia on the cross of ethnic hatreds. Therefore, contemporary colonial context, nevertheless imbued with legal construction and legitimacy-building of European colonialism, would serve as mere background information. Recognition of European colonialism is by no means either presumed or upheld.

In the nineteenth century when China and the Southeast Asia was encountered by forceful and predatory European encroachment in both political and commercial dimensions of their political autonomy and territorial integrity, if not hastily classified, as sovereignty, one among many issue was the imposition of boundaries, boundary lines and boundary areas. To further confuse the picture, other terms, generating more obfuscation, were used interchangeably in the narratives, such as "border (lands)", frontiers and zones of interests and influences.[8] While Southeast Asia was put at the helm of European colonial powers, the making of boundaries was mainly to serve the interests of the metropole, rather than peoples in the local. For the single actor staying relatively insulated from these foreign influences, the Kingdom of Siam (Thailand), the Siamese had exercised a territorial diplomacy to trade remote, peripheral lands for the safety and security of the core in the kingdom.[9] In short, the assignment of boundaries in colonial Southeast Asia was in the hands of the colonial government, for the interests of the metropole and colonial authority, and generally to the detriment of the local population.

One issue nevertheless attracting attention was the concept of frontier, and its implications if it could be applied to the South China Sea issue.

Frontier is different from boundaries. Rather than a clearly defined boundary line generally out of calculation of interests and political calibration, "frontier" can either refer to the political division between two countries or the division between the settled and uninhabited parts within one country.[10] It is the former, not the latter that lends supports to the discussions of the South China Sea issue. Put tersely, political frontier, as different from settlement frontier falling within a state's sovereign domain, has no settled de jure limits, and only disappears when two or more states compete for territory and delimit a definite boundary separating their sovereign domains. These political frontiers mainly are concerned with their physical characteristics, positions, attitudes and policies of flanking states, the influence of the frontier on subsequent development of the cultural landscape and the way in which boundaries were drawn within the frontier.

Several characteristics feature this sort of political frontier. The frontier is outer-oriented and a manifestation of centrifugal forces. Yet the frontier can be an integrating factor, but not a separating one. The frontier, generally remote areas, is harboring their own interests and consciousness different from those of the central government. As runaway elements and centrifugal interests, the frontier nevertheless serves for chances of integration and incorporation of neighbouring zones situated in another sovereign domain. In other words, a frontier provides an excellent opportunity for mutual interpenetration and sway. It is particularly the case as in Southeast Asia when boundaries were generally imposed in a context non-reflective of local realities and practicalities. Further, colonial administration had not established the required administrative apparatus that enabled border land control. Instead, border security was one thin focus of these colonial boundary policies.

Yet one difficulty plaguing the efforts in identifying and defining "frontier" is the given dilemma, that to what degrees is it possible to generalized about the frontier?

This dilemma, on the one hand, is self-proven. A frontier, unlike a boundary, is more a product of history and of political concerns. These two intrinsic characteristics, historical and political, have rendered it difficult to be generalized with quantitative and measurable parameters. Also, following from the historical and political legacies proven to be quintessential to gauge a frontier, a high degree of contingency, expressed in the fluidity of situations in every case and the high dependence on the contextual environment, is one common phenomenon of frontiers. One example could be illustrated in the territorial acquisition of the Russian Tsarist empire from the Chinese Qing empire in late nineteenth century.

The Tsarist Russian had a lifestyle much less different from that of the pastoral nomadic people in the outer-Mongolian domain. The Qing Chinese, instead, had embedded their society and country on agriculture depending much on an intensive and irrigation system. The incompatibility between the Mongol Khan people and the Chinese people, in either lifestyle, culture or other societal aspects, was more sharply demonstrating that as between the Mongol Khan and Russia Tsar. Consequently, the Mongol desert became a zone of separation between the Han-Chinese and Mongol-Khan civilizations, but a zone of contact from which integration forces were larger and impulsive between the Russian Slavic and Mongol Khan. It was in this sense that the Russian expansion in the Far East since the eighteenth and nineteenth centuries was categorized – in addition to conquest – as frontier integration.[11]

From this boundary-frontier misconception, the South China Sea area should be re-evaluated.

The South China Sea as a frontier and a zone of contact

The South China Sea (the SCS or the Sea hereafter) is bordered by China, Indonesia, Malaysia, the Philippines, Taiwan and Vietnam. It covers around 3.3 million km², excluding the Gulf of Tonkin and Thailand. Sometimes referred to as the "Asian Mediterranean", the Sea is surrounded by some most vibrant economies in nowadays with some densely populated metropolitan areas in the coastal regions. Into the Sea drains significant rivers, the Pearl in Guangdong Province in China, the Red in North Vietnam, and the Mekong in South Vietnam. Many smaller rivers characterize East Malaysia and the Philippines. Associated with these onshore water resources are cities hosting millions of people, and immense pressures from the metropolitan sanitation, consumption of proteins from marine products, and comparative pollutions and disturbances upon the coastal, and offshore marine environment.

The Sea also possesses considerable habitat, and spices diversity. Along the Philippines coast, more than 450 coral species have been recorded.[12] Recent estimates also suggest that around 12 percent of the world mangrove forest is located in the countries bordering the Sea. Six species of marine turtles, either listed as endangered or vulnerable on the International Union for Conversation and Nature (IUCN) list, the dugong and several other spices of marine mammals, which are included on the IUCN Red List of Threatened Animals occur in this region.[13] The migratory behaviour of these species are often trans-boundary, thus imposing great challenges to relevant reservation efforts.

These innate geographical characteristics speak much of how the South China Sea had and has continued to be a source of food supply, and a means of intra-regional communication among local communities since pre-colonial era. Much owed to its chokepoint position in the navigation route between the Indian and Pacific Ocean, this region had regularly received an influx of external cultural influences from the Hinduism-Indian and Confucianism-Chinese spheres. These external influences, which realized "Indianization" and "Sinicization", had brought about a degree of cultural unity in this region, where elements from both could be located and conjugations, flattering the regional cultural richness. Besides these two main cultural domains, there were places entrenching their standing relatively untouched by either force. The Philippines, New Guinea islands and offshore islets in Melanesia, constituted a third distinctive segment. They were a conjugation of the Austronesian system and primary tribal cultures. In this picture, trade had also played a dual role. In some aspect, it served as the chief medium of the transmission of Indian and Chinese cultural influences, while it was polarizing in others.[14] The panoramic view of the political map had told much of this polarization. Even before the arrival of European colonial powers and the thrust-upon of the Westphalian concept and practices, this contestable role of "trade" was responsible, to a considerable extent, for this division of intra-regional political economy into an inland-agrarian hydraulic segment, and a riparian or coastal commercial segment.[15] Geographical and cultural characteristics as such have conjured an image of pre-colonial Southeast Asia with local kingdoms and principalities and their interactions featuring limited hierarchical organization, weak internal political and administrative control and blurred and overlapping territorial domains.

In this context, there existed no such concept of "boundaries", and the area bordering two or more polities were configured as zones of interests. These peripheral zones, bettered termed as frontier zones, served to facilitate transitions through which neighbouring powers and influences interpenetrated in a two-way manner. In other words, these zones were more for intermediation and integration, while less for separation as what a formal standardized boundary line mainly had aimed at. Further, rules of neighbouring polities sought to command the loyalty of their subjects and unify their domain. It was rightly argued that rulers had competed for prestige, rather than property; for people, rather than land.[16] Under this context had the concept of "territories" of each particular polity been construed. This loosely defined territorial concept had much implication upon the sparsely located islands, islets and rocks on the South China Sea.

Political legacies set in motion the perceptions of people in this region regarding how "spaces" are to be perceived and construed, and how perceptions are to be applied in political and legal forum for practices and law-making. Among other things, one point for contention is how these political legacies have set in to remould the perceptions towards the sea.[17] At this juncture, it is a fair observation that situating in the traffic chokepoint, the South China Sea could be deemed, in a more consolidated manner, a zone of contact between earlier Southeast Asia and outer worlds with whom extensive trades were frequented and established, namely India and China. In other words, the South China Sea was a frontier zone where contacts were facilitated from the Confucianist-China in the north, the Hinduist-India in the west, and the Malay-Southeast Asian in local principalities.[18]

C Implications

By prescribing the South China Sea as a zone of contact, in which the inherent flexibility of a zone of contact could be retained and put into practices when opportunity presented itself, it not only would be more sustainable because of its compatibility with the still-developing concept of the ASEAN regionalism, but also would help carve a resolution out of current South China Sea quagmire.

Regional order in postwar Asia is embedded in the Westphalian system. Two pillars quintessential to the operation of this system are first, territorial acquisition, and second, the exclusivity of the right to resources entailed by territorial acquisitions.[19] Under this aegis, territoriality in this region, has ridded itself off the inherently Asian characteristics seeing blurring and overlapping sovereign domains. This led to the contestation that the nature of this Westphalian nation-state system necessitates the establishment of a clear boundary that separates the sovereign domain of neighbouring countries. It is thus a fair observation that instead of border security, border control becomes another dimension that calls for efficient and effective management efforts. In this sense, considerations paying heeds to folkloric needs play a critical role for effective border control, which would require communication and cooperation between flanking states.

This logic has lent supporting references when contemplating the South China Sea issues. Two points merit attention.

First, the South China Sea is replete with shoals, reefs, rocks and islets that scatter around the great swathes of waters. Since ancient time, this area had been deemed as a dangerous water, with these land features considered as hazards to navigation and maritime security.[20] Further, these rocks and islets have largely remained uninhabitable, as many of them are submerged at high tide and are only present for fits and starts during low-tide periods. This submerged land feature constitutes one claim in the ongoing South China Sea arbitration initiated by the Philippines in January, 2013.[21] The context of contemporary law of sea has presupposed that territoriality and effective control are two prerequisites to the enjoyment of exclusive rights to resources exploitation.[22] Implications of such actually arouse some predispositions highly likely to mislead the involving national and decision-making authorities. That these land features, being qualified to generate maritime rights and interests, must be able to facilitate onshore human activities.[23] Yet, contemporary international law and Law of the Sea have not spelled out further details about these human activities, some argue that fishing has been one qualified candidate.[24] It is under this context that the neglect of these submerged features, being unable to provide a consistent and effective basis for human activities, in contemporary international law and the Law of the Sea system are self-proven. Their legal status and legally entailed rights and interests of these submerged features remain unclear.

Second, following the first issue, what occurs to a rational mind is the need to re-contemplate the connection, and impacts, of these remote land features to national policy-making. In other words, how real the South China Sea dispute is.

Since 2009, when Vietnam, Malaysia and China submitted Note Verbale to the United Nations Committee for the Delimitation of Continental Shelf, the South China Sea issue was brought back to the front burner again to public attentions. Tensions then went up and down, and have become one potential flashpoint that easily topples over efforts for regional developments in various aspects. While sentiments remain boiling in certain claimant countries, it is a totally different picture in the other. This cleavage demonstrates that with disputed subjects remote in the sea, where no civilian could easily reach and land, the very "emptiness" of these island (as in people's cognition and memory) makes them the ultimate patriotic symbols, or "logos of nationhood in a global media age".[25] The Southeast Asian politicians have much freedom to define what these territorial conflicts mean to their respective populations.

The current quagmire is seeing a tug of war featuring two forces pulled to two reverse extremes. One is the position often pleading the deference to international law and Law of the Sea, as has been upheld by generally western countries. Contrarily, the other is the claim that appeals to historical facts, often with moral contestations that point to the European colonialist and imperialistic suppressions. These polarizing positions only add fuels to the already intensified anxieties in the South China Sea.

II Recasting the South China Sea Disputes: application and implication

A General considerations

The South China Sea has been a chokepoint of maritime communication since the inter-continental "age of commerce" that had initially seen a booming of maritime trades en route this area.[26] As elaborated in Chapter 4, China's claims could be divided to three dimensions, the islands sovereignty contribution, the Exclusive Economic Zoning, and the dash-line claim.[27] The dash-line claim has entailed a concept of jurisdiction right upon maritime spaces, aiming at maritime security and order maintenance. Also, maritime spaces have different denotations for different subjects under various time-spatial contexts. At that time, the sea remained open to all that sailed by and a uniting force that connecting principalities in Southeast Asia and continental dynasties in East and South Asian continent, China and India. As a zone of contact in a critical location, the South China Sea has long been recognized its strategic values in terms of security and defence,[28] rather than the sovereign attribution of islands, rocks and submerged features scattered around. The territorialization of the South China Sea issue is rather a product of contemporary Law of the Sea, whose contributions of maritime utilization are unprecedented, but not totally uncontroversial. The controversy lies in the possible conflict between the Law of the Sea and regional maritime custom and practices, vividly demonstrated in the South China Sea issue. In an area that has its local maritime concepts and practices, the introduction of contemporary Westphalian system of international law inevitably will put these long-standing historic claims and local customs in embarrassment, which has consistently been weakened, undermined, devaluated and even, invalidated eventually.

It is under this reinvented context that current stalemate could be re-contemplated and recast, while the South China Sea, eventually redefined and reinvigorated. Taking one step further, the kinetics among these three concepts merits discussions, so as to prepare for more solidified negotiation agenda and implementation proposal.

B The interactions among these three levels and the regional maritime order

The three dimensions in China's claims are, namely, the islands sovereignty contribution, the Exclusive Economic Zoning, and the dash-line claim. It is also established that the dash-line claim actually has implied a jurisdiction right upon maritime space that would aim at providing maritime security and order maintenance for regional interests. China has demonstrated well that it is not her intention to defy contemporary Law of the Sea regime, by maintaining these claims. Instead, it seeks to redress some inherent structural issues that currently cause troubles in advancing the goal of the maintenance of a sustainable and peaceful maritime order. Further, it is a fair observation that proposal of this syllogistic understanding towards China (PRC)'s position serves as demonstrating evidences, that emerging countries with considerable naval and commercial maritime capacity, wish to adjust rules prescribed in contemporary Law of the Sea regime to better facilitate their interests. The fine-tuning of this established framework, by reviving a long-practised concept in pre-nineteenth century in the China-dominating Asia, constitutes one initial attempt.

A close look of interactions among these three dimensions lends supports to this observation.

1 sovereignty over land features, such as islands, rocks, shoals or others;
2 delimitation of EEZs and continental shelf; and
3 the dash-line claim, implying a jurisdiction right upon maritime spaces.

Inter alia, 3) had been a long-practised concept in a relatively undisturbed manner before the Westphalian concept intervened in this region. Rather, it had not been put into black and white, until early twentieth century, when then Republican Chinese government had learned a modern sense to mind the maritime business and to acquire relevant knowledge. One most vivid and direct outcome was the dash-line claim. 1) and 2) are well-embedded in the postwar regional order with its root deeply stemmed in the Westphalian concepts. UNCLOS is one of its clear manifestations regarding the miscellaneous dimension of marine affairs. A general observation is that before the nineteenth century, when western imperial powers scaled up their encroachment into the East and Southeast Asia, 3) was generally guaranteed under the Chinese-dominating regional system combining a tributary hierarchy and a maritime order when the Chinese empire undertook major responsibilities in maintaining orders on the sea. 1) and 2) had not caught people's attentions. Instead, small islets, rocks and shoals beneath sea level at high tide were regarded impediments to civil navigation,[29] which required a clear delineation on the map. Yet, the situation became somewhat intriguing, in the post-Westphalian era. Even if 3) is guaranteed, 1) and 2) are claimed, but not secured.

In the past two decades after UNCLOS regime entered into force (1994–2014), 3) is generally neglected, while 1) and 2) are stipulated explicitly in the Law of the Sea. In UNCLOS, 1) has been assumed, from which 2) can subsequently be settled. Then, 1) seemingly can be more efficiently safeguarded. Yet, as what is demonstrated in actuality, 3) cannot be necessarily secured, which in turn would overshadow 1) and 2). The South China Sea serves a good example, when claimant countries are strengthening their unilateral measures, so as to reassert their sovereign claims at an expense of impairing and jeopardizing the final settlement of EEZ and continental shelf delimitation.

When we refocus attentions in Asia (under the aegis of the Chinese civilization) and the South China Sea, it is clear that 2) is one ultimate purpose of UNCLOS on which all claimant countries would concur. Yet, even if 1) leads to 2), then 2) would not be secured without 3), under which maritime order could be more effectively managed. In this sense, the formula for a more effective management of regional maritime order seems to institutionalize 1) and 3), so that 2) can be proceeded on smoothly and efficiently.

Yet, it is not to be overlooked that incongruence may arise between these concepts.

Major conflicts may arise between 1) and 3), and in particular in the South China Sea, when land features are dispersed on the great swathes of water. Upon many land features dotted on the sea, their sovereign countries would claim exclusive rights over such land features and spaces prescribed under UNCLOS framework, various maritime zoning such as the 12 miles of territorial waters.[30] Yet, it is not unrealistic that China (PRC), by proclaiming the "sovereign rights upon maritime spaces", would have laid out rules of engagement and management, which might impede claimant countries activities to reach their claimed islets. This concern, while seemingly imminent, not necessarily hits a dead end, should conflicts arise in such occasion.

To allow other sovereigns the right of passage to their enclaves in one's own territorial domain is not an unusual practice in international law jurisprudence. When a significant portion of lands in the non-Christian world was colonized by European powers, this absurdity had become more common as territorial boundaries were then delimited in accordance with colonial powers' delineation, leaving unattended rights and interests of the indigenous people on those lands. In early days of the International Court of Justice, there was a case regarding the particularity of such territorial enclaves and the issue of transit and communication between these enclaves and the sovereign authorities, The *Right of Passage* case[31] between Portugal and India.

Portugal brought a case in the ICJ against India, alleging that custom established a right of transit and communication among three enclaves in Indian territories, Daman, Dadra and Nagar-Aveli.[32] India repudiated, alleging that such a custom did not exist, and, in the alternative, if it did exist, it was only for commercial and governmental communication, not military passage.[33] The Court adopted something of a "split-the-baby" approach, ruling that Portugal possessed a right of transit from Daman to Dadra and Nagar-Aveli through Indian territory, but that such territory was subject to Indian regulation. It also ruled that the right did not include a right to send military forces or arms through Indian territory.[34]

The *Right of Passage* judgment serves as referential evidence that the case before the ICJ may involve public rights, and how the ICJ may decide once the disagreement arises between exclusive sovereignty and inclusive public goods. It also indicates that the ICJ decision can be as flexible and contextual as what situations require, by not continuing to fit factual square pegs into doctrinal round holes. In this case, the ICJ is deliberating on how to facilitate peaceful usage of the passage by those in need (Portugal) without inflicting harms upon territories (India) where these enclaves are located. Therefore, its supreme parameters in this decision are peaceful co-existence of the two ostensibly rivalry countries and sustainable utilization of resources and venues. Such, would make this decision of weighing preferential reference to the South China Sea situation.

By proclaiming a "jurisdiction right upon maritime spaces", China (PRC) may wield its jurisdiction upon great swathes of waters in the South China Sea, where some islands, islets and shoals may fall under other claimants' sovereign control.[35] Yet, the right of transit and communication to these enclaves by their sovereign authorities should be recognized, if only for regular and non-military purposes. Due regards are required not to inflict harms upon the waters under China (PRC)'s sovereign rights, when transit and communication is exercised by other sovereigns.

III Dismissing the South China Sea conundrum

The South China Sea sits at a chokepoint location, connecting the Indian and the Pacific Ocean. More than half of the world's merchant fleets travel through and upwards to the East and Northeast Asian areas, and the rest parts of the globe.[36] The huge volume of seaborne trade marks the significant importance of this passage, where the security environment is further complicated by a complex of different factors.

Maritime security strategies in this region have gone through periodic adjustments. Changes were largely discernible after the end of Cold War, and the 9/11 terrorist attack in early 2000s. By changing their dependence on great powers to withstand maritime invasion during Cold War to self-reliant efforts of maintaining maritime stability, regional countries have developed a clear consciousness of protecting their maritime rights, and cultivating safety and security for these sea lanes of communication.

Despite the increasing trade volumes, maritime security in this area have been overshadowed by a weakly construed regional consensus, which leads to not only unsatisfactory management outcomes, but also vexing issues, like the role of extra-regional states in regional security regimes building, and a confluence of territorial and resource claims over both the narrow marine passage of the Straits of Malacca and more influentially, the South China Sea. Yet, the efforts continue, while the accomplishments wax and wane. The unsatisfactory results also indicate the yearning for weighing political wills that would draw comparative technical supports, a sine qua non to push though regional, as well as international piracy-curbing efforts.

Despite its contribution to a significant portion of food supply to the world and Asian population, fishing in the South China Sea is confronted with a compound of challenges, from security threats arising from disputed maritime

112 *The South China Sea as a frontier*

delimitation, maritime violent activities, dis-unified unilateral fishing regulations, gradually turned aggressive fishermen driven by nationalistic sentiments and their dire economic dismals, and has been overshadowed by domestic economic dismals prevalent in several ASEAN countries.

Yet, regional responses remain quite underdeveloped, out of major concerns such as worries about the resuscitation of foreign invasions that had plagued this region for past centuries. It is in this context that the proposed concept of a "jurisdiction right upon maritime spaces" by China (PRC) could set off a positive atmosphere to forge a regional consensus, and to motivate required political will.

A Modern essence of the "jurisdiction right upon maritime spaces"

A critical issue for the success of this concept is how to accommodate it in contemporary Law of the Sea setting, and how its operation could be feasibly implemented. In other words, to flesh out the modern essence of this concept would be the key to its future success. A general observation is that this modern essence comprises two aspects. On the one hand, a leading actor along with coordinated regional cooperation would better guarantee its due development. On the other, preferential claims may be vested in China (PRC), out of its historical and practical contributions, and of utilitarian concerns of future maritime stability in this region.

i China (PRC)'s preferential claim on maritime security – an evolving progress

Of particular and initial importance is preferential claim vested in China. However, the issue of the Chinese representativeness between the two China(s) – the PRC and the ROC – has went beyond the scope of this article. Rather, the focus here is on the scope and ramification of such preferential leverages.

The proposition is that China (PRC) is in a position to profess a privileged status in the South China Sea issues. Its privileges, as demonstrated in various manifestations, will most likely be a weighing position in agenda-setting and rule-making for marine affairs management, in the design of implementation deployment and in conflict management and dispute settlement whenever tensions rattle the region. Ostensibly preferential in the surface, these privileges are actually in company with responsibilities corresponding to a leadership role. Overall speaking, the underlying concept of China (PRC)'s preferential claim is to assure that national security of both China (PRC) and other claimants in the region, in particular in the maritime scenario, would not be anyhow compromised.

China (PRC), as a regional power, whose civilization and national prowess had used to shape and lead regional developments, is tied in a vital relation with the stability in the South China Sea. As discussed previously, noninterruption of seaborne activities since ancient times had constituted not only an essence to survival for sea-bordering communities, but also a critical yet peaceful connection between then distinguished civilizations in the Orient and the Occident. It is fair to say that a peaceful, or manageable to the least, South China Sea, benefits all those on the same regional boat. It is also in this sense that the leading actor should, and has better to be the regional power, who shares critical stakes similar to all other regional claimants.

Subsequently, the leading regional power would have more credentials in agenda-setting and rule-making scenarios, since its national interests would be at stake along with its regional counterparts. Last but not least, a regional platform for consultation and exchange of opinions before an implementation plan is activated, would serve as a dispute avoidance mechanism and a prerequisite for continuing coordination and enhancement of a regional consensus. In this regard, incumbent settings, such as various levels of working groups, formal and informal dialogues, and inter-state forums in the framework of ASEAN, would be of convenient usage.

Besides the scenarios of agenda-setting and rule-making, conflict management and dispute settlement constitute another focal point. In this sense, one critical issue is how to address the conundrum of the existing unilateral occupation by claimant countries upon land features in the South China Sea.

From a theoretical perspective, by occupying unilaterally these land features, countries are not deemed logically as being vested with the territorial sovereignty over these features. Their effective controls may constitute a weighing portion of evidence of their proclaiming territoriality. Yet, to be accordingly qualified, this administration should be uncontested and uninterrupted. Even if a critical date was ultimately determined, out of either judicial deliberations or an upshot of diplomatic compromises, current unilateral occupation should be regarded, to an utmost extent, a bargaining leverage in future negotiations, and lesser, an instrument of convenience to facilitate conflict management when tension arises.

One critical point is that this concept is not intended to the revival of the famed China-centred tributary system before the Westphalian order making inroads into this region. Rather, the revival of this Asia-intrinsic concept on maritime management in the twenty-first century signals a confluence of the concept of national sovereigns and territoriality originated in the west, and the maritime order in this area where social, cultural and legal values from the Oriental and Occidental system had consistently collided, conflated and converged. In other words, this concept entails, inevitably, corresponding efforts so as to create appropriate means to accommodate those whose interests considered affected.

Accordingly, maritime order management in the South China Sea has dual characteristics. It could be seen as on one hand, the revival of a long-practised regional custom in maritime affairs management, signaling that certain non-western systemic values manage to posit themselves, along the wave of the revival of China and the Oriental values, in the political and legal hierarchy established and shaped by the prevailing Westphalian view. Meanwhile, it is also an innovation in contemporary international legal development with precedential effects for a better convergence of regional, local customs and general, universal practices.

Therefore, it is in this context that regional participation, with a goal aimed ultimately at further levels of cooperation, appears essential in future success of this concept.

ii Regional cooperation

For the second element, a leading actor would better guarantee that resources be efficiently coordinated, and the political will of all participants mobilized. It is not surprising that China (PRC), as a regional great power, may posit its leadership role. Yet, this is not an easy task, in an era when sovereignty remains a cornerstone principle among its ASEAN rivalry counterparts.

Regional efforts in addressing security threats present a relatively more promising story. Yet, it is far from satisfactory. Instead, multilateral efforts initiated by extra regional powers remain dismal. The bleakness of international participation in maritime security regime building in Southeast Asia has multiple root causes. Among them, littoral states' hesitation over possible circumscription upon their sovereignty, and the tussle between littoral states, user states and shippers, rank as two major reasons that further shape the route for efficacious international cooperation.

Bearing in mind this contradiction among ASEAN claimant countries, China (PRC) would need to carefully steer thru between its relations with ASEAN, an ostensibly powerful regional leader, and its ambitions and capacity, which is actually a sine qua non to further unfold all the developments and possibilities. Put differently, it requires Beijing to play the game with one-upmanship, so that its leadership could be welcomed with less perceived threats and more practical benefits. That said, a brief review of current regional cooperation may help sort out a clear picture of what's happening now, what can be hoped for in the future, and what China (PRC) can do to accelerate the proceeding.

Several regional initiatives were facilitated, and some operated with laudable successes. Yet they are flawed with sovereignty concerns and technical issues, such as financial shortcomings and shortage of appropriate equipment.

The regionally indigenous effort is the Malacca Straits Patrol (the MSP), initiated and organized by three littoral states, and, since 2008, Thailand as well.[37] The Patrol was established within the framework of the Malacca Straits Security Initiative, launched as early as in 1992 and strengthened in 2004 when patrols were formally implemented. Yet, the Patrol remains within domestic domain of littoral states respectively. Coordinated rather than joint, the sea patrols were further complemented by the Eyes in the Sky operations in 2005.[38] The Eyes in the Sky operations introduced joint patrols in national and international airspaces over the Straits of Malacca and Singapore. The operation was initiated in 2005 to allow joint air patrols across territorial boundaries for better effectiveness in monitoring and maintaining maritime security and for operational cooperation. The operation tasks are carefully programmed to assuage concerns of invasion of the sovereignty of participating states. A foreign liaison officer is placed on aboard each aircraft to control actions over the waters of that officer's state.

These regional cooperation remains limited in its geographical scope, and embryonic in the depth of cooperation levels. Currently, the patrolling area is on the Malacca and Singapore Strait, and the focus, on traditional security threats, such as maritime robbery and piratic attacks.[39] For great swathes of waters in the South China Sea, cooperation as such is scarce, whereas unilateral national patrols tend to trigger unexpected spark-ups.

Despite the increasing inter-state and regional exchanges, maritime security in the South China Sea has been overshadowed by a weakly construed regional consensus, which leads to not only unsatisfactory management outcomes, but also vexing issues, like the role of extra-regional states in regional security regimes building, and a confluence of territorial and resource claims over both some critical marine passages, such as the Strait of Malacca and more influentially, the South China Sea. Yet efforts continue while the accomplishments wax and wane. The unsatisfactory results also indicate the yearning for weighing political wills that would draw comparative technical supports, from inside and outside, a sine qua non to push through the ultimate goal or perpetual maritime security in the South China Sea.

China (PRC) could ride on this chance to shore up the mobility for regional cooperation, and then to facilitate its leadership role. In due course, China (PRC) would pay heeds to two critical issues. Of initial importance is that China (PRC)'s ambition for future leadership should not conflict with the already existing ASEAN platform, and its role, not defying one crucial major actor, Indonesia. Subsequently, China (PRC) would need to take leads in designing appropriate mechanism so as to accommodate the participation of extra-regional stakeholders. In this regard, the role of the United States, along with its treaty alliances, is worth particular attention. China (PRC) would need to concern how to better roll on its efforts upon the existing conditions and to fine-tune current regulatory framework.

B Implementation conceptual scheme

i Police power with a security focus

As discussed, China (PRC) would need to consider the South China Sea issue from a perspective that draw attentions more on order maintenance, the provision of public goods, with its rights and interests being accommodated with preferential consideration. In due course, cooperation from all regional countries that have an interest, in whatever exposition, in the South China Sea, would make this Chinese approach more justified, with a projection that all would be benefitted therewith. For implementation, a proposal could be attempted, that

China (PRC) may refer to the exercise of police power to furthering the projected accomplishment.

In contemporary legal concept of the power of the government and its justification, police power is one of the three apparatuses[40] available for states to apply coercive forces upon individuals residing within the territorial perimeters of the political unit.[41] Posited on the realization of the legitimacy of government power, this concept has undergone reflections, reconsiderations and a revival of attention, since it was first proposed and more heatedly debated in the domain of the American continent in late nineteenth century.[42] Constitutional legal theorists and positivist in the United States generally share the wisdom that its development went from a more stringent rein to a more generous exposition purported to broaden the governmental function.[43] In the early days of the Union (the North), state regulation was limited by the common law principle of *sic utere tuo ut alienum non laedas* (you should use what is yours so as not to harm what is others').[44]

The implication was that only specified interests and concrete harms were the subjects to be addressed via legitimate regulation that might impose restrictions, or at least prohibitive impacts upon constitutionally prescribed individual liberties. However, sometimes around the turn of the twentieth century, the principle had changed from the old *sic uetere* to the new principle of *salus populi est suprema lex* (the good of the public is the supreme law).[45] This new concept is suggesting that states could regulate as they chose so long as they claimed to be working to promote the public safety, welfare or morality.[46]

This concept is not without criticism. Scholarly discussions and juridical opinions remain heated on its scope and limitation, proper exercise and competing constructions of how a police power of a federal state ought to be evolved.[47] Yet, the point here is how this concept could help construct a useful conceptual scheme to achieve more efficacious marine affairs management. In this regard, a panoramic review of UNCLOS would shed lights on this inquiry, if China (PRC), by proposing a "jurisdiction right upon maritime spaces", could apply this common law concept of police power to further an implementation scheme of marine affairs and conflict management in the South China Sea.

UNCLOS AND THE POLICE POWER CONCEPT

The inquiry here is how should a common law concept, the police power of states' government, help a certain country, China (PRC) to better achieve the purported goal of efficacious marine affairs management, without unjustified expenses at the UNCLOS and Southeast Asian community.

UNCLOS is a bold initiative driven by both empirically exacerbating infringements on the customary maritime freedom and a conflation of growing political wills in national capitals. By conquering intractable issues left by UNCLOS I and II, the regime has achieved not only a comprehensive package of rules in relation to ocean affairs management in, allegedly, all aspects,[48] but also a binding dispute settlement which safeguards the interpretation and application of rights and obligations achieved via negotiations.[49] This sweeping bargain, introducing new subjects, objects, actors and laws into marine spaces, has been hailed as a purported constitution of marine affairs containing one of the largest scales of international bargaining and law-making in postwar era.

In this sense, the proposition is that the common law concept of police power is not egregiously incongruent with the UNCLOS system. Rather, it lends supports to help advancing the UNCLOS regime in both procedural and substantial dimensions.

To develop a neutral police power concept, albeit under different manifestations of leadership that suit demands in different groupings, would help improve and achieve the purported implementation outcome intended in the Law of the Sea regime. It is the exercise of a relatively impartial police power regulatory concept that the flexibility, impartiality and commonality of marine affairs could be best secured. Without further compartmentation of unsettled issues of sovereignties of land features on the sea, this neutral regulatory concept helps facilitate management of maritime affairs to everyone's interests.

Further, this police power concept helps inform one key ethical rule prescribed in Article 300 in UNCLOS, the binding promise to fulfil in good faith all the obligations under the convention and to exercise the rights, jurisdiction and freedoms in a manner which would not constitute an abuse of right.[50] In a legal regime when relative rules and principles are yet to be well-established via international legislative and juridical law-making, the abuse of right concept, also dubbed as a substantial (as compared to its procedural parameter) good faith, help inflict certain practical limitations upon the exercise of rights of sovereign states in the regime.[51] While not exactly embryonic, the UNCLOS regime is far from a mature legal system. It is in this sense that this concept also helps inform the open-endedness of the UNCLOS system.

Yet with a relatively impartial police power concept to help purported implementation outcome in UNCLOS, the worries may arise concerning if the exercise of such police power would easily transgress its reasonableness and appropriateness, absent a mandatory judiciary with a powerful enforcement mechanism in international Law of the Sea community.

In this regard, a flexible approach should be adopted when disputes arise on China (PRC)'s police action enforcement. Multiple means, judicial and non-judicial, should be allowed, while a plethora of occasions be considered. In this sense, a concept of dispute avoidance,[52] along with one of conflict management, constitute the framework of dispute settlement mechanism that helps safeguard this new theme of maritime order in the South China Sea. Significance of this new framework should not be overlooked.

Successful marine affairs management requires a multi-disciplinary approach, which straddles a wide range of topics from marine environment, ocean biology, fishery, mineral resources, hydrography and non-scientific issues, such as cultural heritage under sea level. With so many issues involved, it is indeed a challenging mission for international judiciary to frame political and other demands in terms of justice and substantive equality in international courts. Besides, the practices by international courts are fragmented. It is in this sense that certain mechanism with dispute avoidance function would help insulate frivolous cases, while resolving the conflict before it becomes a reality. Examples include consultation in pre-judicial stage and well-recognized alternative dispute resolution means.[53] Moreover, a framework as such would not run counter to the existing semi-compulsory dispute settlement mechanism in the Law of the Sea regime. Rather, it supplements the semi-compulsory mechanism in Part XV (Settlement of Disputes), Section I (General Provisions), by addressing the prevalent resistance of states of referring disputes with environmental components to a contentious and conflictual procedure. Articles 279 to 285 provides guidance of how these means in the pre-judicial stage be conducted, and how Part XV could set in upon their failures of settling disputes.[54]

Future studies are required, in how this framework could kick off functioning and how the outcomes could be better accommodated in contemporary Law of the Sea setting. Yet this preliminary assessment of this budding police power concept, and a broader dispute settlement framework, signals a new direction in carving ways out of the long-dragging South China Sea dispute.

IV Concluding observation: China's claims towards further legal construction of a "quasi-sovereign" rights in the South China Sea

In the South China Sea, the Law of the Sea cannot effectively solve current the stalemate. One of the biggest hurdles is the conflict between historical claims and contemporary Law of the Sea. In particular, rules regarding EEZ and continental shelf delimitation cannot ameliorate the tension arising from contested maritime territorial claims. Before the settlement of final maritime boundaries, all acts could be justified, for the sake of purported maritime territorial claims. The vacuum in the Law of the Sea regime to clearly define the reasonableness of maritime territorial claim explains, to a major extent, current dilemma in the South China Sea.

Another reason that catalyses this vacuum is one basic principle underlying modern international (inter-state) adjudication institutions. Reflecting Grotius's arguments, contemporary international adjudication institutions generally uphold that law reaching beyond a single state (civitas) should aspire to achieve corrective justice, but not distributive justice.[55] The ICJ practices have largely confirmed this principle. Money damages payments even for corrective purposes are very rarely awarded, let alone being quantified for injury to state interests. It is also in this sense that state responsibilities, along with the articles stipulated by the International Law Commission, have received tepid responses since its inauguration in 2001.[56] This corrective justice logic can be explained by one inherent flaw of international adjudication, the lack of legitimacy of international third-party judiciary in adjudicating disputes between sovereign states, let alone to quantify its judicial decisions into tangible monetary interests. With the continuing supremacy of the concept of state sovereignty, it is hardly optimistic that international judiciary would be quick to deliver decisions on a distributive justice basis, which would in turn help establish a clear connection between Law of the Sea regime and state responsibilities.

The "jurisdiction right upon maritime spaces" may serve as a resolution to current dilemma in the South China Sea, when claimants are competing for resource exploitation and willful occupation of land features. The claim is to focus on maintenance of maritime order that stresses upon uninterruption of maritime activities, a more flexible approach for dispute resolution, and inter-state cooperation on conflict management. This proposal, while professed by China (PRC), would not be able to accomplish if all those interested in this region were not involved. Moreover, its accomplishment would not be achieved at the expense of the defiance of the Law of the Sea regime. In particular, it is not the aim to overwrite the established regime of EEZ and continental shelf in the Law of the Sea. Yet, China (PRC) is in a position to make preferential claims, in not only agenda-setting and rule-making, but also in its practical implementation by exercising a police power, with a major focus on maintenance and restoration of maritime security.

This new approach, seeing China (PRC)'s position from a three-dimensional perception, is to shed new light on how to fit the purported historical rights and interests into contemporary Law of the Sea regime. It is fair to say that by construing the purported historical rights and interests in this way, not only China (PRC), but the region as a whole, would be benefitted from a secured and stabilized maritime order. In this sense, historical right and interest serve to supplement/fortify the Law of the Sea regime, but not a dampening factor.

Yet the South China Sea dispute clearly has shown a picture of diversified interests with sometimes conflicting considerations. Also, how the public perceives this issue depends heavily on the parochial interests of the agents that have the power to mediate access to these sites. One common worry for all those involved is to make a clear distinction between real stakes and those serving for lip service and passionate sentiments that appear as a double-edged sword. The underlying interests are economic, geopolitical and strategic. Yet, they can be easily ratcheted up or down, and to be transformed to emotions with nationalistic significance to suit political calculations for certain politicians. These frames always end up with counterproductive upshots. In this sense, rational thinking and restraints remains the key, as this is exactly what is absent in this region.

Notes

1 Robert L. Solomon, "Boundary Concepts and Practices in Southeast Asia", *World Politics*, 23:1 (October 1970): 1–23; Lee Yong Leng, *Southeast Asia: Essays in Political Geography* (Singapore: National University Press, 1982), 9–16; Leng, "The Colonial Legacy in Southeast Asia: Maritime Boundary Problems", *Contemporary Southeast Asia*, 8:2 (September 1986): 119–130; Amitav Acharya, "Imaging Southeast Asia", in his *The Making of Southeast Asia: International*

Relations of a Region (Ithaca: Cornell University Press, 2013), 51–104; Alastair Lamb, *Asian Frontiers* (New York: Frederick A. Praeger Inc., 1968), 39.
2 Ibid.
3 See, note 1, and also, Carlyle A. Thayer, "The Tyranny of Geography: Vietnamese Strategies to Constrain China in the South China Sea", *Contemporary Southeast Asia: A Journal of International and Strategic Affairs*, 33:3 (December 2011): 348–369; Brantly Womack, "The Spratlys: From Dangerous Ground to Apple of Discord", *Contemporary Southeast Asia*, 33:3 (December 2011): 370–387.
4 J.R. John Robert, Victor Prescott, Gillian and Doreen Triggs, *International Frontiers and Boundaries: Law, Politics and Geography*, (Leiden: Martinus Nijhoff Publishers, 2008), 23–90; J.R.V. Prescott, "Frontiers", in *The Geography of Frontiers and Boundaries* (London: Routledge, 2015), 33–55; Ladis K.D. Kristof, "The Nature of Frontiers and Boundaries", *Annals of the Association of American Geographers*, 49:3 (1959): 269–282.
5 Ibid. In Southeast Asia, frontiers are of many types. Some are zones of separation because of their inaccessibility. Examples are like those in central New Guinea, central Borneo, the Laos-Yunnan-Myanmar area and the Laos-Vietnam area. On the other hand, there are zones of contact where the physical geography is not so difficult, making these frontiers easily crossed between two or more groups of peoples. This contact can involve migration, trade, intermarriage and conflict. In Southeast Asia, areas such as the Lao-Thai border, the Thai-Kampuchean border, the Vietnamese-Kampuchean border and the Sino-Vietnamese border fall into this category.
6 Craig A. Lockard, *Southeast Asia in World History* (New York: Oxford University Press, 2009), Chapter 4 and 5; Amitav Acharya, *The Quest for Identity: International Relations of Southeast Asia* (Singapore: Oxford University Press, 2009), Chapter 1, 17–42.
7 This idea has been a feature of modern history writing since Fernand Braudel's The Mediterranean and the Mediterranean World. In Braudel's words, the sea was "the great divider, the obstacle that had to be overcome". F. Braudel, *The Mediterranean and the Mediterranean World in the Age of Philip II*, 2nd English ed., abridged (London: Harper Collins, 1992), 201.
8 See notes 1 and 4. Also, Thomas H. Holdich, *Political Frontiers and Boundary Making* (New York: Macmillan, 1916), Chapter VI.
9 See notes 1, 4 and 6.
10 See, notes 1 and 4.
11 O. Wæver, "Identities, Communities and Foreign Policy: Discourse Analysis as Foreign Policy Theory", in *Between Nations and Europe: Regionalism, Nationalism and the Politics of Union*, L. Hansen and O. Wæver (eds.) (London: Routledge, 2002), 20–49; C.S. Browning, "Coming Home or Moving Home? 'Westernising' Narratives in Finnish Foreign Policy and the Re-Interpretation of Past Identities", *Cooperation and Conflict* 37:1 (2001): 47–72; A. Roshwald, *Ethnic Nationalism & the Fall of Empires: Central Europe, Russia & the Middle East, 1914–1923* (London and New York: Routledge, 2001); A. Paasi, *Territories, Boundaries and Consciousness: The Changing Geographies of the Finnish-Russian Border* (Chichester: John Wiley & Sons, 1996).
12 K. Sherman and G. Hempel (eds.), 2009. *The UNEP Large Marine Ecosystem Report: A Perspective on Changing Conditions in LMEs of the World's Regional Seas*, UNEP Regional Seas Report and Studies No. 182, United Nations Environment Programme, Nairobi, Kenya, 297.
13 Ibid. More details could be located on the IUCN Red List website, www.iucnredlist.org/, last visited 1 June, 2013.
14 Anthony Reid made the argument concerning the role of trade in due course of regional development in Southeast Asia. "[M]aritime intercourse continued

to link the peoples of Southeast Asia more tightly to one another than to outside influences down to the seventeenth century. The fact that Chinese and Indian influences came to most of the region by maritime trade, not by conquest or colonialization, appeared to ensure that Southeast Asia retained its distinctiveness even while borrowing numerous elements from those large centres. What did not happen (with the partial exception of Vietnam) was that any part of the region established closer relations with China and India than with its neighbours in Southeast Asia". Anthony Reid, "Southeast Asia in the Age of Commerce 1450–1680", in his *The Lands Below the Winds, Volume One* (New Haven: Yale University Press, 1988), 7.

15 See Reid, in note 14. For more discussions of the Southeast Asia regional development, see J. Benda, "The Structure of Southeast Asian History: Some Preliminary Observations", in *Man, State and Society in Contemporary Southeast Asia*, Robert O. Tilman (ed.) (London: Pall Mall Press, 1969), 23–24; Craig Reynolds, "A New Look at Old Southeast Asia", *Journal of ASEAN Studies*, 54:2 (1995): 419–446; Peng Er Lam and Victor Teo, *Southeast Asia between China and Japan* (New Castle, UK: Cambridge Scholars Publishing, 2012); Pandu Utama Manggala, "The Mandala Culture of Anarchy: The Pre-Colonial Southeast Asian International Society", *Journal of ASEAN Studies*, 1:1 (2013): 1–13; Siska Lund, "A Mandala for the Southeast Asian International System", *The Bulletin of the Centre for East-West Cultural and Economic Studies*, 6:1 (2003), Article 2, 1–12; S.J. Tambiah, *Culture, Thought and Social Action: An Anthropological Perspective* (Cambridge: Harvard University Press, 1985), 260; Karl A. Wittfogel, *Oriental Despotism: A Comparative Study of Total Power* (New York: Vintage Books, 1981), Chapter 6.

16 See notes 1, 4 and 6.

17 See Reid, in notes 14 and 15; also, O.W. Wolter, *History, Culture and Religion in Southeast Asian Perspectives*, rev. ed., Cornell University Southeast Asian Program Publications No. 26 (Ithaca: Cornell University Press, 1999); Amitav Acharya, *The Quest for Identity: International Relations of Southeast Asia* (Singapore: Oxford University Press, 2000).

18 See Acharya, in note 17, 30–33.

19 Criticisms that if "international law" had lived up its name as of an "international" characteristic with bipartisan values, so as to make its universal application sensible, are rife. Along with the European expansion to Asia, the issue of application of international law to these non-European, non-Christian local principalities aroused heated debates. Succinctly put, European powers had endeavoured to justify their occupation of territories and colonialization of local societies in Southeast Asia, by deeming these territories as terra nullius, and rejecting the granting of a total international legal personality to these local principalities. As Churchill and Lowe opined, "While there have over the centuries been many documented systems of relations between independent polities, in Africa and Asia and Europe, "international law" as it exists today is the body of law initially generated by the relations between the European States during the period known as "modern" history. Cultural imperialism that may be, but it is an inescapable fact." Robin Rolf Churchill and Alan Vaughan Lowe, *The Law of the Sea* (Manchester: Manchester University Press, 1988), 3–4.

20 Stein Tønnesson, "The South China Sea in the Age of European Decline", *Modern Asian Studies*, 40:1 (2006): 1–57; Tønnesson, "The Paracels: The 'Other' South China Sea Dispute", *Asian Perspective*, 26:4 (2002): 145–169; also, Tønnesson, "The South China Sea: Law Trumps Power", *Asian Survey*, 55:3 (May/June 2015): 455–477.

21 The Philippines submitted the case against China to the Permanent Court of Arbitration to initiate an arbitration. For more information of the progress, see

"The Republic of the Philippines v. The People's Republic of China" in the Permanent Court of Arbitration website, www.pca-cpa.org/shownewsa454.html?nws_id=518&pag_id=1261&ac=view, last visited 20 October, 2015.

22 This is often termed as the "land dominates sea" principle. For more discussions of the law of sea convention, see Chapter 4. Also, Churchill and Lowe, in note 19; M.H. Nordquist (ed.), *United Nations Convention on the Law of the Sea 1982*, vol. 5 (Dordrecht: Martinus Nijhoff Publishers, 1989); L.B. Sohn, "The Importance of the Peaceful Settlement of Disputes: Provisions of the United Nations Convention on the Law of the Sea", in *Entry into Force of the Law of the Sea Convention*, M.H. Nordquist and J.N. Moore (eds.) (The Hague: Nijhoff, 1995), 265–277; J. Charney, "The Implications of Expanding International Dispute Settlement Systems: The 1982 Convention on the Law of the Sea", *American Journal of International Law*, 90 (1996): 69–75; A.E. Boyle, "Dispute Settlement and the Law of the Sea Convention: Problems of Fragmentation and Jurisdiction", *International Comparative Law Quarterly*, 46 (1997): 37–54.

23 See Law of the sea Convention, Part VIII: Regime of Islands, Article 121–123. United Nations Convention on the Law of the Sea (concluded 10 December, 1982, entered into force 16 November, 1994), 1833 U.N.T.S. 397.

24 Keyuan Zou, "China and Maritime Boundary Delimitation: Past, Present and Future", in *Conflict Management and Dispute Settlement in East Asia*, Ramses Amer and Keyuan Zou (eds.) (Farnham, UK: Ashgate, 2013), 149–169; Nong Hong, *UNCLOS and Ocean Dispute Settlement: Law and Politics in the South China Sea* (London: Routledge, 2012), 73.

25 Robert D. Kaplan, "Concer of Civilizations", in *Asia's Cauldron: The South China Sea and the End of a Stable Pacific* (New York: Random House, 2014), chapter IV. Mina Pollmann, "Government Narratives in Maritime Disputes", *The Diplomat*, 10 July 2014, http://thediplomat.com/2014/07/government-narratives-in-maritime-disputes/, last visited 30 August, 2016.

26 See, notes 1, 4 and 6.

27 See Chapter 4, III. The dash-line claim in contemporary international maritime legal order.

28 This has led to some argue that the South China Sea should be valued more from its credits in security and defence considerations, rather than directing the focus mainly on territoriality and sovereignty. Wang Gungwu, "China and the Map of Nine-Dotted Lines", *Strait Times*, 11 July, 2012, p. A23.

29 Guoqiang Li, "Islands and the Historical Studies on China's Sea Territory", *Journal of Yunnan Normal University* (Humanities and Social Sciences ed.), 3 (2010): 21–25; Guozhen Yang and Zhimin Zhou, "The Sea Boundary in Ancient China and the Right of Sea in History", *Journal of Yunnan Normal University* (Humanities and Social Sciences ed.), 42:3 (May 2010): 26–32.

30 See UNCLOS, Article 3(Breadth of the Territorial Sea), in Part I(Territorial Sea and Contiguous Zone), Section 2(Limits of the Territorial Sea).

31 Right of Passage over Indian Territory (Port. v. India), 1960 I.C.J. 6, 9 (12 April).

32 Right of Passage over Indian Territory (1960).

33 Counter-Memorial of India, Right of Passage over Indian Territory (Port. v. India), 1958 I.C.J. Pleadings 146–49 (25 March, 1958).

34 Right of Passage over Indian Territory, 1960 I.C.J. at 40–43.

35 While China(s) also claims that all land features within the dash-line belongs to it, there remains the possibilities that some may fall under other claimants' sovereign claim. Bearing in mind that all five claimant countries have asserted controls upon these land features, albeit to different extents, pending a final settlement, the Right of Passage case situation may, much likely, take place in the South China Sea.

36 The United States Energy Information Administration, "The South China Sea Is an Important World Energy Trade Route", 4 April, 2013, www.eia.gov/todayinenergy/detail.cfm?id=10671, last visited 20 November, 2014; Beina Xu, "South China Sea Tensions", *Council on Foreign Relations*, 14 May, 2014, www.cfr.org/china/south-china-sea-tensions/p29790, last visited 20 November, 2014.

37 Victor Huang, "Building Maritime Security Regime in Southeast Asia: Outsiders Not Welcome", *Naval War College Review*, 61:1 (Winter 2008): 87–105; Simon Sheldon, "Safety and Security in the Malacca Straits: The Limits of Collaboration", *Asian Security*, 7:1 (February 2011): 27–43; Joyce Dela Pena, "Maritime in the Strait of Malacca: Balancing Regional and Extra-Regional Concerns", *Stanford Journal of International Relations*, vol. 10:2 (Spring 2009): 1–8.

38 Huang, "Building Maritime Security Regime in Southeast Asia"; Sheldon, "Safety and Security in the Malacca Straits".

39 There are different definitions of these seaborne criminal acts. Piracy is confined to illegal acts committed for private ends, against another ship, and on the high seas or places outside the jurisdiction of any State. See UNCLOS, Article 101 (Definition of Piracy). For violence occurred within national territorial waters, they are considered as armed robberies against ships defined by the International Maritime Organization in its 26th Assembly Resolution A. 1025. The International Maritime Organization (IMO) 26th Assembly Resolution A. 1025 (26).

40 The other two power regarded as inherent to state powers are the power of eminent domain, and of taxation. Hugh Evander Willis, *Constitutional Law of the United States* (Bloomington, IN: The Principia Press, 1936), 224.

41 This inherent linkage can also be demonstrated in manifestations, such as, by virtue of birth, allegiance, contract or custom.

42 Glenn H. Reynolds and David Kopel, "The Evolving Police Power: Some Observations for a New Century", *Hastings Constitutional Law Quarterly*, 27 (Spring 2000): 511–530; Randy Barnett, "The Proper Scope of the Police Power", *Notre Dame Law Review*, 79 (2004): 429–495; David Garland, "The Limits of the Sovereign State", *The British Journal of Criminology*, 36:4 (Autumn 1996): 445–471; See also, Douglas A. Balog, "Fluoridation of Public Water Systems: Valid Exercise of State Police Power or Constitutional Violation", *14 Pace Envtl. L. Rev.* 645 (1997), Available at: http://digitalcommons.pace.edu/pelr/vol14/iss2/7.

43 Reynolds and Kopel, "The Evolving Police Power"; Barnett, "The Proper Scope of the Police Power"; See also, Ridgway Foley, "Police Power: Sovereignty's Sledgehammer", *The Freeman*, 25:11 (November 1975): 677–687. Available at http://c457332.r32.cf2.rackcdn.com/pdf/the-freeman/november%201975.pdf.

44 Barnett, "The Proper Scope of the Police Power"; Foley, "Police Power".

45 Reynolds and Kopel, "The Evolving Police Power"; Barnett, "The Proper Scope of the Police Power".

46 Barnett, "The Proper Scope of the Police Power"; Foley, "Police Power"; Reynolds and Kopel, "The Evolving Police Power".

47 Barnett, "The Proper Scope of the Police Power"; Foley, "Police Power".

48 The preamble of UNCLOS is explicit in this ambition by stating that "*Prompted* by the desire to settle, in a spirit of mutual understanding and cooperation, *all issues* relating to the Law of the Sea", and ". . .that the problems of ocean space are *closely related* and need to be considered *as a whole*. . .". See UNCLOS Preamble.

49 Negotiations lasting nearly a decade took place in UNCLOS III, covering an ambitious range of issues related to maritime affairs. Also, consensus was adopted in UNCLOS III, instead of majority voting, so as to forge and solidify the

achieved outcome that contains voluminous compromises between parties' rights and obligations.
50 Article 300, UNCLOS. *The Law of the Sea*, Division for Ocean Affairs and the Law of the Sea, Office of Legal Affairs, United Nations, New York, 1997. This neutral police power concept also fleshes out the substantial good faith principle, abuse of right, in the scenario of Law of the Sea.
51 Michael Byers, "Abuse of Rights: An Old Principle, a New Age", *McGill Law Journal*, 47 (2002): 389–431; Georg Schwarzenberger, "Uses and Abuses of the 'Abuse of Right' in International Law", *Transactions of the Grotius Society*, 42 (1956): 147–179, Article SRL www.jstor.org/stable/743132.
52 Cameron Hutchison, "The Duty to Negotiate International Environmental Disputes in Good Faith", *McGill Journal of Sustainable Development Law and Policy*, 2:2 (2006): 117–153; See also, Philippe Sands and Jacqueline Peel, *Principles of International Environmental Law*, 3rd ed. (Cambridge: Cambridge University Press, 2012).
53 Hutchison, "The Duty to Negotiate International Environmental Disputes in Good Faith"; Ilias Plakokefalos, "Prevention Obligations in International Environmental Law", ACIL Research Paper, 2013-12, available at www.acil.uva.nl (Forthcoming in Yearbook of International Environmental Law); Philippe Sands, "Litigating Environmental Disputes: Courts, Tribunals and the Progressive Development of International Environmental Law", *Environmental Policy and Law*, 37:2–3 (2007): 66–78.
54 See UNCLOS, Article 279–285, in Part XV(Settlement of Disputes), Section 1 (General Provisions).
55 Kingsbury, "International Courts".
56 Responsibility of States for Internationally Wrongful Acts. The text can be retrieved from http://legal.un.org/ilc/texts/instruments/english/draft%20articles/9_6_2001.pdf, last visited 20 November, 2014. Text reproduced as it appears in the annex to General Assembly resolution 56/83 of 12 December, 2001, and corrected by document A/56/49(Vol. I)/Corr.4. See Article 30.

7 Echoing the mandala legacy

Rethinking ASEAN engagement in the South China Sea

I Inter-polity relations: a mandalic legacy in Southeast Asia

A *The "mandala" system*

Southeast Asia has long been deemed an integral part of the Sino-centric tributary system in East Asia. Studies since 1980s suggest that this region was far from a backwater, or simply an intermediate area interfacing the Indian and Confucian civilizations. Fierce competition for survival and domination among voluminous regional polities had characterized inter-polity relations in this region throughout the era before the arrival of European colonizers.[1] Against this backdrop, dynamism of inter-polity action-reaction should be considered with a tradition of knowledge in this region, the "mandala" concept.

Put in a geo-political sense, "mandala" refers to a network of inter-polity relations among kings whose principalities are enclosed by circles of allies (mitra), enemies (ari), medium (madhyama) and major (udasina) powers. Situated in the core is the Vijigisu (centre), who also claims universal lordship.

i *Three principles*

Construction of a regional order in the "mandala" context contains three principles: the centre, symmetry and cardinal points. The "centre" was demonstrated in a leader's role/capability as a spiritual center, which earned political allegiance from other chiefs by its highest degree of merits. The political leader could also claim an ideal of cakravartin – universal lordship with highest degree of deity, indicating the realization of the sacred dimension of the "mandala" – humans can connect with the cosmic by centring on the divine spark or essence.

This spiritual-moral ethos provides the ground on which a spiritually sourced meritocracy could be nourished. Chiefs in the mandala circle pay their attribute, namely political allegiance, to the leader because of his spiritual potency and moral sublimes. In return, the leader is to assume the responsibility of protection and order maintenance of the circle. It can also be termed that moral sublime and spiritual deity of the leader is of practical effectiveness so as to conquer possible dampeners. In a word, the leader is to maintain the order in the mandala circle, and to vindicate moral values via his ruling. This is how the "mandala" circle works in managing both its internal and external affairs.

The second principle, symmetry, is believed to be dynamic, depending on contextual situations and contingent demands of the "mandala" circle. A wider geographical view shows that leaders in Southeast Asia may have posited themselves in the centre where the Indian and East Asian world interfaced each other, in various forms of commercial exchanges and religious pilgrimages. An incident provided by Wolters exemplifies how the leader in a "mandala" circle, by applying a symmetrical strategy of security diplomacy, carried out his security and order-maintenance responsibilities.[2] The Ayudhyan King Naresvara offered to help China, in 1592, resist a Japanese invasion under Hideyoshi leadership. Naresvara had seen Japan a powerful enemy in the rearward, and China, a rearward friend. In this sense, Naresvara had demonstrated East Asia under the Chinese civilization had been deemed as a rearward part of his "mandala" circle, and himself, cakravartin, a universal overlord. This example shows how the centre read and applied the symmetry, and had managed to maintain the order inside the "mandala".[3]

Symmetry relates to the third principle, cardinal points, in the sense that different points would influence how symmetry be defined, maintained and reconfigured. In pre-modern era, there existed two cardinal points, trade and security. Since then, trade had played an important role in shaping and reconfiguring regional political landscapes. This is particularly the case in the maritime Southeast Asia, leading to scholarly brainstorming of how local Southeast Asian polities should be conceptualized, defined, and categorized.[4]

In maritime Southeast Asia, port-based mandala circles, or in Kathirithamby-Wells's words, "port-polities", had been thrived on trade practices by which a mandala that incorporated various sub-regions with chiefdoms scattered around sporadically.[5] A network of intelligence that spread around confines of these sub-regions thus became critical to the existence of the mandala circle. This was where trade and security interfaced each other. Intricacy of this trade-security intertwinement was multi-dimensional. Trade brought wealth to the mandala. Meanwhile, cardinal points could be stretched as far as Arabia, Africa and Europe. But, it also generated leeway, thru which security threats would permeate, proliferate and mutate.

Yet, this trade-security intertwinement should not be deemed to overwrite the cakravartin concept, which emphasizes a universal moral conquest, rather than trade facilitation. Rather, trade practices should be deemed as confirmation of the concept, cakravartin. Trade had aided the centre to demonstrate its capability of ruling, in a profit-generating and benefit-sharing manner. Those who came to trade would benefit, materially and spiritually, an achievement that was attributed to the leader's ruling at a comprehensive scale. In other words, trade helped strengthen the leader's ruling upmanship and fortify security promises, in the sense that it provided the leader extra means to deliver both his moral edification and security guarantees. Nevertheless, it was a contingent fact that trade along would inevitably complicate how symmetry was defined, maintained and re-configured. In this sense, this trade-security intertwinement shed insightful lights on how this "mandala" concept helps inform the Southeast Asia regional order nowadays.

II Southeast Asia regionalization: the mandalic ethos reconfigured

The above revelation of how local polities had interacted in pre-modern era depicts a picture very different from what it has been since the end of the Second World War. Differences lie in both external grandeur context, the macrocosm, and internal national setting, the microcosm. Yet, the mandalic legacy has loomed behind regional countries' calculations and subsequent coalitions. Corresponding to a changing external context, there also emerged new cardinal points influencing how the centre is realized and symmetry being practised. Concomitantly, these new contents reconfigure old factors and further complicate operations of a mandalic Southeast Asian regional order in postwar era.

A Challenges Reconstruction

i Challenge I: the centre redefined

One primary feature of the postwar era is the emergence of a new regional order, which is based on the juxtaposition of a supra-national framework of international cooperation, and nation states as atomic actors at the ground level. In other words, two critical factors in this new system, international organizations at the upper level and nation states at the bottom, have challenged the conceptualization and operation of the mandala system.

Challenges lie in two aspects. On the one hand, it is becoming more difficult for the centre to claim ruling legitimacy based on its spiritual potency and moral sublimes. Instead, national authority now earns justifications of ruling legitimacy from a compound of democratic principles, such as protection of civil and human rights, rule of law, and those for modern governance. Besides, there emerges international law that stipulates how statehood is established,[6] while recognitions from international community constitute an important role.[7]

In terms of national management, it is no longer moral trait that accredits legitimacy/deity to the centre. Rather, national developments in a comprehensive scale earn increasing momentum when leadership is debated and its performance, measured. In the postwar era, when Southeast Asian people escaped the shackles of colonialism, they were snarled in the wave of nationalistic renaissance, one that had rendered critical supports to the booming of a new political prototype, sovereign nation states. In this sense, unlike the mandala system, power is measured in terms of lands being grabbed and resources thus exploited, which reflect two important pillars that fortify the Westphalian international system, territorial acquisition and resources monopolization[8] of certain occupant countries. Territories become a critical constituent to nation formation, and lands generally a trophy of inter-nation battles. Meanwhile, nationalism has sneaked in, providing a powerful resource from which national authority can tap on to strengthen its grips of power and ruling legitimacy.

In other words, with the imposition of a new system of inter-state relations supported by Westphalian international law, new cardinal points have emerged. Territory, nationalism, principles of democracy and modern governance – such as human rights, rule of law, transparency, protection of civil liberty/rights and procedural justice – all serve as potential candidates. Yet territory should be deemed as one with relatively weighing importance.

Territory should be highlighted as one new cardinal point that reshapes patterns of symmetries in inter-state relations in Southeast Asia.[9] In short, grabs of land, followed by boundary demarcation, are no longer results of acquired loyalties from other mandalas, when contingent situations change, but powerful evidences that demonstrate effective administration and alleged sovereignty of national authorities. Territorial acquisition also verifies the fact that moral conquest has since succumbed to realistic politicking that speaks more on arms and material obtention.

ii Challenge II: symmetry reconfigured with new cardinal points

The second challenge is the pattern how symmetry is defined and has evolved, at a scale swift and preposterous enough so as to make its confines blurred for consistent predictions. The changing pattern of symmetry should be discussed jointly with the emergence of new cardinal points.[10]

Immediately after the end of the Second World War, the region was overwhelmed by rows of changing geopolitical landscapes, including a burgeoning of newly independent nation states, the advent of Cold War confrontation, regional initiatives for closer cooperation on the economic and social dimension. Political calculations had wriggled restlessly underneath the surface of these regional groupings. Meanwhile, some conventional cardinal points have remained – trade and security – and new one – territory – has developed.

Trade and security have remained capable enough to reshape the pattern of how symmetries are defined and deployed. The former has seen multiplication and evolution, in the sense that economic development is deemed a consensus, and trade, a practical instrument to its achievement. It is the logic on which ASEAN regionalism has been advanced. A brief review of regionalization development would reify this contestation.

It was around 1950s and 1960s that the idea of regional groupings started to substantiate. Before the Association of Southeast Asian Nations (ASEAN) was formalized in 1967, several initiatives were attempted for the purpose of further advancement of regionalization.[11] At their infancies, these countries were imbued with dyadic concerns that closely knitted together due to the festering of Cold War, that of economic development and security. Mahatir's words are worth quoting, "Security is not just a matter of military capability. Nation security is inseparable from political stability, economic success and social harmony. . ."[12]

With this belief, regional countries started to build up new regional orders by focusing on economic development and internal stability, from which regional security could be meaningfully realized. The first attempt was in 1959 when Southeast Asia Friendship and Economic Treaty was sealed between Malaya and Philippines, albeit with a narrow focus limited to economy, trade and education.[13] A subsequent effort was in July 1961, the Association of Southeast Asia that involved three countries, Malaya, Thailand and Philippines.[14] This latter organization was more ambitious, including an array of issues in its agenda. It was to create regional stability and peace, while cultivating cooperation in economic, social science and cultural dimensions among member countries. A third attempt was put into action, shortly after, comprising Malaysia, Philippines and Indonesia.[15] Drawing similar organizational focuses on economic, social sciences and culture, this organization was tasked with a specific mission, to end territorial disputes among three countries. Yet, all attempts were aborted, due to the lack of a holistic view from an organizational perspective and regional interests.

iii The Region – Country Confrontation:
An Anomaly of Symmetry

Failures of these attempts reveal a postwar phenomenon, that of the conflict between national and regional interests, an anomaly of symmetry, which unfortunately had defied the intended goal to nourish both regionalism and localism. While realization of regionalism may come at a price of the relinquishment of state sovereignty, regionalism can also be deemed an advance over the traditional concept of absolute sovereignty.[16] Often driven by wars at a large and comprehensive scale, regionalism in postwar era is generally an immediate reaction to deteriorating external environment and rising security threat wrought by bipolar rivalry because of Cold War. Theoretically, regional stability should have aided these fledgling countries, in maintaining domestic order, which recursively would create an environment conducive to economic development for all. Besides unsettled attitudes and opponent voices favouring self-interested considerations and unilateral moves in national capitals of ASEAN countries, evolution of Southeast Asian regionalism has spoken much of itself.[17]

This anomaly of symmetry in due course of regional integration actually explains ASEAN's weakness in taking the responsibility of the role, "centre". Further, this anomaly of symmetry could be construed from two dyadic issues. They are not only inter-related, but also share the intricacy of an *explanandum-explanans*[18] relation.

First, this country-region conflict – presented in the fact that prioritization of state/national interests paradoxically costs these countries regionalism development – is catalysed/triggered because of two factors, establishment of "new countries" and formation of "Southeast Asia" as a region. Poignantly put, both are imposed processes stipulated largely by colonial powers and extra-regional countries. In other words, state formation was largely an outcome of political maneuvering of powerful actors non-extant geographically. Social responses were triggered, rather than spontaneously sprouted from the bottom that echoed communal demands. The corollary is, sadly, that these new countries and the region – in both a conceptual and nominal sense – appear more a convenient construct and a contingent device for these extra-regional actors.

One example is the geographical term which is now universally recognized, Southeast Asia. The Allied South East Asia Command established in 1943 during the Second World War is believed to be the earliest widely influential use of the geographical term, Southeast Asia.[19] In the immediate postwar era, the Southeast Asia Treaty Organization lent significant supports to the fortification of "Southeast Asia" as a geographical term, with the credits in both nominal and conceptual senses.[20] As McVey insightfully points, that ". . .the coincidence between Southeast Asia's birth as a concept and the triumph of American world power. World War II was important not for the bureaucratic detail of the South East Asia Command but for the fact that the Japanese occupied the region, creating an abrupt break with the era of European domination and making it an object of American attention."[21]

Accordingly, people in this region had been purportedly grouping and branding under specific stipulations that served mainly not the interest of their indigenous communities, but of the powers holding commands militarily, politically and economically. State formation was thus driven by political calculations and contingent demands.[22] In this sense, these new countries would need to spare greater efforts in domestic governance, with foremost priorities emphasized on the converging of national consciousnesses, which is able to nourish tolerances and respects to various ethnic groups and to solicit political allegiance to one central authority. Thus, unified national identities among all constituent ethnic groups are more an educated achievement in this region.

B The New Cardinal Point: Territory

A second explanation to this anomaly of symmetry is contingent on the new cardinal point, territory. This deliberate remapping out of geopolitical concerns and strategic needs not only lead to regrouping of indigenous peoples, but also lend fortifying supports to the development and concretization of territory, as a new cardinal point which is often left contested with considerable potentials of generating more confusions than clarifications.

Before the arrival of the European and the imposition of more systemic and predatory colonial administration, the concept and practice of borderlands and boundaries in Southeast Asia were rather alien to these western invaders. In effect, the ebb and flow of conflicts between coastal people and upland tribes had rendered unstable and undetermined boundaries in Southeast Asia mainland. Boundaries between local kingdoms and dynasties were not stable, non-delimited and non-demarcated. Further, within the region, zones of contact,[23] and in some cases, of separation,[24] and intermittent positional warfare, serve the functional equivalent of borders. Accordingly, the "sovereign" extension of these kingdoms, dynasties and principalities were determined by a power relationship that was always subject to change.[25] Further, the realist context had been that the central authority dwindled as the administration could barely reach into remote territories, whose inhabitants were thus used to this neglect by the alleged central authority and hardly would identify themselves with the lowland political authority. These pre-colonial concepts and practices of boundaries, territory and central authority (if not termed it sovereignty), nevertheless showcased that in pre-modern era, while the essence of central authority was of great importance, its territorial aspect was in fact negotiable.

Yet, along with the arrival of Europeans is the Westphalian international order, which has its premise on two pillar principles, territorial acquisition and monopoly enjoyment of resources on given territories.[26] In short, European colonialists had brought in the Westphalian order which employed an exclusive concept towards how territories being delimited and demarcated.[27] This territorial element was also one critical constituent to how sovereignty being established and identified. In this sense, the four criteria of modern statehood prescribed in the Montevideo Convention lend explicatory supports, in which territory is deemed a sine qua non of modern statehood.[28]

This new cardinal point, territory, serves as a poignant reminding of the prime and foremost challenge that encounters modern nation states in this region. Their dilemmas of becoming a modern polity with a centre that has to acquire ruling legitimacy from new resources – sovereignty, territories, people (ideally a single race), and effective administration, all defined in exclusive terms and attributed to a single centre – are vividly felt. Under this context, it is not surprising that the region has seen quite a few internal conflicts, both inter-state and intra-state, that have territorial, nationalistic or a dyadic origin.[29]

Before regional countries can effectively tackle the chaos wrought by territories, rough and tumble has crept to great swathes of waters in South China Sea, involving not only respective countries, but also ASEAN. To some extent, the increasing involvement of Southeast Asian countries in the South China Sea conundrum is once assimilated as what had been happening in pre-colonial era of old kingdoms,[30] when they keenly looked into the sea as a source of wealth and revenue of royal and dynastic authorities.

III The South China Sea: accommodating mandalic legacies in contemporary Southeast Asia

A ASEAN and the South China Sea issue

When situating ASEAN in the scenario of South China Sea dispute, the first issue is the relations between ASEAN, as a regional organization, and its member countries, as independent sovereign claimants. This is best witnessed in the ongoing debate whether ASEAN should forge a unified position against China in the South China Sea scenario. Yet, recalling that only a handful of countries are claimants, controversies continue. Has ASEAN earned the credits and justification to intervene on behalf of its member countries? How could ASEAN justify its intervening posture under the ethos that it is an organization for all (including non-claimants), and will not cost collective interests because of disputes involving only some of them? In other words, is ASEAN claiming a unified position on behalf of its member countries or of its own?

In this aspect, messages sent via a unified position of ASEAN in South China Sea are manifold. First, it signifies that ASEAN has been able to address anarchy in issues usually overwhelmed by national interests and utilitarian considerations, which are often unilateral and conflicting.[31] Second, certain institutional developments simultaneously are to take place, such as certain extents of power-centralization and institutional capacity which may subsume/take over national sovereignty in some aspects of regional issues. With the enhancement of institutional capacity and corresponding development of stronger institutional leadership, a basis for ASEAN to realize the aspiration to a supra-national legal personality is becoming more reified. Yet, besides institutional establishment, what lie at the crux are two issues sitting at two sides of the coin. On the one hand, it is the legitimacy and competence of ASEAN as the representative of its member countries, both claimant and non-claimant. On the other, has ASEAN been able to assume the role of the centre, reifying its responsibilities without compromising member countries' independence and sovereignty? Whatever the manifestation, it is likely that ASEAN is able to step into scenarios that fall conventionally into member countries' sovereign reign, should it continue to realize regional integration with steady progresses.

i ASEAN assuming the role of "the centre": limitation

The mandalic legacy mandates that a central deity from which power emanates is a critical constituent. The central deity is able to attract chiefdoms and commoners, because it stimulates the exalting experience of enlightenment, and also represents purity and virtuality in its highest form. In this sense, how has this mandalic legacy enlightened on ASEAN's development as the centre in modern context?

Documentary evidences suggest that reflecting mandalic legacies, ASEAN is assuming the role of the "centre", albeit in a partial manner, in modern context. The central role of ASEAN is partial, in the sense that it serves to assist national economic development by establishing a trade-conducive environment, from which certain extents of security can be guaranteed. Yet, the hard side of security, involving military capability and defence requirement, is left largely outside its helm. A row of ASEAN documents supports this contestation.

The founding document, Bangkok Declaration, provides in Article 1 that the goal is to accelerate economic growth, social progress and cultural development.[32] A peaceful and prosperous community would be the aspiration to which all these efforts are directed. Article 2 extends further the promotion of regional peace and stability, via policies in the economic, social, cultural, technical, scientific and administrative fields.[33] An official emphasis on economic development, from which regional economic integration can be realized, is more than apparent.

As a complement to the Bangkok Declaration, the Treaty of Amity and Cooperation (TAC), signed in 1976, could be deemed as a reconfirmation of the goal and principles intended by ASEAN's establishment. The purpose of this treaty is to promote perpetual peace, everlasting amity and cooperation among their peoples which would contribute to their strength, solidarity and closer relationship.[34] Towards this end, it provides a mechanism for the pacific settlement of regional disputes between TAC parties.

The third documentary evidence is the Vision 2020, which was unveiled in December, 1997, by the ASEAN Heads of State and Government.[35] In this document, ASEAN is envisioned to be a community conscious of ties of its history, aware of its cultural heritage and bound by a common regional identity.[36]

These above-mentioned documents, in the initiation moment of ASEAN and a critical juncture of ASEAN's enlargement,[37] have addressed mainly on the development of social and economic dimensions, with the aim to generate and sustain regional stability, which ultimately would achieve the goal of enduring security. Accordingly, what ASEAN has achieved after decades of regionalism development is that of assuming the role and function of the centre, albeit mainly in specific scenarios of economic development and thus-induced security.

Therefore, ASEAN has managed to realize the goal of common security by promoting economic developments, via a smart maneuvering of various forms of symmetries in policy cooperation in various fields. In this sense, inter-state policy cooperation and coordination in the ASEAN framework has revived the trade-security intertwinement in conventional practices of symmetry engrained in pre-modern Southeast Asia, by recasting them as economic growth, social progress and cultural development. The domestic stability of respective sovereigns, which is also deemed a critical constituent of regional security, is to be achieved via a positive dynamism between economic success and security guarantees.

In this aspect, textual contents in Vision 2020 lend explicatory supports to how ASEAN manages to deliver cardinal values reified in the trade/economic-security intertwinement by facilitating policy cooperation and coordination in the ASEAN platform. These cardinal values are reflected in a quadruple framework comprised of four constituents: peace, prosperity, progress and partnership.[38]

Beside this internal dimension of security, the external dimension of security should not be neglected.

To say that ASEAN is neglecting the hard side of security from its integration progress, that of military capability and defence deployment, is hasty. ASEAN is not a military pact, but one that intends to achieve collective security via non-military instruments, such as social and economic means. ASEAN member countries have attempted alternative means in addressing this military/security vacuum by entering into alliance relationships with extra-regional countries, such as United States.[39] Further, collective efforts in the organizational setting of ASEAN have been situated under the egis of United Nations framework since the end of WWII.[40]

However, the fact that ASEAN has not been able to manage the security guarantee has overshadowed ASEAN's engagement in South China Sea issue, in particular when tension continues to escalate, and when claimant countries politicize their contestations, by relying on a new cardinal point that ASEAN is seemingly incapable to handle, territory.

B Challenges of ASEAN in South China Sea issue

i A partially-functioned "centre" v. the totalizing effect of security

One first observation is that there exist two impediments preventing ASEAN from assuming the role of "centre" in handling South China Sea issue.

The first is that ASEAN is clearly limited in handling the security vacuum in South China Sea, thus rendering the role and function of ASEAN as the "centre" in a limited manner. It is able take the helm of issues, such as economic and social development. Yet, ASEAN could not deal with current dilemma in South China Sea that is catalysed by a security vacuum, escalating nationalism and a law-prioritized mindset. However, the trend that security consideration in South China Sea is becoming overwhelming enough so as to engulf efforts in mostly other aspects is signifying that a "totalization" phenomenon is quietly, yet rapidly, transforming the nature of the issue and swerving patterns of symmetries practised by ASEAN claimants. Yet, this totalizing effect – to address mainly the security threat by attaching weighing references to corresponding measures, such as defence diplomacy and military capability development – has become more telling, not of ASEAN's strengths, but shortcomings, the shortage of ASEAN in taking over responsibilities in security guarantees.

This capability, security provision, has been relegated to external sources, previously SEATO mechanism, and later U.S. and United Nations. In other words, while ASEAN has been assuming a satisfactory role in delivering material interests in non-military development in the region, its incompetence in assuming the role that deliver security guarantee has become one fragile point, the Achilles Heel from which extra-regional powers would be able to intervene and interfere in regional affairs.

Before 2009, ASEAN still had some leverages, capping the risks of tension escalation.[41] However, this institutional incompetence of ASEAN in addressing security threats wrought by South China Sea tensions, has reached a limit when the issue gets further complicated after 2009.[42] Ever since, South China Sea issue has continued to deteriorate. It is under this context that regional maritime order has become more fragmented and maritime security, further deteriorated. ASEAN incompetence thus is becoming more realistically felt.

ii A partially functioned "centre" v. the new cardinal point "territory"

The second impediment is ASEAN's incompetence in handling the new cardinal point, territory, and its corresponding patterns of symmetries. This lies mainly in the lack of wills, but not necessarily out of institutional shortcomings. Territory has become a critical constituent in forging legal personalities of these newly established countries, as enshrined in Montevideo Convention.[43] It is also one important source for national authorities to earn legitimacy credits for their rulings. This perception, territorial integrity and supremacy, was deemed quintessential to realize modern statehood for these countries. Accordingly, one pillar principle of ASEAN, "non-interference", can be seen as a clear reflection. In practice, ASEAN has shown consistence in upholding this principle, in whenever occasions of territorial-relevant issues. One latest example is the Thai-Cambodia border clashes extended from July 2008 until February 2011.[44] Despite criticism that ASEAN had waited too long to intervene, this restraint nevertheless has reified this self-imposed restriction and consistent respect of ASEAN to territory-relevant issues.

Yet, recent developments, seeing an intertwinement of territorial integrity and national identification of claimants do not bode well the prospect of South China Sea disputes. Lacking the will in handling territory-relevant issues, ASEAN would be further debilitated if narratives are further politicized, naming these territories one critical constituent to national identification of claimants. Vietnam serves as an example. For one thing, Vietnam's South China Sea claims strengthen the ruling legitimacy of Vietnam Communist Party, to save Vietnam from a powerful rivalry, China, which aimed at further encroachment of Vietnam's territories. Second, it signifies a long quest of the Vietnamese for self-identification, which can explain not only where they were from, but also direct the way they are to progress.[45] Particularly, it is Paracel Islands dispute, which Hanoi can cultivate ruling legitimacies after the 1976 unification, and to consolidate a new generation national identity.[46]

This dilemma confirms again the influence of mandalic legacies in modern Southeast Asia. Every country is operated by following these mandala legacies. Every national authority would claim itself, cakravartin, a universal lord, so that no one is more superior and capable to judge and intervene into others' internal affairs. This explains ASEAN's predilection to the route of informality, of eschewing legal formulations and legally binding commitments. Yet, it does not help in solving territory-relevant issues, let alone highly politicized South China Sea territorial disputes.

IV Conclusion: recasting ASEAN's South China Sea engagement

A *ASEAN facing leadership competence competition*

Retrospect of how state (dynasties and municipalities then) interact in pre-modern era shows that contemporary dichotomy in Southeast Asian practices in economic and security matters, often deemed an anomaly, has its historical roots and cultural explanations. The mandala system of regional order has left behind profound legacies, which continues to be one underlying reason explaining the action-reaction dynamism among ASEAN countries.

These legacies have loomed large in various aspects: that of ASEAN's partial achievement to be the "centre" able to exercise institutional powers and moral persuasion to tackle sensitive issues, like South China Sea disputes; that of incompetence of ASEAN and member countries to construe and leverage on the newly emerged cardinal point of territory; that of the contradiction between ASEAN's role as the "centre" and national authority of member countries as one with unchallengeable sovereignty; and that of the dichotomy of economic and security matters, which nevertheless are tied by a dyadic interrelation.

These impediments not only have explained the ineffectiveness and limitation of ASEAN in handling the South China Sea issue, but also denote the challenge to ASEAN in its further pursuit of regional integration. The challenge is mostly demonstrated in the looming competition for leadership competence between ASEAN and other "centres" thriving from external sources of legitimacy. These other "centres" have cast weighing influences in ASEAN's further developments in economics and security scenarios, and even one concerning normative authority. Of relevant importance to the South China Sea issue is scenarios of security and normative authority.

Yet, this should not be attributed to ASEAN's institutional failure, rather than a prevailing phenomenon globe wide. The whole world has become more integrated, in the sense that issues in one scenario, and certain regions, may have their impacts rippling further beyond their geographic and conventional confines. To some extent, this phenomenon can be deemed as collaborative labour division, as countries or organizations have delegated some sorts of decision-making authorities to external "centres", when situations require. Scholars in international law scenario describe this from the lens of national sovereignty evolution.[47] Globalization has further concretized this outsourcing of sovereignty, or authority delegation of decision-making authority to international institutional mechanism, business actors and even civil movement advocates.

This is what has happened in ASEAN's engagement in South China Sea issue, in particular in the scenario of maritime security and norm-making authority. For the security issue, maritime order has been further aggravated due to unilateral activities and politicized narratives aspiring to territorial pursuits and identification re-configuration. Room for negotiation and compromise is quickly shrinking. As of now, no single ruling authority can afford being bent down in their South China Sea claims. This is further catalysed as some claimants utilize territorial claims as a means for reconfiguration of national identity. In this aspect, ASEAN lacks the consciousness as the "centre" and corresponding moral potency to tackle impacts wrought by the new cardinal point, territory, extravagant politicizing narratives and corresponding symmetries practiced by claimant countries.

Similar incompetence of ASEAN is also poignantly felt in handling a dominating role of law.

Law has been elevated to a paramount status with an unchallengeable authority. A legal solution, with institutional guarantees, is more sustainable. Yet, this trend of a law-prioritized mindset, if not law dictatorship, is worrisome. For ASEAN claimants, legalist narratives create the illusion that law of sea and international law can be one panacea, the magic wand that not only could resolve the dispute, but also wipe off inherent intricacies engrained in regional order – power asymmetry and multilateral relationships. Moreover, a dangerous conglomeration of this over-judicialization of claimants' contestation and the over-politicization of their policy narratives is on the making, seeing a growing intertwinement of law and politics which further catalyses South China Sea confrontations.

In this aspect, what requires reconsideration is the debate whether ASEAN should converge a unified position. A hasty conclusion in this only makes the ASEAN approach of informality and non-bindingness in handling regional issues only too credible.

This is actually where mandalic legacies could lend ASEAN explicatory supports. ASEAN is reflecting the legacy of the centre. This centre role is becoming more symbolic, which has functioned to connect regional members in informal ways, with an aspiration of regional security and autonomy. To some extents, in a world where the Westphalian system has largely stipulated how inter-state relations be displayed/depicted, existence of the centre that serves not any more than reifying a symbolic consciousness of autonomy and independence of the region is becoming more indispensable to further regional development. Situating in a traffic chokepoint seeing cultural conglomerations, it is only in this non-physical/spiritual terms that Southeast Asia could be deemed a centre, having its own landscape where a historical processes of interaction between people and the environment are made and shaped. Therefore, ASEAN has achieved concrete outcomes in regional integration and development in an informal setting that counters the European experience.[48] From this perspective, ASEAN's unity should be applauded. The unity is demonstrated not much in a unified position, but in their resilience of upholding ASEAN consistently as a centre. This manifestation, standing together, has become one primary way of members to honour ASEAN's engagement in South China Sea issues, to demonstrate the unity in the face of external threats.[49]

Notes

1 "Mandala" is seen a tradition of knowledge in Southeast Asia, comprises two constituents, a religious diagram connoting both Hinduist and Buddhist heritages, and a doctrine shaping traditional Southeast Asian inter-polity relations. For more discussions, see, Stanley J. Tambiah, "The Galactic Polity in Southeast Asia", in *Culture, Thought and Social Action*, Stanley J. Tambiah (ed.) (Cambridge, MA: Harvard University Press, 1985), 252–286; Tambiah, "The Galactic Polity", in *World Conqueror and World Renouncer: A Study of Religion and Polity in Thailand against a Historical Background* (Cambridge: Cambridge University Press, 1976), 102–131; Giuseppe Tucci, *The Theory and Practice of the Mandala*

(Mineola, NY.: Dover, 2001), 1–20; Robert Heine-Geldern, "Concept of State and Kinship in Southeast Asia", *Far Eastern Quarterly*, 2 (1942): 15–30; Lawrence P. Briggs, "The Ancient Khmer Empire", *Transactions of the American Philosophical Society*, N.S., 41 (1951): 1–295; G. Coedes, *The Indianized States of Southeast Asia* (Honolulu: East-West Center Press), 3–13, 14–35; G. Carter Bentley, "Indigenous States of Southeast Asia", *Annual Review of Anthropology*, 15 (1986): 275–305. Also, see Oliver W. Wolters, "Ayudhya and the Rearward Part of the World", *Journal of the Royal Asiatic Society*, 3–4 (1968): 166–178; Wolters, *History, Culture and Religion in Southeast Asian Perspectives* (Singapore: Institute of Southeast Asian Studies, 1982), Chapter 2, 16–33; Wolters, *History, Culture and Religion in Southeast Asian Perspectives*, rev. ed. (Ithaca, NY: Southeast Asian Program Publications (SEAP), 1999), Chapter 2, 27–40; M. Shu, "Hegemon and Instability: Pre-Colonial Southeast Asia under the Tribute System", *Waseda Institute for Advanced Studies Research Bulletin*, 4 (2012): 45–62.
2 Supra, note 1, Wolters, "Ayudhya and the Rearward Part of the World".
3 Another case is foreign relations of the Majapahit empire with a couple of polities which were duly placed in the geopolitical mandala of Majapahit in 13th and 14th centuries, so that the empire could deploy friends to contain enemies. This mandala consisted of circles of mitra (friends) – Champa, Syangka and Ayudhya, ari (enemies) – The Mongol, Chola Dynasty, madhyama (medium power) – Ayudhya, and Udasina (major power) – China (Ming Dynasty). Majapahit maintained good relations with friendly polities – like Champa and Syangka, so that enemies were assured counterbalanced – Mongol and Chola. It also managed to accommodate the interests of middle power – Ayudhya. See, Slamet Muljana, *A Story of Majapahit* (Singapore: National University of Singapore Press, 1976), 136, 144–146.
4 See more discussions in Francois Gipouloux, *The Asian Mediterranean: Port Cities and Trading Networks in China, Japan and Southeast Asia, 13th-21st Century* (Cheltenham: Edward Elgar Publishing, 2011); Anthony Reid, *Southeast Asia in the Age of Commerce, 1450–1680: The Lands Below the Winds* (New Haven: Yale University Press, 1990); J. Kathirithamby-Wells, "Introduction: An Overview", in *The Southeast Asian Port and Polity: Rise and Demise*, J. Kathirithamby-Wells and J. Villiers (eds.) (Singapore: National University of Singapore, 1990), 1–16; Christie J. Wisseman, "Trade and State Formation in the Malay Peninsula and Sumatra, 300 A.C. – A.D. 700", in *The Southeast Asian Port and Polity: Rise and Demise*, J. Kathirithamby-Wells and J. Villiers (eds.) (Singapore: National University of Singapore, 1990), 39–60; Wisseman, "State Formation in Early Maritime Southeast Asia: A Consideration of the Theories and the Data", *Bijdragen tot de Taal-, Land- en Volkenkunde*, 151:2 (1995): 235–288.
5 Ibid, Kathirithamby-Wells, "Introduction", 3–4.
6 Criteria of modern statehood are stipulated, such as sovereignty over certain peoples, upon given territories, and a government exercising effective administration within and without national boundaries. The Montevideo Convention on Rights and Duties of States (Montevideo Convention), 26 December, 1933, 165 LNTS 19. Article 1 prescribes the four qualifications to vest a state with a legal personality in international law: a permanent population, a defined territory, government and capacity to enter into relations with the other states.
7 The role and impact of recognition from the international community constitute another thorn in the flesh to the succession regime. Following the creation of new states, in whatever manifestation, whether foreign recognition should be regarded as a constituent factor, or one with merely declaratory effect to the establishment of new states, find respective supports in state practices. Simply put, decisions whether to grant formal recognition are tinged with a murky

confluence of legal and political considerations in the law of recognition. For a brief review of the evolution of the law (including theories of state, the basis of obligation, sovereignty, recognition, and succession...etc.), see Malcom Shaw, *International Law*, 6th ed. (Cambridge: Cambridge University Press, 2008); Ian Brownlie, *Principles of Public International Law*, 7th ed. (Oxford: Oxford University Press, 2008); James Crawford, *The Creation of States in International Law*, 2th ed. (Oxford: Clarendon Press, 2006); Antonio Cassese, *International Law*, 2nd ed. (Oxford: Oxford University Press, 2005); Also, see M.J. Peterson, "Recognition of Governments Should Not Be Abolished", *The American Journal of International Law*, 77:1 (January 1983): 31–50; See also, "Revolutions, Treaties and State Successions", *The Yale Law Journal*, 76:8 (July 1967): 1669–1687; Matthew Craven, *The Decolonization of International Law: State Succession and the Law of Treaties* (Oxford: Oxford University Press, 2007), 23–29; Craven, "The Problem of State Succession and the Identity of States under International Law", *European Journal of International Law*, 9 (1998): 142–162.
8 See more discussions in, Antony Anghie, *Imperialism, Sovereignty and the Making of International Law* (New York: Cambridge University Press, 2007), 32–114; Anghie, "The Evolution of International Law: Colonial and Postcolonial Realities", *Third World Quarterly*, 27:5 (2006): 739–753; Prasenjit Duara, "The New Imperialism and the Post-Colonial Developmental State: Manchukuo in Comparative Perspective", *The Asia-Pacific Journal*, 4:1 (2006): 1–18; Duara, *Decolonization: Perspectives from Now and Then* (New York and London: Routledge, 2004), 1–20, 78–100.
9 More discussions will be pursued in next section.
10 It is argued in previous discussions that territory, nationalism, principles of democracy and modern governance – such as human rights, rule of law, transparency, protection of civil liberty/rights, procedural justice – all serve as potential candidates of new cardinal points.
11 Johan Saravanamuttu, *The Dilemma of Independence Two Decades of Malaysia's Foreign Policy 1957–1977* (Penang: Penerbitan Universiti Sains Malaysia, 1983), 42–43; K.S. Nathan, "Law and Politics in the Vietnam Conflict: An Appraisal of the Geneva Accords (1954) and Paris Agreements (1973)", in *Historical Essays on Remembering 25th Year Anniversary of University Malaya History Department*, Muhammad Abu Bakar, Amarjit Kaur and Abdullah Zakaria Ghazali (eds.) (Kuala Lumpur: The Malaysia History Society, 1984), 515; Nicholas Tarling, "From SEAFET and ASA: Precursors of ASEAN", *International Journal of Asia Pacific Studies*, 3:1 (2007): 1–14; Mohamad F. Keling, Hishamudin Md. Som, Mohamad Nasir Saludin, Md. Shukri Shuib and Mohd Na'eim Ajis, "The Development of ASEAN from Historical Approach", *Asian Social Science*, 7:7 (July 2011): 169–189.
12 Abdul Razak and Abdullah Baginda, "National Security Issues in Malaysian Foreign Policy", in *Malaysian Foreign Policy, Issues and Perspective*, Mohamad Azhari Karim, Lewellyn D. Howell and Grace Okuda (eds.) (Kuala Lumpur: Institut Tadbrian Awam Negara, 1990), 39.
13 Supra, note 11.
14 This was the Association of Southeast Asia. Supra, note 11 and 12.
15 The organization was called MAPHILINDO, whose objective was to create cooperation in the field of economy, culture and social sciences. Supra, note 11 and 12. Also, Russell H. Fified, "National and Regional Interest in ASEAN Competition and Cooperation in International Politics", Occasional Paper, No. 57, Institute of Southeast Asian Studies, Singapore, 1979, 6–9; M. Patmanathan, *Reading in Malaysia Foreign Policy* (Kuala Lumpur: University Malaya Press, 1980), 23.

16 K.R. Singh, "Regionalism: Past and Present", in *The Troubled Region: Issues of Peace and Development in Southeast Asia*, Parimal Kumar Das (ed.) (London: Sage, 1987), 61. Also, a theory lends supplementary references when Southeast Asian regionalism is considered – Diffusion as an outcome of regional integration. W.P. Avery, "Extra-Regional Transfer of Integrative Behavior", *International Organization*, 27:4 (1973): 549–556. This theory suggests that the decision for particular institutional designs is not exclusively determined by regional dynamics but at least partly influenced by the institutional and policy decisions of other regional organizations. It further argues that a full account of regional integration processes needs to take diffusion processes into consideration. See more discussions in, David Strang and John D. Meyer, "Institutional Conditions for Diffusion", *Theory and Society*, 22 (1993): 487–511; David Levi-Faur, "The Global Diffusion of Regulatory Capitalism", *Annals of the American Academy of Political and Social Science*, 598 (2005): 12–32; Zachary Elkins and Beth Simmons, "On Waves, Clusters and Diffusion: A Conceptual Framework", *Annals of the American Academy of Political and Social Science*, 598 (2005): 33–51; Covadonga Meseguer, *Learning, Policy Making and Market Reforms* (Cambridge, UK: Cambridge University Press, 2009).
17 Key factors motivating more advanced regionalism in Southeast Asia are stability of regional politics, peace objective, regional conflict solution, security guarantee, economic development and cooperation.
18 An explanandum (a Latin term) is a phenomenon that is to be explained and its explanans is the explanation of that phenomenon.
19 Eric C. Thompson, *Southeast Asia, in International Encyclopedia of Human Geography*, vol. 10, Kitchin R. Thrift (ed.) (Oxford: Elsevier, 2009), 248–254; Grant Evans, "Between the Global and the Local There Are Regions, Culture Areas, and National States: A Review Article", *Journal of Southeast Asian Studies*, 33:1 (February 2002): 147–162.
20 In September of 1954, the United States, France, Great Britain, New Zealand, Australia, the Philippines, Thailand and Pakistan formed the Southeast Asia Treaty Organization, or SEATO. United States Department of State, Office of The Historian, *Southeast Asia Treaty Organization (SEATO), 1954*, https://history.state.gov/milestones/1953–1960/seato, last visited 15 April, 2016.
21 Ruth McVey, "Change and Continuity in Southeast Asian Studies", *Journal of Southeast Asian Studies*, 26:1 (1995): 1–9, doi: 10.1017/S0022463400010432.
22 Tim Harper, "A Long View on the Great Asian War", in *Legacies of World War II in South and East Asia*, David Koh Wee Hock (ed.) (Singapore: Institute of Southeast Asian Studies, 2007), 7–25.
23 *International Frontiers and Boundaries: Law, Politics and Geography*, J.R. John Robert, Victor Prescott, Gillian and Doreen Triggs (Leiden: Martinus Nijhoff Publishers, 2008), 23–90; J.R.V. Prescott, *The Geography of Frontiers and Boundaries* (London and New York: Routledge, 2015), 33–55; Ladis K.D. Kristof, "The Nature of Frontiers and Boundaries", *Annals of the Association of American Geographers*, 49:3 (1959): 269–282.
24 Ibid. In Southeast Asia, frontiers are of many types. Some are zones of separation because of their inaccessibility. Examples are like those in central New Guinea, central Borneo, the Laos-Yunnan-Myanmar area and the Laos-Vietnam area. On the other hand, there are zones of contact where the physical geography is not so difficult, making these frontiers easily crossed between two or more groups of peoples. This contact can involve migration, trade, intermarriage and conflict. In Southeast Asia, areas such as the Lao-Thai border, the Thai-Kampuchean border, the Vietnamese-Kampuchean border and the Sino-Vietnamese border fall into this category.

25 Craig A. Lockard, *Southeast Asia in World History* (New York: Oxford University Press, 2009), Chapter 4 and 5; Amitav Acharya, *The Quest for Identity: International Relations of Southeast Asia* (Singapore: Oxford University Press, 2009), Chapter 1, 17–42.
26 Supra, note 8.
27 Generally when territories/boundaries are designated, four stages can be identified, namely, allocation or definition, delimitation, demarcation and administration. Yet, in Southeast Asia, the evolution of boundaries in Southeast Asia has not followed the classical model of an international boundary. It is poignantly observed that due to the political discontinuity created by the intervention of European colonial powers, the evolution of boundaries in Southeast Asia has seen a discursive development, which is not pursued in a lineal order. See, Robert L. Solomon, "Boundary Concepts and Practices in Southeast Asia", *World Politics*, 23:1 (October 1970): 1–23; Lee Yong Leng, *Southeast Asia: Essays in Political Geography* (Singapore: National University Press, 1982), 9–16; Lee Yong Leng, "The Colonial Legacy in Southeast Asia: Maritime Boundary Problems", *Contemporary Southeast Asia*, 8:2 (September 1986): 119–130; Amitav Acharya, "Imaging Southeast Asia", in his *The Making of Southeast Asia: International Relations of a Region* (Ithaca: Cornell University Press, 2013), 51–104; Alastair Lamb, *Asian Frontiers* (New York: Frederick A. Praeger Inc., 1968), 39.
28 Supra, note 6.
29 Vietnam invaded Cambodia in 1979. Kevin Doyle, "Vietnam's Forgotten Cambodian War", *BBC*, 14 September, 2014, www.bbc.com/news/world-asia-29106034, last visited 30 August, 2016. The latest was in early 2011, when border clashes between Thailand and Cambodia, near the temple internationally known as Preah Vihear. Jason Szep and Ambica Ahuja, "Thai, Cambodia Troops Clash Again on Disputed Border", *Reuters*, 6 February, 2011, www.reuters.com/article/us-thailand-cambodia-idUSTRE7151K320110206, last visited 30 August, 2016.
30 See, note 1, and also, Carlyle A. Thayer, "The Tyranny of Geography: Vietnamese Strategies to Constrain China in the South China Sea", *Contemporary Southeast Asia: A Journal of International and Strategic Affairs*, 33:3 (December 2011): 348–369; Brantly Womack, "The Spratlys: From Dangerous Ground to Apple of Discord", *Contemporary Southeast Asia*, 33:3 (December 2011): 370–387.
31 Anarchy has been a contentious concept, and the focus of debates in international relation studies. Proponents, largely in the realist school, accept/recognize the condition of anarchy, but argue that this does not necessarily preclude order beyond the reign of respective sovereign countries. Opponents, mainly in the liberalist school, deem anarchy as incompatible with order, which can only be realized by the existence of governance, of one sort or another, that replaces this anarchical disorder. Besides, there are also voices that reject these dichotomic positions that assume an exclusive relation between anarchy and hierarchy. Lake identifies different forms of hierarchical relations by using "degrees of hierarchy" that is situated in a single dimensional continuum between total anarchy and complete hierarchy. Yet, when recasting these thoughts to modern Southeast Asian context, this anarchy-hierarchy relation touches upon if ASEAN has, or would be able to assume the role and function of the "centre", from which powers, in both conceptual and realistic manifestation, can be emanated and respected. G. Evans and J. Newnham, *The Penguin Dictionary of International Relations* (London: Penguin, 1998), 19, 224; D. Lake, *Hierarchy in International Relations* (Ithaca and London: Cornell University Press, 2009), Chapter 2: International Hierarchy.
32 The ASEAN Declaration (Bangkok Declaration), adopted by the Foreign Ministers at the 1st ASEAN Ministerial Meeting in Bangkok, Thailand on 8 August,

1967, www.asean.org/the-asean-declaration-bangkok-declaration-bangkok-8-august-1967/, last visited 15 April, 2016]. See, Article 1.
33 Ibid., Article 2.
34 1976 Treaty of Amity and Cooperation in Southeast Asia, adopted by the Heads of State/Government at the 1st ASEAN Summit in Bali, Indonesia, 24 February, 1976, http://cil.nus.edu.sg/rp/pdf/1976%20Treaty%20of%20Amity%20and%20Cooperation%20in%20Southeast%20Asia-pdf.pdf, last visited 15 April, 2016.
35 1997 ASEAN Vision 2020, adopted by ASEAN Heads of State/Government at the 2nd Informal Summit in Kuala Lumpur, Malaysia, 15 December, 1997, http://cil.nus.edu.sg/rp/pdf/1997%20ASEAN%20Vision%202020-pdf.pdf, last visited 15 April, 2016.
36 Ibid.
37 After the end of Cold War in 1991, ASEAN's membership increased through the participation of communist countries of Indochina. Vietnam decided to join ASEAN on 23 July, 1995, whose entry consequently influenced other Indochina countries to follow suit, Laos entered in 1997, followed by Myanmar and Cambodia in 1999. Mohammed Nasrudin, ASEAN and Administration, "Regional Threats", *Pemikir*, 41 (July–September 2005): 103.
38 Supra, note 35.
39 In 1954, the Philippines and Thailand entered into the Southeast Asian Treaty Organization (SEATO) with a couple of countries, all located outside Southeast Asia, for the purpose of prevent communism from gaining ground in the region. Other regional countries declined to join in SEATO for a variety of reasons. Malaya was embarrassed to forward support to the treaty due to its previous political tensions with U.K. Indonesia and Burma (Myanmar) favoured to maintain their neutrality, which they later endorsed in the Bandung Conference in 1955. Vietnam, Laos and Cambodia were prevented from joining any international military alliance because of the terms of the Geneva Agreements of 1954 signed after the fall of French Indochina. Despite institutional shortages such as the lack of a SEATO force, the treaty had rendered helps to regional countries in fortifying their military capabilities in combating against communism threat.
40 This is another alternative that ASEAN member countries could rely on for security guarantee, the United Nations framework. U.N. framework had laid down the platform on which post-WWII international order could be established. It also serves as a security safeguard mechanism, which aims at delivering basic security guarantee of a regional order free from devastative, engulfing war. In this sense, ASEAN has aimed to encourage peace and political stability founded by the principles of United Nations. Therefore, ASEAN members should comply with rules and regulations laid out in U.N. Charter when building regional ties and inter-state cooperation.
41 The Declaration of Conduct reached between ASEAN and China in 2002, and a Declaration of ASEAN Concord was issued in the 7th ASEAN Plus Three Summit in 2003, serve two examples. 2002 Declaration of The Conduct of Parties in The South China Sea, adopted by the Foreign Ministers of ASEAN and the People's Republic of China at the 8th ASEAN Summit in Phnom Penh, Cambodia on 4 November, 2002; Declaration of ASEAN Concord II (Bali Concord II), signed on 7 October, 2003 in Bali, Indonesia by the Heads of State/Government.
42 To meet the deadline, 2009, set up by the Committee of the Limits of Continental Shelf, Vietnam, Malaysia, China and the Philippines submitted their claims with corresponding documents and graphs. Commission on the Limits of the Continental Shelf, Outer limits of the continental shelf beyond 200 nautical

miles from the baselines: Submissions to the Commission: Joint submission by Malaysia and the Socialist Republic of Viet Nam, 3 May, 2011 (updated), www.un.org/depts/los/clcs_new/submissions_files/submission_mysvnm_33_2009.htm, last visited 20 April, 2016.
43 Supra, note 6.
44 Waging Peace: ASEAN and The Thai-Cambodian Border Conflict, International Crisis Group Report, No. 215, 6 December, 2011.
45 Accordingly, it is understandable that Vietnamese claims are imbued with historical justifications, nationalistic sentiments, realistic considerations prioritizing compliance to international norm, and state-authorized propaganda directed to domestic audience in order to converge recognition to a resilient and self-preserving Vietnamese self-image.
46 Teh-Kuang Chang, "China's Claim of Sovereignty Over Spratly and Paracel Islands: A Historical and Legal Perspective", *Case Western Reserve Journal of International Law*, 23:3 (1991): 399–420; David Scott, "Conflict Irresolution in the South China Sea", *Asian Survey*, 52:6 (2012): 1019–1042; Stein Tonnesson, "The Paracels: The Other South China Sea Dispute", *Asian Survey*, 26:4 (2002): 145–169.
47 The concept sovereignty is re-configured in due course when national communities become more diversified, albeit under the context of a more intensified globalization phenomenon. Intellectual brainstorming of "sovereignty", gathers further momentum quickly. For example, Christoph Rudolph argues for "sovereignty bargain", when various facets of sovereignty are engaged. Robert Jackson made a distinction between negative and positive sovereignty, as the former describes formal conditions, the latter indicates the substantive capacity to enjoy liberty and interests of sovereignty. Christopher Rudolph, "Sovereignty and Territorial Borders in a Global Age", *International Studies Review*, 7:1 (March 2005): 1–20, at 4–9, 12–15; Robert Jackson, "The Weight of Ideas in Decolonization: Normative Change in International Relations", in *Ideas and Foreign Policy*, Judith Goldstein and Robert Keohane (eds.) (Ithaca: Cornell University Press, 1993), 111–138.
48 Sovereign state in the Westphalian system has been inscribed as one of ASEAN constitutive norms. This is criticized as constituting huge impediments towards greater efficiency and deeper integration. See, Shaun Narine, "ASEAN in the Twenty-First Century: A Sceptical Review", *Cambridge Review of International Affairs*, 22:3 (2009): 369–386; John Ravenhill, "Fighting Irrelevance: An Economic Community, with ASEAN Characteristics", *Pacific Review*, 21:4 (2008): 469–506. For more discussions in ASEAN model of regional integration, see, Amitav Acharya, *Whose Ideas Matter? Agency Power in Asian Regionalism* (Ithaca: Cornell University Press, 2009); Alice Ba, *[Re]Negotiating East and Southeast Asia Region, Regionalism, and the Association of Southeast Asian Nations* (Stanford: Stanford University Press, 2009); Benjamin Goldsmith, "A Liberal Peace in Asia", *Journal of Peace Research*, 44:1 (2007): 5–27; Yoram Haftel, "Designing for Peace: Regional Integration Arrangements, Institutional Variation, and Militarized Interstate Dispute", *International Organization*, 61:1 (2007): 217–237; Johnson I. Alastair, "The Myth of the ASEAN Way? Explaining the Evolution of ASEAN Regional Forum", in *Imperfect Unions, Security Institutions Over Time and Space*, Helga Haftendorn, Robert Keohane and Celeste Wallander (eds.) (Oxford: Oxford University Press, 1999), 287–324.
49 Allan Gyngell, *Looking Outwards: ASEAN's External Relations, in Understanding ASEAN*, Alison Broinowski (ed.) (London: Macmillan Press, 1983), 116.

8 From the periphery
State succession and the South China Sea disputes

I A Revisionist Approach: new categorization of the South China Sea dispute

As elaborated in Chapter 5, China's claims could be divided to three dimensions, the islands sovereignty contribution, the Exclusive Economic Zoning, and the dash-line claim.[1] The dash-line claim has long attracted scholarly and public attention, but no corresponding studies of the numerous islands scattered around the South China Sea. However, a more delicate reading of the voluminous islands and islets is justified, in the sense that their different roots have actually posted them under different contexts that require different strategies and negotiation agenda.

In construing China (PRC)'s South China Sea claims, one should not be careless enough to ignore the distinction Beijing made among the three subsets in the land features in the South China Sea. While implicitly, nuances among these three subsets in terms of China (PRC)'s justification and practices, reveal its unique perspective regarding the role of international law, and China (PRC)'s position in the constructed political and legal hierarchy.

China (PRC) has, in fact, categorized the South China Sea issues in three subsets, the Paracel Islands against the Socialist Republic of Vietnam (SRV, Vietnam), the Itu Aba and the Pratas Islands currently under Taiwan (ROC)'s control, and all other land features that cover disputed subjects in the ongoing arbitration. In a nutshell, the Paracel and Itu Aba Islands concern more than just maritime zoning and resource enjoyment. Instead, they should be studied in a broader context, when successions of governments (or states) take place at different timing and with varying conditions. These successions occur in both Vietnam and China. The focus of this chapter will be the Chinese case. Both cases suggest that a clear line between succession of governments or of states – namely, creation of new states following the demise of old one – is blurred. Yet the Chinese succession has evolved on. The progress of this ongoing Chinese succession will generate significant impacts on China (PRC) and Taiwan (ROC)'s claims in South China Sea issues.

It is in this context that the Paracel and Itu Aba Islands should be categorized separately from the rest of islands and islets in South China Sea, such as the

Spratly Islands. The Paracel Islands dispute is related to the Vietnamese succession that occurred in 1976, while the Itu Aba Island, the Chinese succession which continues to develop up to the present.

A The Paracel Islands: not just an island-sovereignty dispute

China (PRC) bases its claim upon the Paracel Islands on two bases, the nine-dash line and the maritime clash that recovered the Paracels from then Democratic Republic of Vietnam (DRV, North Vietnam) in 1974.[2] As indicated, for the dash-line claim, an interpretation that better serves both China(s)' interests is required, upon the cooperation between China (PRC) and Taiwan (ROC).

For the maritime clash in 1974, it could be viewed as a reaffirmation of China (PRC)'s territorial statement made by then Prime Minister Zhou in 1958,[3] and also a countermeasure to DRV's repudiation on its concurring statement made by its Prime Minister, Phạm Văn Đồng, in 1958,[4] in which DRV explicitly supported China (PRC)'s position.

Yet, these reasonings are not totally sound and free of criticism. Two flaws exist. On the one hand, whether the SRV inherited the DRV's positions in the Paracel Islands require more detailed considerations. Maritime clashes occurred in 1974, and between the DRV and China (PRC), leading to China (PRC)'s reclaiming of the Paracel Islands that came into the control of the Republic of Vietnam (South Vietnam) in 1973.[5] In 1975, unification of North and South Vietnam led to the emergence of a new country, the SRV. Despite voluminous scholarly debates yet to be settled, on this Vietnamese unification, it is widely accepted in the international community that it is more an episode of state succession, not a murky one of simply, changes of governments.[6]

In this sense, the clean-slate theory, concerning the relations between the new state and treaty rights and obligations committed by its predecessor when state succession occurs, is applicable in a general term.[7] Put differently, whether the new state, the SRV in this occasion, is deemed, without doubts, to inherit the rights and obligations committed by the DRV, should be governed by the clean-slate theory, in which a general exemption would be applied to the new state.[8] Accordingly, the SRV should not be deemed, for granted, as inheriting all rights and obligations committed by its predecessor DRV government, unless it has made explicit commitments therewith. In this sense, whether China (PRC)'s justification of recovering the Paracel Islands against the DRV could be unequivocally applied to the SRV remains an open question.

On the other hand, China (PRC) enmeshed itself in embarrassment by having recourse to use of force, but not peaceful means, to solve disputes with DRV in 1974. The key was if the use of force had been outlawed, which was recognized then as a customary international law. A row of international documents lend supports to this observation that peaceful means should be prioritized and trumpet forceful measures in international dispute settlement.

In normative scenarios, this goal is upheld with supreme esteem. In Article 2(4) and 33 in the United Nations Charter, this goal is reaffirmed from both a

146 *State succession and the disputes*

holistic perspective, along with detailed delineations of what constitute peaceful means.[9] States are encouraged to settle their disputes via negotiation, enquiry, mediation, conciliation, arbitration, judicial settlement, resort to regional agencies or arrangements or other peaceful means of their own choice.[10]

Besides hard laws such as the UN Charter, this goal is reconfirmed repeatedly in a series of international documents and treaty regimes that do not contain as many party members as the UN regime. Examples are plenty, such as the General Assembly Resolution 2625 (XXV), Declaration on Principles of International Law Concerning Friendly Relations and Co-Operation among States in Accordance with the Charter of the United Nations.[11] The document solemnly proclaimed principles emphasizing that states shall refrain from the threat or use of force in territorial-related disputes, and shall recourse to peaceful means for dispute settlement so that international peace, security and justice would not be endangered.[12]

Another international treaty also provides weighing evidence to this trendy development. In Article 49 in the Responsibility of States for Internationally Wrongful Acts (the State Responsibility Acts), object and limits of countermeasures an injured state is allowed to adopt are clearly stipulated.[13] In short, to induce compliance of the obligation in dispute, and the resumption of performance of the obligations in question, are two supreme goals enshrined in the State Responsibility Acts. Meanwhile, general principles such as proportionality, necessity and to employ counter-measure as the last resort, are applied, incurring considerable restrictions on this exceptional means of dispute settlement by states.[14] In this sense, modern international adjudication is living up what Grotius had argued centuries ago about the function of international adjudication, law reaching beyond a single state (civitas) should aspire to achieve corrective justice, but not distributive justice.[15]

It is sound and clear that in 1974, when China (PRC) had acceded into the international community,[16] prohibition of use of force while settling disputes by peaceful means has become a part of customary international law. States in the international community had generally recognized and accepted its legal status, as soft laws that generated moral responsibilities as well as legal binding forces after its long and established practices. As a result, by using force to solve the Paracel disputes with then DRV government, even as a countermeasure to the DRV's repudiation of its pre-claimed position in a1958 Statement, it is difficult to fully insulate China (PRC) from international skepticism on its commitments and political wills on vindicating its international undertakings.

B *The Pratas and Itu Aba Islands*

The second subset is the Pratas and Itu Aba Islands currently under effective control of Taiwan (ROC). The status of Taiwan (ROC)'s claim upon these features cannot be comprehended, absent considerations of issues of state and government succession. Put differently, explorations of Taiwan (ROC)'s claim, control and legal implications on the Pratas and Itu Aba Islands would be a prerequisite to understand China (PRC)'s position. More details will be laid out in section II, when state and government succession are studied in scholarly depth and practical feasibility. Nevertheless, a primary observation is that China (PRC) seemingly has regarded the Pratas Islands as an area with no disputes.[17] A settled consensus, as perceived by Beijing, is that the Pratas has been recovered even before the dash-line map was drawn,[18] and generally, has not been the target of the South China Sea spats. If only disputes arise upon the Pratas Islands, it may be likely to fall within the ambit of the "one China" conundrum. In this sense, the thorn in the flesh may not be only the sovereignty and maritime interests derived therefrom, but also the yet-to-be-settled battle of the Chinese representativeness between China (PRC) and Taiwan (ROC).

Similar situations take place in the Itu Aba Island. Those arguments and reasoning applied to the Pratas Island could be referred to the Itu Aba Island as well. Yet for the Itu Aba Island, things get thornier. Issues such as if it could and should be separated from, as a single episode, the Spratly Islands may constitute a tough challenge. In section II, more details will be examined, with attempts to provide reasoned and reasonable explanations of why this occasion would be possible, and why Taiwan (ROC) may consider amend its claim to be more focused on its continuing and effective control upon the Pratas and Itu Aba Islands.

II The Drama of Two China(s): succession and recognition

A Succession and Recognition

In the wake of worldwide expansion of European international law beginning in the eighteenth and nineteenth centuries, one phenomenon that cast profound impacts on the non-European world is the concept and corresponding emergence of "nation state". Emphasizing the ethnic pureness of the governed in a clearly defined territory, this concept nevertheless brought challenges and had seen dramatic reorganization of the Oriental world order at different levels. In the larger geopolitical context, the dissolution of the Austro-Hungarian Empire was one major factor underlying the mushrooming upheavals. In East Asia, the Qing dynasty in the Chinese mainland had its catastrophic countdown of not only centuries-long glories of civilization, but supremacy in the regional political hierarchy. At the micro level, the vicissitude of ancient dynasties in the Indo-China peninsular had consumed much energy and resource which could have been dedicated to the establishment of a new order. Amid the turmoil, the entailing development of mushrooming newly established nation states is further complicated by a body of international law on state succession alleged to be creating more confusion than clarification.

International law distinguishes succession laws into two categories, state succession and that of governments.[19] This categorization has not met serious objections, when legal scholars agree generally that the later would inflict lesser influences upon international order. The successor government is to uphold international commitments and treaty obligations made by previous administrations.[20] On the contrary, the former is viewed with more leniency, in the sense that interests of new states have been assumed in diversification with their parent states.[21] State succession may involve intractable issues, such as the right of self-determination of peoples in some areas of the original territories, and if the legality and legitimacy of the way that establish the new state should be brought into enquires.[22] Further, there exists government succession that entails changes at all dimensions with revolutionary characteristics. Even its title and identity as a state is not changed, the nature of this kind of succession generates confusion, when attempting to define treaty rights and obligations to be succeeded by this new government. In this regard, the Chinese case that had seen a split of governance across the Taiwan Strait since 1949, and a change of international recognition of the Chinese representativeness, is posing great challenging to succession theories in international law.

Yet challenges do not stop there. The role and impact of recognition from the international community constitute another thorn in the flesh in the succession regime. Whether foreign recognition should be regarded as a constituent factor, or one with merely declaratory function, to the establishment of new states, find respective supports in state practices.[23] Simply put, decisions whether to grant formal recognition are tinged with a murky confluence of legal and political considerations in the law of recognition.

The question whether to grant formal recognition to a new state or government long attracts controversy. In a general sense, de jure recognition to the new government is stronger, while de facto one is more tentative and deeply connected with the fact if effective administration of certain territories has been well established.[24] De facto recognition is thus provisional, and aims at facilitating the reality with operational rules, so that administration effects upon certain territories by the de facto government could be secured. It is thus giving the recognizing state rooms to act expediently, and constitutes a rebuttable position which could be fine-tuned depending on circumstantial political facts and its interests.

The criteria that facilitate the granting of recognition have undergone fundamental changes. The effectivism perspective that prioritizes administration of a defined territory is one example.[25] In the nineteenth century, this principle was upheld with crown importance, along with great distinctions by foreign states and courts in recognized and unrecognized states.[26] In the twentieth century, as international cooperation deepens, recognition is gradually tinged with sympathy or hostility to the new state by the granting state. As a result, prolonged non-recognition becomes more common, as ideological lineage weighs in to influence the decision. Legal assertion thus diverges from the reality, to the extent that the effectivist view, originally upheld by few countries, such as the UK and Switzerland, had been marginalized when ideological rivalry divided the East and West hemispheres during Cold War. Yet, effectivism regained its attractions when the end of Cold War shuffled again the world order in early

1990s. The British and Swiss were later rejoined by an increasing number of states, leading to a revival of effectivism and pragmatism perspective.[27] Yet, it will be a premature judgment to depict this change as an outlook of the demise of the long prevailing concept of "nation state".

Another issue is the formation of international organizations after the Second World War, and the relation between their membership and implication of recognition.[28] Generally, membership with international organizations seeing a large volume of state members in the international community would constitute a convincing evidence of its capacity and qualification as being deemed a sovereign state. For instance, the membership of the U.N. is one example. However, the U.N. membership is not of decisive influence in some cases either. Both Israel and Arab states are members in the U.N. However, it does not change Arab non-recognition of the Israel State. Nevertheless, when a State affirms the U.N. membership of an entity, needless to say, recognition occurs.

The quest for a body of more clearly-defined rules remains unsettled. Yet, it is in this context that the Chinese case helps shed lights on the succession and recognition issues, and also in the intractable South China Sea dispute.

B Difficulties in the China-Taiwan case in the South China Sea dispute

The Chinese case of succession and recognition shed new lights on the development of relevant international law. Its uniqueness lies in the divergence between legal assertion, state practices and the reality with profound political concerns. The difficulties lie in both succession and recognition. For the former, a cleavage is clearly discerned between state practices and legal pronouncements. The Republic of China government (better known as Taiwan) continues to entertain substantial exchanges without formal recognitions with the international community. Despite the widely accepted "one China" policy, these long-practised informal exchanges with Taiwan thus raise doubts if de facto recognition via these substantial relations has remoulded and fortified its separate international legal identity. Comparatively, the recognition issue is no less easier. International practices have long been blurred in granting de jure or de facto recognition to the Taiwanese government. States tend to give the credit to the Taiwan policy of the People's Republic of China government, while treating Taiwan as a political entity with a separate international legal personality. This is the sphere when de facto recognition may conflict with de jure one, in particular in sensitive issues such as Taiwan's procurement of defence equipment from the U.S. and Taiwan's participation in a plethora of international cooperation.

In the long-dragging South China Sea disputes, the murky Chinese story in succession and recognition has also spillover effect. The focus is, without surprises, on Taiwan claims that share proportionate similarity with those of China, and on the implication of how this assimilation impacts on future development of this issue.

150 *State succession and the disputes*

i The intricacy of the Chinese case of succession and recognition

Despite that a comprehensive study could better explain the murky Chinese story of succession and recognition, some words are helpful before delving into the conundrum in the South China Sea.

In the Chinese case, despite critical issues of both normative force and realistic practicality remain, the position held by PRC asserts that it is a case of changes of government, while the state of China remains, with its international legal personality being left untouched. The international community has seemingly accepted this position, when discussions of lingering issues, such as the international personality and identity of the ROC government, have lain relatively dormant in recent years. The inquiry if it is an establishment of a new state is rarely raised at present. Put differently, the state of China remains, amid the turmoil of administration change that took place as a result of a painstaking civil war which is yet to see an official rapprochement between Beijing (the People's Republic of China government, PRC) and Taipei (the Republic of China government, ROC). international documents, along with practices of state that cast weighing influence lend evidentiary support to this observation. Of primary significance is the General Assembly Resolution 2758, mandating the expulsion of the Taiwanese government from the United Nations, and the take-over of the seat by the Chinese government.[29] Its wording, as reflecting the position of the international community, was clearly crafted to indicate that the Chinese case is one of government changes, from the Chiang administration in Taiwan to the People's Republic of China in the mainland.[30] Another example is the delicacy of U.S. crafting on its positions and subsequent state practices on Taiwan's international status.

The official position of Washington on the Taiwan issue is largely informed by a series of inter-governmental documents including joint communiques and exchanges of political statements between China and the U.S.[31] Inter alia, approaches by the executive organ opened the debates if the U.S. had treated Taipei, not as what the succession theory suggested a local affiliation to the PRC, but a de facto entity having the attributes of a state or government. In an official memorandum, the President stated that ". . .whenever any law, regulation, or order of the United States refers to a foreign country, nation state, government, or similar entity, departments and agencies shall construe those terms and apply those laws, regulations, or orders to include Taiwan."[32] To further strengthen this line of argument, Washington had not seen it necessary to obtain Beijing's approval before furthering exchanges with Taiwan. Should Washington uphold the Chinese case as one of government succession with genuineness of intentions, it would risk placing U.S. Taiwan policy under Beijing's wills.

In this sense, Taiwan (the ROC government) had enjoyed de jure recognition as the legitimate Chinese representative from the international community before the admission of PRC government in the U.N. in 1971. Yet, after 1971, the status and identity of ROC, becomes a focus of heated debates. Cleavages exist in this issue. In formality, the PRC government in Beijing as the solely legitimate Chinese representative has gained wide acceptance, to which Taipei (the ROC government) is viewed as a local entity in a somewhat loose affiliation to the central government in Beijing. In actuality, some rooms are created, giving Taiwan a dubious role of a political entity having the attributes of a state or government in certain scenarios. As a result, the ROC government in Taiwan has enjoyed de facto recognition, to a certain extent, from the international community as a self-ruling political entity with its effective control vested upon a definite territory including the Formosa Island, and several adjacent islets.

ii The determinant factor: territory and administration

The status of the ROC government in Taiwan as a self-ruling entity which enjoys, in an implicit manner, de facto recognition from the international community has earned fortifying evidence in the following two dimensions. The first determinant factor is a territory separate from that under the effective control of the PRC. The second is the capacity of the ROC government to conduct and engage in exchanges, formal and informal, with the international community.

For the former, despite the lingering belligerent status across the Taiwan Strait and looming dangers of the threat of the use of force by the PRC, the ROC government has been able to sustain its administration upon the Formosa Islands and its adjacent islets separate from the domain under PRC control. The effective administration upon a separate and independent territory becomes one preferable criterion for an increasing probability to earn recognition. Yet, the administration requires being settled and the likeness of continuation.[33] It is in this context that the Tobar Doctrine is worth mentioning, according to which an unconstitutional change of the government should be recognized only when the people accept it.[34] Despite its anachronistic origin used by the United States in Central America for the purpose to protect stability of regional order, the requirement of constitutional legitimacy of the government finds some echoes in the strong support to democratic politics.[35] In this sense, Taiwan's democratization movement, starting from the 1980s with its climax peaked in mid-1990s when universal suffrage was realized in the presidential election, lend strong supports to the constitutional legitimacy requirement of the ROC government in Taiwan.

For the latter, the ROC administration in Taiwan is an example of how the concept of "sovereignty" has evolved to see new development that a multi-faceted angle should be adopted when viewing state sovereignty in a world informed by mushrooming international cooperation. Put differently, in the wave of the expansive globalization and increasing international cooperation in breadth and depth, sovereignty has become more segmented into various dimensions,[36] which interact with each other with both conciliatory and contradicting effects. In Taiwan's case, bargains of various dimensions of sovereignty are demonstrating. Instances are plenty, in the specificity of Taiwan's situations. Sovereign function in border administration has been loosen off, so as to facilitate economic engagement, inwards and outwards, at regional and global levels, for the purpose that sovereignty in providing good governance, to promote general well-beings of the people, could be effectively delivered.[37] Subsequently, it is a positive interaction that after domestic good governance has largely been secured via these international economic exchanges, it then helps fortify the legal status of ROC, to act as one polity with an independent legal personality in future occasions of international participation.

Having established that the ROC government in Taiwan has enjoyed de facto recognition and has operated as a political entity enjoying a separate international legal identity in the Formosa Island area, an inquiry arises upon the relation between the PRC and the ROC government in the South China Sea issue, in which both have laid sovereign claims. The issue gets further complicated when both claims refer to one identical subject, sharing a high degree of similarity in the contents. Amid the blurring international practices that see the Chinese case as both state and government succession depending on the viewers' national interests and the specificity of scenarios, the South China Sea issue actually opens an window of opportunity for both China(s) to reconsider their claims while exploring further cooperation possibilities.

C The Drama of Two China(s) in the South China Sea theatre

i Taiwan's South China Sea claims: from de-jure-ist to de-facto-ist

Both China and Taiwan lay sovereign claims in the South China Sea. Sovereignty upon land features aside, both uphold a dash-line map issued originally in 1947.[38] Despite minor adjustments resulted in the PRC negotiations with then Democratic Republic of Vietnam (North Vietnam, 1945–1976), their dash-line claims overlap significantly and share with each other a high degree of similarity.[39] In this sense, Beijing held the position, on the basis of government succession of ROC by PRC, that Taipei's South China Sea claims are subsumed into that of the PRC. It is interesting to note that China has yet to put it in an official formality, regarding its absorption of Taiwan's South China Sea claims.[40] Rather, China relies on the succession argument, opining that whatever claims made by ROC have been equivalently succeeded by the PRC government after 1949.[41]

That said, a minor point, but not trivial, is whether a general legal principle, the non-retroactivity of law, is also applicable to the recognition of a newly established government.[42] Flowing from this inquiry, in the Chinese case, the intricacy falls on if PRC, as the legitimate Chinese government, could enjoy formal recognition in a retrospective manner, tracing all the way back at its establishment in 1949. The answer, either positively or negatively, would inflict fundamental changes on the status of ROC before and after its withdrawal from the U.N. in 1971, and also on its South China Sea claims.

De jure recognition is logically stronger, while de facto recognition usually is provisional. In this sense, relations between claims made by the de jure and de facto government, in particular, when these claims are largely the same, should be construed on this basis. The PRC government, with de jure recognition as the legitimate Chinese government, would trumpet the ROC government in major international occasions and activities. Consequently, PRC's South China Sea claim has overwritten that of ROC, to the extent that those, seeing a rivalry confrontation between the two, would ultimately give credits, in both legal and political scenarios, to PRC's claims. Accordingly, the nine-dash line claim by PRC has subsumed ROC's 11-dash line claim. Similar legal effects apply to the ROC's sovereignty claims upon land features in the South China Sea. Contrarily, the ROC claim may function to shore up the PRC's, should their claims focus on one identical subject and similar arguments.

Therefore, this reasoning helps declassify ROC's South China Sea claims, and its relations with that of PRC. However, the drama does not stop here. While ROC's South China Sea claim has largely been subsumed with that of PRC, this absorption would stop short of ROC claims upon the Pratas, and the Itu Aba Islands (the Taiping Islands). In other words, ROC claims upon the Pratas and Itu Aba Islands should be viewed respectively, earning rooms for ROC to claim its sovereignty independent from PRC.

Two points support this observation. The Pratas and Itu Aba Islands have come into ROC's effective control since March 1947,[43] to which the PRC has not made official protests.[44] In other words, PRC has, after decades of its muteness on this issue, forwarded acquiescence towards ROC claims upon the Pratas and Itu Aba Islands. ROC claims upon these land features thus, should be singled out from other parts that have been absorbed. Meanwhile, Taiwan's claims are further fortified by the following facts. ROC, acting as a government with de facto recognition in territories separate from those under PRC's control, is possessed with an independent international legal personality and is able to make effective claims, should they not conflict with that made by PRC.

Further, PRC has not formally objected to ROC claims upon these land features, in an official and explicit manner. The reiteration of government succession and relevant issues by the PRC government, as a general position, should not be extensively explained to cover, in a straight and forthright manner, ROC claims upon the Pratas and Itu Aba Islands. Rather, a restrictive perspective should be adopted when construing the impact of government succession upon issues involving both ROC and PRC in international occasions or disputes. The logic is simple. When disputes exist and other parties are involved, the views of both China(s) constitute their respective claim, their perceptions of the facts. Nevertheless, their perspectives aside, the reality is also shaped by other parties' positions presented in both words and deeds. A close examination reveals that other claimants have dealt with the two China(s) differently in the South China

Sea issue. In this sense, it is an oversimplification to overlook the fact and its entailing profound impacts of the two China(s) governments and their nuanced sovereign claims in the South China Sea.

The fact that other disputants, in particular Vietnam, have launched formal protests to ROC's control upon the Pratas and Itu Aba Islands for decades after 1971,[45] cast intriguing impacts upon the relations between ROC and PRC claims. On one hand, Vietnam's protests implicate that it has viewed Taiwan (ROC)'s claims distinctively from that of China (PRC). This understanding has entailed its implied recognition of Taiwan (ROC), as an independent sovereign able to assert territorial claims in the South China Sea. On the other, Vietnam's calculations dwell on tapping upon the spilt governance across the Taiwan Strait. The legitimacy and legal forces of China (PRC)'s claim would be questioned. The unsettled Chinese recognition problem, being brought back from the burner after decades since 1970s, would largely overwhelm and further complicate this already chaotic conundrum. To Beijing, it would need to fight a war between Scylla and Charybdis, a least-hoped for scenario on the Beijing's agenda list.

Whether this manoeuvring to separate ROC control and claim upon the Pratas and Itu Aba Islands from that of PRC is one intentional outcome, or a mere inadvertent upshot, the outcome, rather than raison d'être, is of more weighing importance in the legal reasoning. In this sense, grey zones indeed exist, giving the ROC claims upon the Pratas and Itu Aba Islands room for making an independent claim not incorporated by PRC.

Another point, strengthening separate claims by ROC upon the Pratas and Itu Aba Islands, is that ROC is relatively less confronted with formal protests by claimants other than Vietnam in relevant international forum upon its effective administration over said subjects.[46] For the Pratas Islands, ever since ROC reclaimed it from the Japanese occupation in 1947, other disputants have largely neglected ROC's administration, by not raising inquiries in a formal sense in relevant international forum. No formal discussions, let alone protests, have been launched either. For the Itu Aba Islands, the Philippines had once occupied the island in 1956, who was soon expelled by ROC naval forces.[47] Thereafter, Manila issued a formal apology to the ROC government and reiterated its recognition of ROC's sovereignty over the Itu Aba Island. After the ROC government was expulsed from its U.N. seats in 1971, ROC claim and presence over the Itu Aba Islands also has not attracted much attention from other disputants and the international community. It may be argued that if these intermittent challenges brought by Vietnam had constituted legal impediments towards Taiwan (ROC)'s effective administration upon the Pratas and Itu Aba Islands. In one sense, Taiwan (ROC)'s efforts to obtain territorial titles under the theory of prescription may be impeded. On the contrary, these challenges may re-mould Taiwan (ROC)'s claim as an independent claimant, as only an independent sovereign can assert territorial claim.

III Concluding observations

The intractable nature of the South China Sea issue is self-demonstrating, as it covers, superficially, sovereignty attribution of land features, maritime resources utilization and maritime delimitation. Fundamentally, the battle of Chinese representativeness and debates on the dash-line claim, which predate the development of the Law of the Sea regime, becomes revived again in the wave of escalating tensions. Leaving aside the suspicion if Beijing intended to discard, or to remould contemporary Law of the Sea regime, by solving the dispute solely by political wrestling, its position that the South China Sea dispute has went beyond the scope of the Law of the Sea deserves some credits.

With a close look of China and Taiwan's positions, the South China Sea dispute reflects a mission unaccomplished for the two China(s) in their transitions to a modern nation state. Challenges are presented in the following dimensions: an unfinished revolutionary civil war, a battle to secure the Chinese independence in various aspects against external pressures, and a yet-to-be-accomplished mission of modernization, remoulding this ancient civilization into a modern state.

Positions of PRC in different grouping of land features in the South China Sea reveal that the South China Sea concerns not only material interests, such as marine resources utilization, but also, intangible issues implicating certain unfinished missions. The Paracel Island dispute marks the PRC's struggles to secure respects from the rivalry disputant and international community. The PRC's efforts to earn international recognition, as an independent sovereign laying claim upon the Paracel Islands, are far from accomplished. Further, this also relates to the challenge of modernization of China, which, as presented in the South China Sea dispute, denotes a smooth integration of the PRC into contemporary international Law of the Sea regime.

The Pratas and Itu Aba Islands dispute remains a thorn in the flesh to the PRC. It still lies under Taiwan's control, and the two have yet to reach a solution to the pending issue of separate governance across the Taiwan Strait. Possibilities of turmoil in the Pratas and Itu Aba Islands still exist, should the cross-strait relations turn sour in the future. In this sense, the Chinese civil war continues to haunt both Taiwan and China, sending a grudging reminding of the unfinished business of Chinese struggles to accomplish revolution in its domestic terrain. Also, the remaining debates on the dash-line claim demonstrate further great efforts are still required, for a smooth incorporation into contemporary international political and legal system.

For the ROC, challenges are no easier. Major issues are presented in earning itself room to participate in the South China Sea dispute, while separating its claims from those made by the PRC. Even with the fact that states tend to treat Taiwan as a polity enjoying de facto recognition separate from China, Taipei is enmeshed in the dilemma as its claims are largely absorbed into Beijing's position, posing more difficulties on its future efforts for a ROC South China Sea claim independent from the PRC. In this sense, the ROC's struggle

156 *State succession and the disputes*

to accomplish revolution in the Chinese domain is yet to be accomplished. Without de jure recognition from the international community, the ROC's independence as a sovereign remains insecure and unjustified. The pending issue for a modern interpretation of the dash-line claim also poses challenges on the ROC, as an indispensable party initiating and continuing to hold this dash-line claim.

The unfinished Chinese stories in the South China Sea battle thus raises following inquiries. Should Taiwan, the ROC, be admitted to future South China Sea dispute? With a positive answer, the formality of Taiwan's participation is a headache to Beijing, and an issue of great concerns of major extra-regional power, such as the U.S. Taking one step further, will the unfinished, but temporarily kept under the lid, battle for Chinese representativeness extend to the South China Sea scenario? Would the spill-over further exacerbate the dispute, how and to what extent?

These remaining issues have not loomed far. It is time for China and Taiwan to take a second and serious thought, before the fact becomes a reality.

Notes

1 See Chapter 5, III. The Dash-Line Claim in Contemporary International Maritime Legal Order.
2 "1974 China-Vietnam(Democratic Republic of Vietnam) Maritime Clashes in the Paracel Islands", *I-Feng News*, 07 March, 2008, last visited 10 November, 2014.
3 Lizhou Sun, "Vietnam Back and Fill in the South China Sea Islands: Prime Minister in Democratic Republic of Vietnam Once Recognized China (PRC)'s Sovereignty upon the South China Sea Islands", *Renming News*, 18 July, 2011, last visited 10 November, 2014; 4 Zhonghua Renmin Gonghe Guo Duiwai Guanxi Wenjian Ji [Collection of Documents on the Foreign Relations of the People's Republic of China] (1956–1957), At 61–62 (1961); 5 Zhonghua Renmin Gonghe Guo Duiwai Guanxi Wenjian Ji [Collection of Documents on the Foreign Relations of the People's Republic of China] (1958), at 162–163 (1959). The declaration was approved by the Standing Committee of the People's Congress on 4 September, 1958, thus making it part of Chinese law.
4 "The Phan Van Dong Statement in 1956: The Democratic Republic of Vietnam Affirmed Its Recognition to the Sovereignty Claim of the People's Republic of China on the Spratley Islands" [1956 年"范文同"声明：越南承认中国对南沙享有主权], *The State Council Gazette* (Guowuyuan Gongbao), 43 (1956). The statement is reprinted and can be retrieved from, *I-Feng News*(凤凰网), 17 May, 2010, http://news.ifeng.com/history/special/zhengyankanyuenan/detail_2010_05/17/1524689_0.shtml, last visited 10 January, 2015.
5 You Hong-Bo, "US Reaction to the Paracels Battle between PRC and South Vietnam", *Southeast Asian Affairs*, 3 (2011): 20–28; Duowei News, "Never Forgotten: The 1974 Maritime Clashes in the Paracel Islands" [尚未被遺忘：1974年中越西沙海戰紀實], 18 May, 2014, http://history.dwnews.com/big5/news/2014-05-18/59472327.html, last visited 10 January, 2015.
6 The Vietnam case requires a more comprehensive study which would go beyond the scope of this article. Yet the murky confluence of state continuity, state creation, succession and identity of the newly established one suggests that recognition from the international community has cast a great sway in the status

of this newly formed state. In this sense, the Vietnam case is more definitely not a case of government change, but one of state succession. See, Christian J. Tams and Antonios Tzanakopoulos (eds.), *Research Handbook on the Law of Treaties* (Cheltenham, UK: Edward Elgar Publishing, 2014), 505–540; Konrad G. Bühler, *State Succession and Membership in International Organizations: Legal Theories versus Political Pragmatism* (Leiden: Martinus Nijhoff, 2001), 93–114.
7 Carsten Ebenroth and Matthew Kemner, "The Enduring Political Nature of Questions of State Succession and Secession and the Quest for Objective Standards", *University of Pennsylvania Journal of International Economic Law*, 17:3 (Fall 1996): 756–759; Robert Sloane, "The Policies of State Succession: Harmonizing Self-Determination and Global Order in the Twenty-First Century", *Fordham International Law Journal*, 30 (2007): 1288–1317.
8 Bühler, *State Succession and Membership in International Organizations*; J.H.W. Verzijl, *International Law in Historical Perspective: State Succession* (Leiden: Martinus Nijhoff, 1974), 229–321.
9 Charter of the United Nations, 26 June, 1945, 59 Stat. 1031, T.S. 993, 3 Bevans 1153, entered into force 24 October, 1945, Article 2(4) and 33.
10 U.N. Charter, Article 33. There are series of international documents reaffirming this principle of peaceful resolution of disputes. For instance, 1970 Declaration on Principles of International Law Concerning Friendly Relations and Co-operation among States in accordance with the Charter of the United Nations. United Nations General Assembly Resolution 2625, GA Res. 2625 / UN GAOR, 25th Sess., Supp. No. 28 / UN Doc. A/8028 (1970)121. The document is available at: www.unhcr.org/refworld/topic,459d17822,459d17a82,3dda1fl04,0.html, last visited 10 January, 2015.
11 "United Nations General Assembly: Resolution 2625 (XXV) Declaration on Principles of International Law Concerning Friendly Relations and Co-Operation among States in Accordance with the Charter of the United Nations", *The American Journal of International Law*, 65:1 (January 1971): 243–251.
12 Ibid.
13 Draft Articles of Responsibility of States for Internationally Wrongful Acts, Annex to General Assembly Resolution 56/83 (12 December 2001), reproduced in *Yearbook of the International Law Commission, 2001*, vol. 2, Part 2.
14 Ian Brownlie, "The Peaceful Settlement of International Disputes", *Chinese Journal of International Law*, 8:2 (2009): 267–283; Gaetano Arangio-Ruiz, "Counter-Measures and Amicable Dispute Settlement Means in the Implementation of State Responsibility: A Crucial Issue before the International Law Commission", *European Journal of International Law*, 5 (1994): 20–53.
15 Benedict Kingsbury, "International Courts: Uneven Judicialization in Global Order", in *The Cambridge Companion to International Law*, James Crawford and Martti Koskenniemi (eds.) (Cambridge: Cambridge University Press, 2012), 202–228.
16 United Nations, General Assembly Resolution, 2758. G.A. Res. 2758, 26 U.N. GAOR, Supp. (No. 29) 2, U.N. Doc. A/8429 (1971). The text can be retrieved from UN website, http://daccess-dds-ny.un.org/doc/RESOLUTION/GEN/NR0/327/74/IMG/NR032774.pdf?OpenElement, last visited 10 December, 2014.
17 Ever since the South China Sea issue has been brought above the table, China, as well as other claimants rarely addresses their attentions upon the Pratas Islands. They neither issue formal protests to Taiwan (ROC)'s control over it, nor brought this issue to the formal negotiation forum.
18 In an exhibition regarding historical archives and documents of the South China Sea issue held by the ROC government in October 2014, records show that ROC had taken over the Pratas Islands in 1947. The ROC navy stationed in

158 *State succession and the disputes*

the Pratas Islands in March, 1947. Jiazhen Xie, "Taiwan Hold First Exhibition on South China Sea Documents" [首次南海史料展 檔案照片珍貴], *Central News Agency*, 1 September, 2014, www.cna.com.tw/news/aipl/201409010163-1.aspx, last visited 10 January, 2015.

19 Matthew Craven, "The Problem of State Succession and the Identity of States under International Law", *European Journal of International Law*, 9 (1998): 142–162; Ebenroth and Kemner, "The Enduring Political Nature of Questions of State Succession and Secession and the Quest for Objective Standards".

20 Craven, "The Problem of State Succession and the Identity of States under International Law"; Ebenroth and Kemner, "The Enduring Political Nature of Questions of State Succession and Secession and the Quest for Objective Standards". See also discussions on recent cases and impacts on the theoretical development. Mario Martini and Matthias Damm, "Succession of States in the EU", *Ancilla Iuris* (2014): 159–181, this article can be retrieved from www.anci.ch/beitrag/martini_damm_succession, last visited 10 January, 2015; "New European Union Rules on International Succession/Inheritance", *PLMJ Informative Note*, July 2004, this note can be retrieved from www.plmj.com/xms/files/newsletters/2014/Julho/NEW_EUROPEAN_UNION_RULES_ON_INTERNATIONAL_SUCCESSIONINHERITANCE.pdf, last visited 10 January 2015; "State Succession to the Immovable Assets of Former Yugoslavia", International Crisis Group, Bosnia Report, No. 20, 20 February 1997. The document can be retrieved from, www.crisisgroup.org/~/media/Files/europe/Bosnia%206.pdf, last visited 10 January 2015.

21 Craven, "The Problem of State Succession and the Identity of States under International Law"; Ebenroth and Kemner, "The Enduring Political Nature of Questions of State Succession and Secession and the Quest for Objective Standards". Also, see Matthew Craven, *The Decolonization of International Law: State Succession and the Law of Treaties* (Oxford: Oxford University Press, 2007), 23–29.

22 M.J. Peterson, "Recognition of Governments Should Not Be Abolished", *The American Journal of International Law*, 77:1 (January 1983): 31–50; See also, "Revolutions, Treaties and State Successions", *The Yale Law Journal*, 76:8 (July 1967): 1669–1687, URL: www.jstor.org/stable/795056.

23 Craven, "The Problem of State Succession and the Identity of States under International Law"; Ebenroth and Kemner, "The Enduring Political Nature of Questions of State Succession and Secession and the Quest for Objective Standards"; Craven, "The Decolonization of International Law".

24 In reality, the source of criticism of the U.N. practice with regard to succession to membership is not the internal rules of the organization, but rather rooted in the doctrinal uncertainty in international law about the criteria for the extinction, identity and continuity of States. It is the preliminary question of determining whether an international person has ceased to exist or a new one has been created, not the application of the governing principles, which is mostly guided by political and pragmatic considerations and, thus, often highly controversial.

25 J.H. Verzijl, *International Law in Historical Perspective Leiden*, vol. 7 (The Netherlands: A.W. Sijthoff, 1974); Peterson, "Recognition of Governments Should Not Be Abolished"; See also Chris Naticchia, "Recognizing States and Governments", *Canadian Journal of Philosophy*, 35:1 (March 2005): 27–82, rethinking the generally upheld justice-based account of recognition and the one favoured by the author, the pragmatic account. The latter holds that political entities ought to be recognized as states if and only if cooperating with them and giving them international support would be the best means of achieving peace and justice among and within them.

State succession and the disputes 159

26 Peterson, "Recognition of Governments Should Not Be Abolished".
27 Instead of the end of Cold War, another factor to fuel the revival is the deepened and broadened international cooperation at a variety of issues. To better facilitate international cooperation, the concept of "non-state actors or polities" becomes more popular in regional and international organizations aiming at specific subjects of a more neutral and non-political characteristic. The fishery organization serves as one example.
28 Bühler, "State Succession and Membership in International Organizations"; Qerim Qerimi* and Suzana Krasniqi, "Theories and Practice of State Succession to Bilateral Treaties: The Recent Experience of Kosovo", *German Law Journal*, 14:9 (2013): 1639–1660; Martini and Damm, "Succession of States in the EU".
29 See United Nations, General Assembly Resolution, 2758 (1971).
30 Ibid. The wording reads "Recognizing that the representatives of the Government of the People's Republic of China are the only lawful representatives of China to the United Nations. . .", and "Decides to restore all its rights to the People's Republic of China. . ." "to expel forthwith the representatives of Chiang Kai-Shek from the place which they unlawfully occupied at the United Nations. . .".
31 Five key documents are of particular importance: the Shanghai Communique in 1972, the Normalization Communique in 1979, the Taiwan Relations Act in 1979 (enacted by the U.S. Congress), the Six Assurances to the ROC government in 1982, and the Communique in 17 August in 1982 regarding U.S. arm sales to Taiwan. Shirley Kan, "China/Taiwan: Evolution of the 'One China' Policy – Key Statements from Washington, Beijing, and Taipei", *CRS* (RL 30341), 10 October, 2014. The report can be retrieved from www.fas.org/sgp/crs/row/RL30341.pdf, last visited 10 December, 2014.
32 Presidential Memorandum of 30 December, 1978, Relations with the People on Taiwan, 44 Fed. Reg. 1075(1979).
33 Malcom Shaw, *International Law*, 6th ed. (Cambridge: Cambridge University Press, 2008), 446.
34 Ibid., 457.
35 One great contribution of democracy lies in the legitimacy vested by the electorate upon the elected. While it requires other conditions to make an efficient democratic system, this vested interests of legitimacy wrought by democratization upon an originally authoritarian government is of weighing significance in transition periods of many newly-independent states.
36 Christopher Rudolph, "Sovereignty and Territorial Borders in a Global Age", *International Studies Review*, 7:1 (March 2005): 1–20, at 4–9, 12–15; Robert Jackson, "The Weight of Ideas in Decolonization: Normative Change in International Relations", in *Ideas and Foreign Policy*, Judith Goldstein and Robert Keohane (eds.) (Ithaca: Cornell University Press, 1993), 111–138. Christopher Rudolph argues for "sovereignty bargain", when various facets of sovereignty are engaged. Robert Jackson made a distinction between negative and positive sovereignty, as the former describes formal conditions, the latter indicates the substantive capacity to enjoy liberty and interests of sovereignty.
37 For this argument dubbed as "sovereignty bargain", see Rudolph, "Sovereignty and Territorial Borders in a Global Age", 4–9, 12–15; Stephen D. Krasner, *Sovereignty: Organized Hypocrisy* (Princeton: Princeton University Press, 1999); Stephen D. Krasner, "Troubled Societies, Outlaw States, and Gradations of Sovereignty", (working paper, presented to the "Christopher Browne Center for International Politics", University of Pennsylvania, 5 February, 2004). The paper can be read on https://bc.sas.upenn.edu/system/files/Krasner_02.05.04.pdf, last visited 20 February, 2014.

160   *State succession and the disputes*

38 The Republic of Taiwan asserted an 11-dash line claim which was drawn in 1947. The People's Republic of China (the mainland, PRC) upheld a nine-dash line claim, which succeeded and had substituted, as it asserted, the ROC's dash-line claim. Yet, the ROC has maintained its 11-dash line claim till present, despite it has not given rooms in either negotiation or arbitration forum. There are plenty of scholarly research, official statements and position papers about China's position in the South China Sea issues. Yet, an article may be one with state of the art, which is co-authored by a Chinese judge currently serving in the International Tribunal for the Law of the Sea(ITLOS) and a law professor in Qinghua University in Beijing, China, and published in American Journal of International Law in 2013. Zhihuo Gao and Bingbing Jia, "The Nine-Dash Line in the South China Sea: History, Status, and Implications", *The American Journal of International Law*, 107:1 (January 2013): 98–124.
39 Scholarly accounts place the publication date from 1946 to 1948. For simplicity, this study refers to the "1947 map." See, e.g., M. Sheng-Ti Gau, "The U-Shaped Line and a Categorization of the Ocean Disputes in the South China Sea," *Ocean Development & International Law*, 43:1 (2012): 57–69, at 58 (stating the map was "first published" by the Republic of China in December 1946); K.-H. Wang, "The ROC's Maritime Claims and Practices with Special Reference to the South China Sea," *Ocean Development & International Law*, 41 (2010): 237–252, at 243 (stating the map was "released" in 1947); Jinming Lee and Dexia Lee, "The Dotted Line on the Chinese Map of the South China Sea: A Note," *Ocean Development & International Law*, 34 (2003): 287–295, at 290 (stating the map was "printed" in 1947 and "published" in February 1948).
40 On the contrary, the White Paper issued by PRC on 25 September, 2012, could be viewed, as serving the function that officially proclaimed that ROC's sovereign claims over the Diaoyu/Diaoyutai/Senkaku Islands were subsumed into the PRC's claim. . . .
41 This position has not been put into official statements, despite that it has long been upheld by Chinese scholars.
42 Peterson, "Recognition of Governments Should Not Be Abolished"; Quincy Wright, "The Chinese Recognition Problem", *The American Journal of International Law*, 49:3 (July 1955): 320–338.
43 Gau, "The U-Shaped Line and a Categorization of the Ocean Disputes in the South China Sea"; Wang, "The ROC's Maritime Claims and Practices with Special Reference to the South China Sea"; See also, Xie, "Taiwan Hold First Exhibition on South China Sea Documents", Central News Agency.
44 Taiwan (ROC) has been excluded from the South China Sea forum since its withdrawal from the U.N. in 1971. China (PRC) and other claimants also share the tacit understanding that Taiwan (ROC)'s participation is conditioned upon the recognition of "one China" policy, under which its claim is largely subsumed with that of China (PRC). In this sense, other claimants view Taiwan (ROC)'s claim as supplementary to that of China (PRC). Therefore, no specific attentions are drawn to Taiwan (ROC)'s claims for two reasons: for the fear that separation of China (PRC) and Taiwan (ROC)'s claims would irritate Beijing, and that giving room for Taiwan (ROC) would strengthen China (PRC)'s claim, thus disadvantaging other claimants' positions.
45 Cheng-Yi Lin, A Decade of South China Sea Islands Claimants' Policies, *Asia Pacific Forum*, no.19 (March 2003), 1–11; Reginald Chua and Mary Kwang, "Hanoi Again Calls for Formal Talks on Spratly Islands", *Straits Times*, 24 July, 1992, p. 20.
46 Other claimants have rarely launched protests against Taiwan (ROC)'s administration upon the Pratas and Itu Aba Islands in relevant international forum.

Records show that they had not issued formal diplomatic protests to the Taiwan (ROC) government either.
47 Gau, "The U-Shaped Line and a Categorization of the Ocean Disputes in the South China Sea"; Wang, "The ROC's Maritime Claims and Practices with Special Reference to the South China Sea"; Lee and Lee, "The Dotted Line on the Chinese Map of the South China Sea: A Note".

Conclusion

The South China Sea issue possesses, arguably, the greatest potential to easily ignite furious sentiments among regional claimant countries. The tension gets further deteriorated, when more actors, mostly extra-regional not bordering South China Sea, are involved, in various forms of manifestations. Succinctly put, developments of the South China Sea issue, up to present days, can be vividly described with two terms, over-judicialization and over-politicization.

The issue is getting over-judicialized, in the sense that the dispute has not become, ostensibly, more substantiated until further development of the Law of the Sea was sealed in the 1980s. Not defying contributions of the Law of the Sea regime, maritime order in South China Sea becomes further segregated, overshadowed by self-willed state activities under the name of contestation of their sovereign claims. In other words, law of sea cannot solve the stalemate in South China Sea, suggesting the dilemma of transplanting the Westphalian-minded international law system in a region that was nourished from a set of values with different origins and characteristics. It is what the first part of this book is devoted, the retrospect of maritime order and practices in the region.

Discussions are unfolded, revealing the underdevelopment of maritime consciousness of countries in this region, due to a compound of factors, such as continuous wars and civil conflicts, territorial cessions to western countries that created serious hurdles to national sovereignty, unawareness of the importance of maritime zoning and strategic deployment, and lack of knowledge in maritime policy making and coordination among regional countries. The lack of maritime consciousness and corresponding strategies also set the scene of enduring neglect to issues of maritime resource conservation and environmental protection. In this aspect, the depletion of fishery resource serves one astonishing example. The dire reality of a fishery dying-out has posed imminent threats unescapable to everyone in this region.

On the contrary, it is a fair observation that the South China Sea issue has become over-politicized.

Since 2009, when Vietnam, Malaysia and China submitted Note Verbale to the United Nations Committee for the Delimitation of Continental Shelf, the South China Sea issue was brought back to the front burner again for public attention. Tensions then went up and down, and have become one potential flashpoint that easily topples over efforts for regional developments in various aspects. While sentiments remain boiling in certain claimant countries, it is a totally different picture in the other. This cleavage demonstrates that with disputed subjects remote in the sea, where no civilian could easily reach and land, the very "emptiness" of these island (as in people's cognition and memory) makes them the ultimate patriotic symbols, or "logos of nationhood in a global media age".[1] Southeast Asian politicians have much freedom to define what these territorial conflicts mean to their respective populations.

It is in this sense that the South China Sea issue has become overtly politicized and highly vulnerable to external influences. Tensions went up and down, and have become a potential flashpoint that easily topples over efforts of all those concerned. Their political wills are made attenuated concurrently. While sentiments remain boiling in certain claimants, it is a totally different picture in the other. The South China Sea issue thus clearly shows a picture of diversified interests with sometimes conflicting considerations.

To sum up, the developing intractableness of South China Sea issue, in particular, complexity of the dash-line claim, indicates how the intertwinement of law and politics has actually informed and shaped inter-state disputes.

As explained by Tønnesson, law has remoulded the South China Sea issue in terms of governmental behaviour, policy discourses and patterns for inter-state dialogues and dispute resolution.[2] Law has, on one hand, accentuated disputes by inducing contestation of overlapping claims, encouraging claimants' behaviour of asserting sovereignty rights, while failed to clarify certain key issues.[3] However, law has made contributions too, by alleviating the danger of war and constraining claimants from resorting to use of force. One further notable impact is that law and legal justification have become one king clause that all claimants would have embarked on. In past decades since the South China Sea issue was brought back to the front burner in 1990s, law has penetrated diplomatize and policy discourse of all claimants. The emphasis is with such a frequency, that any resolution beyond international law becomes increasingly unlikely and unimaginable. Succinctly put, a trend of overt judicialization is taking place, which in turn is shrinking the alternative and room for dispute resolution in the future.[4]

This law factor has set in to reshape diplomatic practices and policy promulgation of the claimant states. Yet, inquiries remain, as if their policy discourse and position argument are reflecting genuine legalistic thinking, or boiling down to the ground, a mere opportunistic political maneuvering under the disguise of a legal overture. Put sharply, doing law and thinking about law are two things, with polarizingly different reasons/raison d'être, distinctive outcomes and impacts.

Take one step further, legalistic thinking informing claimants' discourses and positions actually reveals one structural issue that has confronted newly-independent countries after the Second World War, and subsequent decades seeing hard struggles against imperialist predation and colonial suppression. Simply put, the issue regards the incongruence between international legal and political order – nourished and developed in an underbed of Christian tradition

164 *Conclusion*

and an account of missionary practices – and indigenous culture, tradition and perspectives to how governance is being projected and should be performed at both domestic and regional levels.

With this increasing intractableness of the dispute, a concept of a "jurisdiction right upon maritime spaces" is proposed in the second part of the book. This concept has its origin which can be traced back to pre-colonial era before European power arrived with a gamut of weaponries. In other words, to recontemplate this concept in incumbent context is the resuscitation of a regional custom and a traditional practice which may support efforts in the quest for sustainable and effective resolutions in South China Sea. Yet, this revitalized concept of a "jurisdiction right" is not aimed at defying the contemporary Law of the Sea regime and general international law. Rather, it is to strengthen and assist its implementation, in the sense that how maritime zoning stipulated in law of sea regime can be meticulously evaluated, duly executed and rationally observed. Meanwhile, this concept provides an alternative solution to imminent crisis of the lack of public goods, such as maritime security vacuum in South China Sea. More efforts are required to flesh out implementation details of this concept and action plans.

Yet as this concept is established on the projection to the provision of regional public goods, one best scenario is to get all those holding stakes in South China Sea on aboard. This is the main reason that the last two chapters are devoted to a long-neglected actor, also a claimant, Taiwan (the Republic of China, ROC) and its South China Sea dilemma. Due to the particularities of its political status, Taiwan (ROC)'s South China Sea claims should be re-evaluated, under the context of state succession and realistic considerations, such as its participation in contemporary law of sea regime and international law.

This book hopes to contribute conceptual and practical insights invaluable to the field of law, history and politics. It points to the way how the lingering unresolved issues underlying China's practices in pursuing its South China Sea claims construct contemporary dilemma, and necessitates new ways of thinking about the right and interest of actors and referents, about what interests at stake are, and the kinds of redefinition and transformations in global legal-cum-political discourses are needed to confront challenges in South China Sea. Further, the explicit conceptual construction of the relation between legal and non-legal factors, for instance the relations among history, law and politics, is a much needed intellectual project that still remains nascent. In this sense, this book hopes to contribute to an emerging and still disparate field of studies that pushes the boundaries of international legal thought, taking into account the long-neglected non-western culture legacies and traditional values that increasingly define contemporary conflicts globe-wide.

The Aftermath Development of The South China Sea Arbitration Award

On 12 July, 2016, the Tribunal established under Annex VII in the Law of the Sea Convention issued the award for the first South China Sea arbitration. This award is sending a timely message, of how the globe has become flattened, and contemporary world order, drastically reconfigured. The Tribunal adopts a strict approach when making decisions on certain critical issues, such as the historic right and the island/rock definition. The Tribunal's deliberations pose further inquiries if it could deliver its responsibilities as a special tribunal for a special legal regime, that of norm-advancement, regime maintenance and coordination among various scenarios in the framework of public international law. The award actually gives China a chance of refining its claim, particularly the nine-dash line claim.

In the face of an arbitral award that upholds almost all submissions made by the Philippines, the statement issued by the Chinese government immediately after the award on 12 July (712 statement) indicated that this was never the ultimate outcome of their disputes. In the 712 statement, China made further efforts to clarify its claims: sovereignty claims over the four major island groups, claims of Exclusive Economic Zone and Continental Shelf based on sovereignties over these islands, and historic rights in the South China Sea. Despite the fact that the Tribunal has left at the hands of China further deliberation of the content and scope of the nine-dash line claim, China has not mentioned this "nine-dash line" claim in its subsequent documents and announcements.

A hasty conclusion should thus be avoided that the nine-dash line claim is being nullified by the award. Rather, the award helps refine China's nine-dash line claim. Before the arbitration, the nine-dash line claim is serving a dual function, as a line stipulating a Chinese standard of maritime zoning in the South China Sea, and itself, a line for maritime boundary. The award has repudiated that China cannot assert a historic right over natural resource by claiming the nine-dash line. Rather, resource utilization and apportion should follow the maritime zoning standard established in the Convention. In this sense, the Tribunal has denounced one function of the nine-dash line claim, that of establishing maritime-zoning for the purpose of resource apportioning in the South China Sea. For the line to serve other purposes, the Tribunal has left it open for the Chinese government's deliberation.

That said, the nine-dash line claim is being put in a grey zone. It is because of this ambiguity that some new thoughts on the nine-dash line claim deserve reconsiderations, for the purposes of re-deliberating and re-calibrating the content and scope of the nine-dash line claim. China will need to reconsider the original purpose and possible projection of this nine-dash line claim. Sophisticated management tactics will help facilitate the success of this deliberation.

The nine-dash line was drawn with considerations mainly for defense purposes. Against this backdrop, the line is intended to be security-relevant, and less resource-oriented. Further, it intends to denote China's sovereignty claims over the four island groups within the line. The resource-related dimension actually has become more substantiated at a later stage when the fishing technology gets further developed around the end of 20th century. It is in this context that when re-fleshing the content of the nine-dash line claim, the resource-related dimension should not be over-emphasized, not only because the award has rejected the resource right based on the nine-dash lien claim, but also the fact that China has in many previous occasions re-affirmed the resource apportioning system established based on the maritime zoning system of Exclusive Economic Zone and Continental Shelf in the Convention.

The arbitration has come to an end, but a new era is opened. China is now facing criticisms from all over the world, but also new opportunities to trim down unnecessary details in its claims, re-calibrate its policy goal and re-evaluate its strategic tactics in this enduring South China Sea battle. The South China Sea dispute has become highly politicized. Yet, the reality is, by not being able to tackle the South China Sea issue, China's regional relations and relevant policies, such as the 21st century Maritime Silk Road plan, may run the risk of being further attenuated, dis-credited and to the extreme, debilitated. Creative thinking, senses of rationality and practicality and an open-mind attitude are what is mostly required for sustainable and beneficial resolutions. Before these facts turn to be dire realities, they'd better be dealt with meticulously and seriously.

Notes

1 Robert D. Kaplan, "Concer of Civilizations", in *Asia's Cauldron: The South China Sea and the End of a Stable Pacific* (New York: Random House, 2014), chapter IV. Mina Pollmann, "Government Narratives in Maritime Disputes", *The Diplomat*, 10 July 2014, http://thediplomat.com/2014/07/government-narratives-in-maritime-disputes/, last visited 30 August, 2016.
2 Stein Tønnesson, "The South China Sea: Law Trumps Power", *Asian Survey*, 55:3 (2015): 455–477.
3 The Law of Sea Convention has left certain issues in deliberate vagueness. This is so because the consensus was reached among a plenty of countries with diversified national interests and calculations. One of the most notable issues is the island regime prescribed from Article 121–123. Definitions of islands are crafted with vague words, and distinctions between an island and a rock, unclear. Other issues that require further clarification and amendment, if necessary, are like historical rights and the effect of declarations made under Article 298. United Nations Conventions on the Law of the Sea, adopted on 10 December, 1982, 1833 UNTS 3 (1994), 21 ILM 1261(1982).
4 Yet, Tønnesson holds a different opinion, ". . .the Law of the Sea sets clear limits to what a solution can look like". Also, Yann-Huei Song and Stein Tønnesson, "The Impact of the Law of the Sea Convention on Conflict and Conflict Management in the South China Sea", *Ocean Development and International Law Journal*, 44:3 (2013): 235–269.

Index

Association of Southeast Asian Nations (ASEAN) 1, 5, 47–8, 60, 89, 106, 112–14, 125, 128–9, 131–7

bilateral agreement 46, 48
border 3, 4, 5, 7, 8, 12–14, 24, 25, 31, 32, 37, 38, 40, 45, 56–8, 62, 101–7, 113, 130, 135, 152; control 25, 31–2, 58, 68, 107; evolution of 12–14; lands 24–5, 31–2, 68, 104, 130; zone 5
border security concept 24, 31–2, 104, 107
boundaries 2, 3, 4, 5, 11, 12–14, 24–5, 28, 31–3, 45, 46–50, 56, 58–63, 65–7, 78, 79, 80, 87, 90, 92, 93, 101–6, 110, 114, 118, 128, 130, 131; demarcation 31, 128; evolution of 101; maritime 46–50, 60–1, 65–7, 93; open-ended 58–60, 90, 92–3
boundary-making 12–14

cardinal point 125–8, 130–1, 133–5; symmetry 125–6, 128–31; territory 130–1, 135–6
centre 12, 24, 27, 39, 46, 53, 55, 56, 59, 65, 76, 113, 125–7, 129, 131, 132–5
China (PRC) 53–4, 60–7, 79, 89–93, 109–12, 114–17, 119, 144–7, 150–4; dash-line claim 60–7, 89–92; maritime security 112–14; Paracel islands 145–6; regional cooperation 114–15
Chinese sovereign consciousness 20–3
claims sovereignty 60, 62
coastal defence 14–15, 20, 22, 91
Cold War 111, 128–9, 148
colonial encounter 7–16

colonial powers 23–4, 32–3, 37, 110, 129
conflict management 9, 88, 90–1, 112–13, 116–17, 119

dash-line claim 2–4, 53–67, 82, 85, 87, 89–90, 93, 108–9, 144–5, 152–3, 155–6; China (PRC) 60–7, 89–92; dual functions of 65–7; inherent uniqueness 61–7; in international maritime legal order 54–60; in maritime legal order 60–7; maritime spaces and 89–92; origin and early history 53–4
de facto 3, 5, 22, 148–53, 155; government 5, 148, 153; recognition 148–9, 151–3, 155
de jure 3, 5, 103, 148, 149, 150, 152–3, 156; government 3, 5, 153; recognition 148, 150, 153, 156
dispute resolution 28, 39, 87–8, 92, 118–19, 163
dispute settlement 112–13, 146

European Colonialism 102–3
exclusive economic zone (EEZ) 2, 49, 60, 63–4, 68, 77, 79–89, 91–2, 108–9, 144; claims 45, 79–80; *personae* jurisdiction 83–7; *ratione materiae* 83–7; recontemplating 88–9

fishery resource management 46–8
fishing activities 4, 25, 37–50, 57, 80, 84–8, 92, 94, 107, 111–12; history 38–9; unreported 39–41, 43
flag states 85–8, 91, 93; responsibilities 85, 88, 91–2
frontier 101–19; political 103–4
function, dual 65–7

illegal, unregulated and unreported (IUU) fishing 39–44, 47, 50, 85–6
illicit fishing 37, 39–42, 44–6; definition 39–40, 44; *vs.* IUU 41–4
Itu Aba Islands 146–7, 153–5

Japan 3, 14, 21, 26–30, 39, 47, 49, 62, 126; Chinese claim against 25–9
jurisdictions 41, 45, 59, 61, 66, 76, 84–6, 89–93, 108–9, 111–12, 116–17, 119, 164; coastal State 64, 83; maritime spaces 89–92; proposal of 77–94

Malay/Nusantara 55–9
mandala 5, 55–7, 59, 67, 125–35
mandala circle 125–6
mandalic legacies 125–37
mare liberum concept 77–8
maritime boundary 48–50
maritime consciousness 21, 22–3, 24–9; European colonial context 24–5; Japanese pursuit, for international status 25–6; Japanese pursuit, for national identity 26–9
maritime delimitation 48, 63–8, 79–80, 155
maritime law-making 10–11
maritime order 54–60; on Grotian ideal 77–8; in Westphalian system 76–7
maritime security 22, 107–9, 111–12, 115, 119, 134, 136
maritime Southeast Asia 126

Paracel Islands 16, 26, 144–5, 155
People's Republic of China *see* China (PRC)
police power 115–17, 119; common law concept of 116–17
Pratas Islands 16, 144, 146–7, 153–5

Qing government 14–15, 20–2

ratione materiae jurisdiction 83–5, 90–2
ratione personae jurisdiction 58, 78, 85, 86, 91
recognition 11, 14, 39, 103, 127, 147–54
regional fishery management organizations 42–3
regionalism 129
Republican government 22–3, 29–30
Republic of China (ROC) claims 153–4
RFMOs *see* regional fishery management organizations

Sino-French war 21–2
Sino-Japanese wars 21, 29
South China Sea 1–6, 7, 10, 11, 14–16, 23, 24–32, 37, 38, 40, 44, 46, 49, 50, 53–63, 65–7, 79, 80, 82, 87–91, 101–118, 125, 131, 132, 134–5, 144, 147, 149, 150, 152–4; area 14, 58, 104; ASEAN and 131–7; boundary concept, evolution of 101–2; China-Taiwan case, difficulties in 149–52; claims 31, 136, 144, 153, 164; colonial expansion 7–8; conundrum, dismissing 111–18; dispute categorization, revisionist approach 144–7; disputes, application and implication 108–11; disputes, international treaties 29–32; fishing in 37–50; frontiers 101–19; illicit fishing in 44–6; issues 28–9, 37, 60, 89, 102–3, 107–8, 115, 131, 134, 136, 152, 155, 162–3; Law of the Sea regime and 79; mandalic legacy in 125–7; open-ended boundary 58–60; quasi-sovereign rights in 118–19; recasting 14–16; refining 14–16; regional-international order 54–8; regionalization, mandalic ethos 127–31; state succession and 144–56; Taiwan's claims 152–4; territorialization, trend of 30–2; zoning of maritime spaces 79–81
Southeast Asia Treaty Organization 130
sovereign claims 27, 29–30, 60, 110, 152, 162
sovereign rights 37, 61, 63–4, 66, 79, 83–4, 88, 110–11
space 2, 4–6, 14, 24–5, 38, 41, 53, 55–9, 61, 63–5, 76–7, 79–80, 82–3, 87, 89–92, 101, 106, 108–12, 114, 116, 117
spatial jurisdiction 59, 84–5, 88, 90–2
State Responsibility Acts 146
succession 3, 5, 16, 144–53
symmetry 125–30, 133–7

Taiwan (ROC) 1, 2, 3, 5, 30, 53–4, 60, 62, 144–7, 150, 154
territorial acquisition 31, 58, 104, 106, 127–8, 131
territorialization 30, 32–3, 89, 108
territorial rights 3, 12–14, 28, 30–2, 57, 87
territory 3, 12, 16, 31, 58–9, 83, 90, 102, 110, 128, 130–1, 134–6, 147, 148, 151

trade 7–10, 20, 24–6, 55, 58, 76, 91, 103, 105–6, 108, 111, 126–9, 132, 133
Treaty of Peace 30

unequal treaty 22
United Nations Convention on the Law of the Sea (UNCLOS) 41, 60–1, 80–1, 93, 109–10, 116–17
uti possiditus principle 31

Vietnam, Democratic Republic of (DRV) 145–6, 152
Vietnam, Socialist Republic of (SRV) 144–5

Westphalian concepts 32, 88, 105, 109

zoning system 77–9, 83, 85, 87, 90, 92–3